NONVERBAL BEHAVIOR

Applications and Cultural Implications

NONVERBAL BEHAVIOR

Applications and Cultural Implications

edited by

Aaron Wolfgang

Department of Applied Psychology
Ontario Institute for Studies in Education
University of Toronto

ACADEMIC PRESS

New York   San Francisco   London
A Subsidiary of Harcourt Brace Jovanovich, Publishers

1979

ACADEMIC PRESS, INC.
111 Fifth Avenue, New York, New York 10003

United Kingdom Edition published by
ACADEMIC PRESS, INC. (LONDON) LTD.
24/28 Oval Road, London NW1 7DX

Library of Congress Cataloging in Publication Data

International Conference on Non-Verbal Behavior,
    Ontario Institute for Studies in Education, 1976.
    Nonverbal behavior.

    1. Nonverbal communication (Psychology)—Congresses.
2. Cross-cultural studies—Congresses.   I. Wolfgang,
Aaron.   II. Title.
BF637.C45157   1976   152.3′84   79-12056
ISBN 0-12-761350-1

PRINTED IN THE UNITED STATES OF AMERICA

79 80 81 82   9 8 7 6 5 4 3 2 1

with love to

Lisa, Deborah, Heidi, and Kurt.

CONTENTS

List of Contributors   ix
Foreword: Edward T. Hall   xi
Preface   xix
Introduction   xxi

PART 1:   PERSPECTIVES

On Communicational Processes   1
    Albert E. Scheflen

Universals in Human Expressive Behavior   17
    Irenäus Eibl-Eibesfeldt

Facial Expression, Emotion, and Motivation   31
    Carroll E. Izard

The State of the Art:
Past and Present Trends in Body Movement Research   51
    Martha Davis

PART 2:   RESEARCH APPLICATIONS

Measuring Sensitivity to Nonverbal Communication:
The PONS Test   67
    Robert Rosenthal, Judith A. Hall, Dane Archer,
    M. Robin DiMatteo, and Peter L. Rogers

Talking Down:
Some Cultural Sources of Miscommunication of Interracial Interviews   99
   Frederick Erickson

Therapist Training in Nonverbal Behavior:
Toward a Curriculum   127
   Peter Waxer

New Developments in the Analysis of Social Skills   139
   Michael Argyle

PART 3: APPLICATIONS OF NONVERBAL
BEHAVIOR IN TEACHING

The Teacher and Nonverbal Behavior in the Multicultural
Classroom   159
   Aaron Wolfgang

Social Contexts for Ethnic Borders and School Failure   175
   Ray P. McDermott and Kenneth Gospodinoff

Teaching and Nonverbal Behavior   197
   Charles M. Galloway

Common Misconceptions about Nonverbal Communication:
Implications for Training   209
   Robert M. Soucie

PART 4: CONCLUSION

Conclusion   219
   Aaron Wolfgang

Index   221

LIST OF CONTRIBUTORS

Numbers in parentheses indicate the pages on which the authors' contributions begin.

Dane Archer (67)
Department of Sociology, University of California, Santa Cruz, California 95060

Michael Argyle (139)
Department of Experimental Psychology, University of Oxford, South Parks Road, Oxford OX1 3UD, England

Martha Davis (51)
The Institute for Nonverbal Communication Research, New York, New York 10024

M. Robin DiMatteo (67)
Department of Psychology, University of California, Riverside, California 92037

Irenäus Eibl-Eibesfeldt (17)
Arbeitsgruppe für Humanethologie, AM Max-Planck-Institute fur Verhaltensphysiologie, 8136 Percha/Sternberg, Enzianstrasse, Postfach 49, Germany

Frederick Erickson (99)
Graduate School of Education, Harvard University, Longfellow Hall, Appian Way, Cambridge, Massachusetts 02138

Charles Galloway (197)
The Ohio State University, College of Education, Columbus, Ohio 43210

Kenneth Gospodinoff (175)
The Rockefeller University, New York, New York 10021

Edward T. Hall* (xi)
   Department of Anthropology, Northwestern University, Evanston, Illinois 60201

Judith A. Hall (67)
   Department of Psychology, The Johns Hopkins University, Baltimore, Maryland 21218

Carroll E. Izard (31)
   Department of Psychology, University of Delaware, College of Arts and Science, Newark, Delaware 19711

Ray P. McDermott (175)
   The Rockefeller University, New York, New York 10021

Peter L. Rogers (67)
   School of Public Health, Harvard University, Cambridge, Massachusetts 02138

Robert Rosenthal (67)
   Department of Psychology and Social Relations, Harvard University, William James Hall, Cambridge, Massachusetts 02138

Albert E. Scheflen (1)
   Albert Einstein College of Medicine, Bronx, New York 10461

Robert Soucie (209)
   Department of Applied Arts, Seneca College, Toronto, Canada

Peter Waxer (127)
   Counselling and Development Centre, York University, Downsview, Ontario M3J 1P3, Canada

Aaron Wolfgang (159, 219)
   Department of Applied Psychology, Ontario Institute for Studies in Education, Toronto, Ontario M5S 1V6, Canada

* Present Address:
642 Camino Lejo, Santa Fe, New Mexico 87501

FOREWORD

CULTURAL MODELS IN TRANSCULTURAL COMMUNICATION

Edward T. Hall

The challenge of understanding nonverbal behavior in a multicultural setting evokes a variety of images and questions concerning the nature of culture, culture contact, and communication. Let me state at the beginning that there is no agreement among the experts on any one of these, which simply means we are contemplating a developing science.

Culture is, of course, man's primary mode of coding information in a way that enables him to cope with an increasingly complex life. In addition to everything else, one might also say culture is a set of solutions to *past* problems and challenges and is therefore *past* oriented, and as a consequence, short in its inventory of solutions to *future* problems—which is what this book is all about. Culture contact has seldom brought out the best in man. This is not to say that warm, close relationships have not occurred. They have, but they have not been as common as one would hope. I speak from long and sometimes painful experience in this and have dedicated most of my life to reducing the distortions and, hence, at least some of the pain of intercultural relations.

Communication, like culture, is one of those terms about which there is very little agreement. My definition is that *communication is always a transaction,* and that culture and communication are very closely linked in the real world. Communication involves *information,* which is a component of both culture and communication and will ultimately be linked to mass and energy in physics. Information is apparently the only way to organize the "stuff of life"—beginning with DNA–RNA chains and ending with nonverbal communication, language, and culture. We see, therefore, that at one level at least culture can be equated with some very basic processes.

Because of the predominately out-of-awareness aspect of culture, much more must be learned than is now known if humans are to be effective in communicating to each other, particularly across the chasms that separate cultures, which results in a situation in which much of what happens between people of different cultures can be likened to roulette, for chance is a larger element than design. I say chance, because it is frequently so difficult in an intercultural encounter to predict what one's opposite number is going to do next. The reasons for this are too complex to go into here, but they are outlined in my most recent book (Beyond Culture, Hall, 1976).

Paradoxically, it is my belief that diversity in ethnicity is one of the greatest assets any country can have. "No matter how hard man tries, it is impossible for him to divest himself of his own culture, for it has penetrated to the roots of his nervous system and determines how he perceives the world" (The Hidden Dimension, Hall, 1966). In the U.S. we have wasted thousands of man-years and untold billions trying to "rub out" the ethnic identity of our minority groups. (It is their "out-of-phase" nonverbal systems that seem to bother people.) In the process we have destroyed the formal values of many ethnic communities and denied ourselves the strength of our own diversity.

The erosion of formal values has created enormous problems in the U.S. If one reviews the history of education in the American Indian groups or the Spanish American populations in the southwest, one is struck by the abysmal failure of our efforts to superimpose one culture's values on another. Today North American youth from all groups are suffering a loss of identity, for which there are multiple causes, but surely we do not need to compound the problem by denying the formal value of our many minorities.

What can really be learned from other cultures? Mostly more about the things that one's own culture takes for granted and how arbitrarily the world is structured by that same culture. What have I learned in this process? A good deal, but not really enough. Most of the time I feel as though I had yet to go to the first grade in school and had managed to master only the alphabet and some of the principal characters of "the language of culture." I feel this way because in my judgment culture provides ways of organizing and managing, in the sense that Drucker (1970) uses the term, the tremendous diversity of talents present in the human race. But in so doing, culture takes on incredible mass, which like the iceberg is only partially visible unless one looks beneath the surface. It is this mass that makes cultures so difficult to change in the deep sense. Superficial changes can be rapid but the basic fabric of culture—the mental processes—changes slowly. It is the hidden mass of ethnicity on which modern ships of state so frequently flounder.

Apart from political and economic reasons, there are definable reasons why human beings of different cultural backgrounds have so much trouble with each other.

(1) The models that are developed and used as cultures change gradually, grow out of date or may have been defective in the first place. That is, they do not match, mesh, or are incongruent with the basic nature of the human organism (Hall, 1976).

(2) When cultural elements are borrowed (which they inevitably are), there may be a mismatch between the borrowed item and the borrowing culture. A case in point is the wide American automobile in the narrow, traditional streets of Tokyo, Paris, Rome, or an Italian hill town; or the Anglo Saxon legal system imposed on a Spanish colonial base in New Mexico.

(3) Man's extensions—both material as well as nonmaterial—have a way of taking over according to a system of internal dynamics that is their very own, a process which I have termed extension–transference (Hall, 1976). *Man becomes the slave of his own creations.* One has only to look at our modern cities to see what I mean.

(4) They fail to read correctly each other's nonverbal behavior.

Man must learn to balance judiciously the first three and recognize the fourth for what it is; that is, his inner nature with the conceptual models of culture, the foreign element as a disruptive force, and the cancerlike growth of his extensions. This is a gargantuan task, and while I have no doubt that the human species will ultimately manage its affairs wisely, it is going to require the cooperative efforts of all of us. Otherwise, we may end up like the dawn men, homos *Robustus Australopithecus* and *Australopithecus Africanus,* in the stomachs of saber tooth tigers. But this time, unlike the early man who became extinct, we will have created our own tiger.

Technology is a force in human affairs that began as a panacea and has become a menace that threatens to destroy us. Technology is taking over the world and man is becoming its slave instead of its master. This happens on the micro as well as the macro level. It is something all of us can observe every day. A perfectly peaceful and generally contented human being frequently becomes a demon as soon as he gets behind the wheel of an automobile. Any anger or frustration he is experiencing is suddenly amplified a hundred times over by the machine just as a gun amplifies the power and range of the arm and hand to hit. In addition, modern technology makes us helpless and dependent and seals us off not only from each other but from the earth as well.

Two great lessons can be learned from our experience with such common extensions as the automobile and public housing. To understand the implications of these experiences, let us begin with the small child. In the course of my life I have had many opportunities to observe children, small and large, attempting to master the tasks they must perform as adults. Take the simple matter of tying one's shoes. At a certain point most children will push the adult's hands away as the child seeks to establish autonomy over his own body. Cultures vary, of course, in the degree to which they permit this to happen. But the fact remains that on the individual, the group or national level, people do seem to have a built-in urge to be masters of their own fate. This need for autonomy is balanced by a complimentary drive to be taken care of. The drive to be taken care of fits the psychological needs of many modern institutions because the temptation of the bureaucrat, the architect, and city planner as well as the large industrialists is to *manage* peoples' lives for them.

The contrasting pair—*autonomy* and *dependence*–seems to be worldwide, transcultural, and omnipresent among humans. In North America there is great pride in individual autonomy, yet we permit our automobile manufacturers to swaddle us in the infantile comfort of a machine that does everything for us. This is not only bad for people, both physically and psychologically, but wasteful of materials and labor (such machines are expensive to build and maintain). There are unforeseen but important consequences of machines of this sort. It is helpful to remember that in machines one can find many parallels with language. There are parts that combine into wholes, for example, and both are extensions. My own research has identified a type of human being who depends very much on muscular feedback from his body to fix information in his brain. Such people, though they may have excellent minds, are disoriented by the American car because it insulates them too successfully from the surface of the road, and they have no way of fixing the continuity of the earth's surface with the continuity that constitutes their lifestream as it is laid down in their central nervous system. German, Italian, and Japanese sports cars, in contrast, send a different set of messages to those who code information using proprioceptive rather than visual and auditory channels.

As the reader can perceive, the model I am working from departs from the conventional mold of words and political–economical acts and is fixed more on what people *do* as a consequence of their culture. I have chosen to emphasize technology because it is thought to be universally applicable, which it clearly is not. It is this image of the transferability of material things (including architecture) that is potentially lethal. Like a time bomb, it can so radically alter the fabric of life as to make it unrecognizable and, in so doing, also destroy the continuity of life.

I make these statements as a result of over a half a century of observation of other cultures as well as my own. While I was growing up in New Mexico, I observed the process of change in the lifestyle of the Spanish villagers and the Navajo Indians from a life with a minimum of gadgets to one that is almost totally mechanized. In my younger years, the whole inventory amounted to little more than horse gear, wagons, axes and saws, shovels, cast iron stoves, leather boots, shoes, and machine-woven clothes. It is this long perspective on material culture systems as they evolved into their present form that enables me to draw conclusions about how to handle and integrate material culture so as to avoid (insofar as possible) some of the pitfalls occasioned by technology (be it home grown or imported, it makes little difference).

All over the industrialized world there have been a series of little-publicized and, therefore, little-known public and private housing disasters. Four years ago when Mildred Hall and I were interviewing town planners in England, several of them commented on what they felt was a world-wide epidemic of vandalism. English youths would take the trains out of London and smash and burn anything that they could destroy in a project like Thames Mead, before it was ever completed. The buildings were "communicating" to them. (It is a mistake to think of nonverbal communication as simply an extension of language, because *everything* communicates and has meaning.) In the United States the recent past is replete with incidents in which youths from middle class, as well as poor families, have gone on destructive sprees. Much of what happened in both Britain and the United States was a "message'' directed at an unresponsive system. My example only illustrates part of the point I am about to make which is that *when human beings rebel and destroy their habitat, it is usually due to a failure to find a correct balance between autonomy and dependency needs of the people.*

In Hong Kong housing we find a move in the right direction. I cannot properly reproduce the incredibly complex and subtle administrative structures, as well as the guiding principles that make Hong Kong public housing work. I am not even sure that it really works as well as I think it does. I can only look at it from the viewpoint of my own experience. It certainly seems more successful than many public housing attempts in the United States in which high-rise complexes were built with little regard for such basic human needs as the necessity to supervise children during play. In Hong Kong, people were given the architectural equivalent of the Model-T Ford instead of a complete, finished apartment: four cement walls, some electrical outlets, and pipes but no fixtures. To make the place habitable, the tenants had to provide their own amenities. Thus they could do without interference from a meddling bureaucracy. Those who proved to be responsible and industrious were later rewarded by an opportunity to move into even more desirable quarters. Nurseries and playrooms for small children were provided on every other floor so that mothers were not tied to a fixed space a hundred or more feet from ground level. It is important to note that the *very strong Chinese family, along with its control over its members, is partially responsible for the success of the Hong Kong projects.* In this case, autonomy was given to the family to improve its environment, but not to the individual.

I had planned to write a few words about the fact that each culture has developed over the years a unique inventory of talents, things that they do well and with ease. Mostly because of communication difficulties, the peoples of the world have yet to learn how to tap the talents of other ethnic groups. This is particularly unfortunate when the ethnic groups live inside one's political boundaries. Not to be allowed to use one's talents is not only frustrating, but can drive people mad (Fromm-Reichman, 1950). There must always be a proper balance between the autonomy and dependency needs of people. It is also important to identify the position of autonomy units in the social organization of the society. In the United States, for those groups of Northern European extraction, it is the *individual* who seeks autonomy. For those groups whose ancestors came from Southern Europe, there is the strong pull of a large *family unit,* namely, the extended family. Everything revolves around this one crucial contrast between individual and family, for it is the context in which all communications occur. For example, Americans brought up in the North European Calvinist tradition feel it is good for both the individual and the state to "make it on his own" without help from family and friends. In fact, the use of influence on the wrong sort is called nepotism. Americans of Mediterranean heritage place much more emphasis on human relations. Their binding ties to family and friends make it mandatory that one do what one can to help any member in need by getting him a job, for the function of power and prestige in these instances is to help those you love and trust. To the South European, the North European looks hard and inhumane, whereas the North European, the Mediterranean type, seems corrupt.

There must be several hundred distinctions of this sort that need to be identified and understood if we are to be successful in reading correctly each others behavior. So far, mankind has had very little experience developing and actively using cultural insights as a way of building harmony in this world. He has spent much too much time and energy on the political and economic side of life; I do not see much hope in either area, whereas I do see hope in the cultural, particularly when it is viewed as a supercommunication system.

To summarize my remarks: It is quite evident that culture, for the most part, has been oriented toward the past and has had as one of its principal functions the provision of models so that the members of a given culture would have clearcut ways of relating to each other. To my knowledge, no culture has developed special skills in relating to outsiders in any term other than its own. Nowhere do we find well-developed techniques for dealing with the *covert* cultures of others (i.e., their nonverbal culture). As a consequence, man's experience in the intercultural field has been fraught with difficulties because people use different ''silent languages'' (Hall, 1959), most of which function outside of conscious awareness. Yet human beings need each other precisely because the essence of so much of culture *is* its out-of-awareness character. One of the principal sources of information about one's own culture is how members of that culture respond when interacting with other cultures. Culture has also provided a way of managing the incredible diversity of talents possessed by mankind. All cultures could do a much better job of allowing these talents to flourish and finding new ways for utilizing man's diverse skills.

Large sections of Europe, Japan, and North America, particularly the cities, have been devoured by the automobile. People's lifestyles are being destroyed by technology before our very eyes. I think much more should be known about the impact of technology, not only because it alters things radically in a physical sense, but because of the deep and indelible inprint it places on *all* communications. One of the unforseen consequences of technology has been the destruction of the balance between man's *autonomy* and *dependency* needs as technology takes over. The history of technology has been the history of the seduction of mankind. While it has not been all bad, neither has it been all good. In housing, in automobiles, and machines in general, it would seem to be important to structure things *so that people have a voice and play an active part in what they use and produce.* Otherwise, they are apt to either turn against their environment and destroy it violently, or turn their rage inward, thereby destroying themselves through neurosis and psychosis. Those societies, cultures, and ethnic groups that still have many of their traditional institutions intact can still avoid some of the pitfalls of the overdeveloped countries. Clearly, technology will be with us for years to come. It should be used with wisdom and caution, however, because it has proved to be a mixed blessing. Mankind can do better. We can stop relying on technology to solve all problems and start to learn much more than we have in the past *from each other.*

References

Drucker, P. *Technology, Management and Society*. New York: Harper & Row, 1970.

Hall, E. T. *Beyond Culture*. Garden City, New York: Doubleday & Company, Inc., 1976.

Hall, E. T. *The Hidden Dimension*. Garden City, New York: Doubleday & Company, Inc., 1966.

Hall, E. T. *The Silent Language*. Garden City, New York: Doubleday & Company, Inc., 1959.

Fromm-Reichmann, F. *Principles of Intensive Psychotherapy*. Chicago: University of Chicago Press, 1950.

PREFACE

The primary objectives of this book are to help bring about an understanding of the role of nonverbal behavior in interpersonal and intercultural communictions, to gain a broad perspective of the field of nonverbal behavior by investigating knowledge gained, the development of theory, and issues, and to explore possible applications of nonverbal behavior in such areas as teaching, counseling, or therapy. The distinguished contributors to this book who come from a variety of disciplines, such as anthropology, psychology, ethology, psychiatry, and education and from different parts of the world bring both an interdisciplinary and international perspective to this field. It is hoped that such a perspective as presented in this book not only underscores the *diversity* of approaches and thinking in this field but also the need for *integration* and possible *applications* of knowledge in this field.

This book would be informative and of value to educators, practitioners, researchers, and students of human communication. The references deal directly or indirectly with the importance of nonverbal behavior in interpersonal communication in a variety of situations. The readings from this volume could be used as a text or supplemental text for either graduate or more advanced undergraduate courses that deal specifically with nonverbal behavior or more generally with interpersonal and/or interculture communication.

The contributors presented papers at the International Conference on Nonverbal Behavior held at the Ontario Institute for Studies in Education, Toronto, Ontario in May 1976. The papers in this book are an outgrowth of this conference. The specific topic areas of this publication were privately suggested by the editor and represent the contributors' current thinking on nonverbal behavior.

INTRODUCTION

Aaron Wolfgang

Some of the underlying issues and questions the authors in this book deal with are: Are there universals in human expressive behavior such as greeting behavior, facial expressions, and fundamental emotions? In what ways are these emotions related to motivation and individual behavior? How are culture, nonverbal, and verbal behavior related? What role does nonverbal behavior play in intercultural communication? How important is nonverbal behavior in teaching, counseling, or therapy? What role does nonverbal behavior play in the multicultural classroom or in interracial interview situations? What are some of the common misconceptions about nonverbal behavior? Will increased knowledge about peoples' nonverbal behavior result in an invasion of their privacy and manipulation? What does the research show in nonverbal behavior and how applicable is it? What does the future hold for the study of nonverbal behavior? These issues and questions as well as others will be discussed from a multidisciplinary perspective.

As the writings in this book show, the field of nonverbal behavior is diverse and mushrooming. The diversity in the field is also reflected in the methods, approaches, and behaviors selected for study. For some, diversity and uncertainty in a relatively new field is disturbing, and for others, a welcome breath of fresh air. Such diversity in the field is not surprising when considering the varied backgrounds of the investigators with each bringing forth his or her unique input to this field.

In Part 1, Scheflen argues against taking a piecemeal approach in studying nonverbal behavior or for that matter in studying behavior in general. He calls for a more integrated, event-centered approach that would avoid the tendency in the social sciences toward doctrinal splinter theories, reductionism, fragmentation, reification, and dichotomies, such as studying word and nonword behavior as separate entities. Scheflen offers us an alternate epistemological approach, a field view or structural paradigm for understanding human communication.

Eibl-Eibesfeldt, a former student of Konrad Lorenz, focuses in his paper on expressive behaviors that transcend culture, or are universal, and uses naturalistic observation to collect his data. He studies and films unstaged social interactions among people primarily from the vanishing cultures of the world in such places as Africa, Borneo, Samoa, Brazil, and the Philippines. Eibl-Eibesfeldt presents evidence that indicates that there are biological foundations for the universal expressive behaviors he has found. For instance, he has shown that children who are deaf and blind as well as being without arms show similar expressive patterns of behavior as anger, happiness, and joy as do children with their senses intact. He stresses that universal expressive nonverbal behaviors such as the smile, eyebrow flash, coyness behavior serve an important positive function in that it allows people to transcend the constraints of their culture and serves as a basis for intercultural communication.

Izard presents evidence like Eibl-Eibesfeldt for the universality of expressive behavior through his cross-cultural studies of fundamental emotions and facial expressions. He is one of the very few psychologists to work in this area. Izard postulates that the fundamental emotions are subserved by innate neural mechanisms. Unlike Eibl-Eibesfeldt, Izard focuses on individual behavior and has developed a theory of emotions. His main thesis is that emotions motivate thought and action. In his paper, Izard shows us the relationship between nonverbal behavior, particularly facial expressions and emotions, and then the relationship between emotion, motivation, and behavior. He also discusses the implications of emotional expression and facial cues in psychological assessment, adjustment, and psychotherapy.

Martha Davis believes like Scheflen that ways must be developed in nonverbal communication research for understanding how the various categories and levels of nonverbal behavior interrelate. In her chapter she gives us a comprehensive overview and perspective of the field. She describes both past and present research trends, funding patterns, and sources for funding of nonverbal research. In dealing with the questions of application of nonverbal behavior, Davis gives us a variety of suggestions and techniques that individuals can use to train themselves to be more sensitive in their understanding of nonverbal behavior and how to glean more from the research literature.

In Part 2, both Erickson and Rosenthal and his colleagues describe their use of film and/or videotape in their research and its applications. Rosenthal et al. use film as an instrument or stimulus for measuring sensitivity to nonverbal behavior, whereas Erickson uses it to unobtrusively capture naturally occurring events, such as job interviews, involving individuals of various ethnic and racial combinations. He studied through slow motion analysis of film characteristic ways of speaking and listening among blacks and whites in an interview situation and found that their styles of listening and speaking are quite different. This he says may be related to cultural differences between blacks and whites in the timing of kinesic activity (e.g., head nods, eye contact) and speech that reflects understanding and paying attention. Erickson shows how these differences put both at odds with one another where white counselors or interviewers may appear to be talking down to blacks, whereas blacks may appear to be not listening or understanding the white speaker. The implications of his findings for educational policy and practice are discussed.

Introduction

Rosenthal and his colleagues give us an extensive report of their recent work on the PONS test. They introduce the PONS test that was designed to measure an individual's sensitivity to various nonverbal channels and show its roots in and implications for theory, research, and applications. They found that a number of groups (e.g., cross-cultural, psychopathological, sex, and age) showed differential ability in interpreting information transmitted through the different nonverbal channels measured by the PONS test. Some of the implications of these results are discussed. In looking to the future, the authors want to ultimately develop accurate measurements of each individual's relative ability to send and receive information in each of the several nonverbal channels and to be better able to predict the outcome of social interactions.

Waxer examines the ways that knowledge from research of nonverbal behavior can be utilized in therapy, counseling, and social interactions. He shows us the ways that the counselor or therapist's nonverbal behaviors are important, for example, in establishing initial rapport, facilitating therapy, and modeling. Waxer also shows how the clients' nonverbal behaviors reveal their psychological state and discusses how the therapist can utilize the clients nonverbal cues for basic diagnosis, for assessment of therapeutic progress, and for counselor and therapist effectiveness. He stresses the need for more basic research in this area and discusses some possibilities and issues in developing a counselor training program that focuses on nonverbal behavior.

Michael Argyle shares with us some new developments in the analysis of social skills. He proposes a social skills model, describes several important functions of nonverbal behavior, as well as the reasons humans use nonverbal behavior. He goes on to discuss a new approach to the analysis of social skills using the analogy of games, and shows us over 20 different ways social performance can fail, all of which have been found in neurotic patients. Argyle describes the different methods or approaches that have been used in training individuals to improve their social skills as well as the approach that he and his colleagues have developed at Oxford for treating patients and for professional social skills training. In this program nonverbal behavior plays an important role.

In Part 3, the focus is on the possible applications and importance of nonverbal behavior in teaching in general and in the multicultural classroom. Wolfgang describes ways teachers or potential teachers can be sensitized to the importance of understanding the role of nonverbal behavior in communication, in general, and, in particular, its impact in the multicultural classroom. He takes the position that teachers communicate simultaneously on at least three levels when teaching students from other cultures, i.e., on the *verbal, nonverbal,* and *cultural levels.* He discusses ways teachers can learn about their nonverbal communication styles and ways communication and learning styles of immigrant students from the West Indies, Hong Kong, and Southern Italy may come into conflict with teachers' expectations. Recommendations for teaching training as well as some possible fruitful areas of research are discussed.

McDermott and Gospodinoff argue that constant miscommunication between

xxiii

rity group children is *no accident* and that communication code
ected by differences in language, dialect, and nonverbal behavior
y reasons for minority group children having difficulty, misbehav-
school. Instead, they argue that these communication code differ-
up by teachers and students, because they are rewarding, functional, and adaptive for both when considering the circumstances in which they are
brought together and asked to teach and learn. The authors give classroom examples
from their research in observing minority school children learning to read as well as
research from others to underscore their argument.

In turning from the multicultural classroom to the general question of teaching
and nonverbal behavior, Galloway focuses on ways of helping teachers become
more aware of their influences and effects on others through their nonverbal communication patterns. He poses four key questions as follows:

(1) Am I aware of my nonverbal behaviors?
(2) Am I willing to take responsibility for my nonverbal influences and effects?
(3) Am I aware of the nonverbal messages of others?
(4) Am I willing to be influenced by nonverbal messages?

Galloway proposes a model for understanding the appearances of nonverbal
phenomena in the classroom and discusses 10 dimensions of nonverbal activity that
affect classroom life.

Soucie in his paper attempts to clarify for us some of the popular misconceptions
people have about nonverbal communication. Soucie discusses the issue of nonverbal training and examines several common misconceptions about nonverbal communication and how these misconceptions confuse and complicate the training issues. The four misconceptions Soucie discusses and attempts to disprove are that:
(1) nonverbal behavior is a very minor part of interpersonal communication; (2)
while there is a great deal to learn about nonverbal communication, sheer life experiences implicty teach us all we need to know about it; (3) too much knowledge
of nonverbal communication will create a direct threat to our privacy and, therefore,
formal training in nonverbal communication would be a mistake; (4) specific nonverbal behaviors have specific invariable, dictionarylike meanings.

PART 1: PERSPECTIVES

ON COMMUNICATIONAL PROCESSES

Albert E. Scheflen

Albert Einstein College of Medicine

We face a serious problem in trying to understand "nonverbal communication." There is no systems reality to the category and no agreement about what it includes but this problem stems from a broader one. We have the same trouble with the concept of communication itself, in fact, the whole field is a hodgepodge of diverse models and points of view. I believe that an integrative definition of communication itself has a higher priority than the contribution of more data. So this paper has been composed in an attempt to do so.

In my opinion our multidoctrinal confusion stems from a very ancient and pervasive problem in the conception of science itself. The classical epistemology that underlies biology, psychology, and sociology is inappropriate for the comprehension of communication as process. I think this point can be made by a critical analysis of our classical theories of communication at three levels of perspective and will be discussed in Part I. If this be so, we must make an epistemological shift to an alternative way of conceiving phenomena. Fortunately this shift has already been made in some sciences so we know how to do it. Part II will deal with this alternate perspective that has begun to bring us a picture of communicational structure.

This emerging view of communicational process does have some serious shortcomings. It neglects the role of people and neural processes in communication. Therefore, I must discuss how these important matters can be put back in the picture, otherwise we will change from one simplistic conception to another and fail to achieve a comprehensive view.

PART I. THE PROBLEM OF OUR CLASSICAL APPROACHES

Various doctrinal schools have contributed diverse conceptions of "nonverbal" communication and communication. I will first make a critical analysis of these approaches at three levels of perspective.

1

Problems of the Category: Nonverbal

The term "nonverbal" implies a dichotomy between processes that are not verbal and processes that are made up of words. But there is no activity that is made up purely of words; even written language consists of *patterns* of words and system of codified markers. And speech is composed of such patterns together with codified sets of changes in stress, pitch, stops, and vocal qualities. In fact, much of our gesticulation is almost invariably speech related, so we cannot attribute a systematic reality to a category of verbal behavior. On this account alone we cannot deal meaningfully with a category of "nonverbal communication." To make this dichotomy is like speaking of indole and nonindole biochemistry or of parathyroid and nonparathyroid physiology.

But we will still have problems even if we compose a broader category of non-language communication. The problem is that nonspeech behavior is a vast, ill defined, and unbounded set of activities that can include anything anyone wants it to include. It includes, to be sure, some gestures, postures, touch, interpersonal distance, and other dimensions that are interactional; but tennis and warfare are interactional too. And for that matter painting, cooking, cognition, and metabolism also have some relation to social processes.

It would be helpful if we could delineate the boundaries of our science. But nonlanguage communication is a dimension of communication in general so we cannot define it until we agree about what communication itself is all about. So I must turn to the larger issue before I can go on.

Problems in Our Concept of Communication

There is no agreement about the inclusiveness of the field of communication either. At its narrowest the process consists of displays or expressions or of an exchange of messages. More broadly the subject is described as a complex sequence of interactions. But people relate in many ways that are not simply interactional in turns and face-to-face configurations. So in some positions the term "communication" includes all of the actions that animals or people share. Finally, some theorists have extended the definition to suborganismic processes and spoken of hormonal and neural communication.

But the problem of boundaries is not the only difficulty with our conventional theories of communication. Each of these also has its own lingo, its own focus of observation, its own methodologies, and its own explanatory principles. On this account we lack agreement about the very nature of human communication.

There are now about five widely used models of communication. Two of these are event-centered views of process that I will discuss later in the paper. The other three are animal- or people-centered. They have been contributed by the classical, animal- or people-centered sciences: biology or psychology, or by sociology which is centered upon groups. These three models can be termed, respectively, an expressional, a reactional, and an interactional model.

An expressional and a reactional models focus upon one person or one animal and ignore the others as if communication was the activity of a single organism. So these are in fact models of how an organism *participates* in communication, they are not models of communication itself. In taking such a view, the observer imagines the participant as (1) a subject who is expressing something or (2) as an object who is perceiving something and reacting to it as a response. In more complex versions the participant is visualized as both responding and expressing. Examples are the S-O-R variants of classical psychology and the psychodynamic model of psychoanalysis.

In an interactional model, the observer shifts his or her view of communication *from* one person *to* another. The process of communication is then visualized as a sequence of actions and reactions *between* the participants. One person or animal expresses, the other responds, and so on. We could outline these classical approaches as follows:

Individual-centered views
    A → expresses or → A reacts (or both)

Interactional models
    A and B respond to each other. A ⇌ B

There is yet another way to describe communication within these classical models. *One can say that communication is that which is expressed.* If one believes for instance that the behavior of human relations is instinctual, one says that communication *is* instinctual. Thus doctrinalists variously say that communication is instinctive, learned, cultural, social, emotional defensive, etc. In such views it is assumed that the favorite explanatory principles of a particular school of thought characterize communication and make up its content.

This sort of disciplinary reductionism narrows our view of communication. It seems obvious that people do participate in communication by expression *and* response and that they also interact. It also seems obvious that human behavior is genetic, cultural, psychological, *and* social in accordance with what classical viewpoints we use to conceive it. So communication is not one of these characterizations but all of them—and more.

The Problem of Epistemology

In the main a particular epistemology or way of conceiving has long dominated philosophy, scholarship, and research in Western civilization. There are other Western epistemologies I will mention later on, so I must designate the one I will criticize here. It is sometimes called "Aristotelian," but in my opinion this is most unfair to Aristotle so I will call if "Aristotelian*ism*".[1] I will use this term much more broadly than its usage in logical positivism where it is equivalent to doing science by armchair philosophy. In fact, it is my opinion that the logical positivists are the contemporary Aristotelianists in spite of their insistence on objectivity.

In order to criticize the conceptual processes of Aristotelianism, I must first describe them. I will not pretend to be fair-minded in doing so, since I am not writing an impartial history of science. I am trying instead to jar us out of attachment to this epistemology in order to set a broader stage for our conceptual endeavors. Its steps may be quite useful for studying the nature and composition of organisms but it is unsuited to study the organization of behavioral processes.

The conceptual processes of Aristotelianism can be described in mneumonic terms by speaking of its three "Rs": reductionism, reification, and real truth.

Reductionism

In exploration of any complex phenomenon it is tactically useful to break down one's observation into simpler and simpler elements. But there is a particular way to do this in Aristotelianism. The parts are conceived of things or people (represented by nouns); actions (represented by verbs), and various other components such as qualities (represented by adjectives and adverbs). These phenomenological types of components are then listed, categorized, and classified. One type of component is then singled out for selective study. Since things or people are considered more important, the sciences of man that evolved with Aristotelianism are thing- or person-centered. They pay relatively little attention to actions, conditions, and other phenomenological components.

The Aristotelianist is now in a bag. One cannot reintegrate a picture of a total phenomena when the reduction has taken us to a list of incomparable components. Indeed little attempt is made to reintegrate these components. The tactic of reduction becomes the total strategy of such sciences, and tactics for synthesis are not developed. This practice is reductionism.

The reductions of Aristotelianism do not stop with reducing a complex phenomenon to a view of the things or people who appear in the phenomenon. It makes further steps in reduction. Of all celestial bodies one is the central or main body.

---

[1] Aristotle described the reduction of complex phenomena to substances, actions, conditions, qualities, quantities, and so forth. Of these he claimed that substances (physicalistic forms) were the most important. He also advocated the doctrine of real and absolute truth. On these bases followers since the Middle Ages have made an "ism" of some of these conceptual practices. But Aristotle elsewhere said many other things about procedures of investigation. For instance he also advocated holistic descriptions in space and time and thus anticipated Einstein. Followers seem addicted to oversimplification and the evolution of isms. Like Marx, who late in life said he was not a Marxist, Aristotle might nowadays say he was not an Aristotelianist.

In Ptolmetic astronomy this one was the earth; after Copernicus it was the sun. In a group of people one is most important. That one is the villain, the "dominant" male, the initiator of interaction, the prime mover, or the cause of it all.

Aristotelian reductions are likely to continue still further in an atomistic direction. In an anatomical series a person is reduced to a genetic organism, then to an organ like brain, and even to a brain area. In heuristic reduction a person is reduced to psyche and soma and then psyche is reduced to hypothetical parts like ego and id. The reduction is guided by a belief in some essence or main part. When this one is "found" the others are slighted or ignored altogether.

Reification

So entrenched is the notion of a main or causative subject that we automatically try to find it in any phenomenon that we examine. If there is no evident thing or person in the phenomenon, we implicate a subject of causal importance who is outside of the phenomenon. Action-at-a-distance is an example. Or we make up an unseen subject. God is an example. Or we conceive of an unseen thing within the organisms of the observational field. In the seventeenth century, for example, it was postulated that a little man within the sperm cells explained reproduction. In the twentieth, we postulated a humunculus in the cerebral cortex. Someone had to read Tolman's cognitive maps.

There is another way of postulating an unseen causative subject. *When a theorist makes up an explanatory principle to account for a phenomenon, his followers conceive of the explanatory principle as a thing with some human traits.* Aristotle once said that a falling body accelerates because it gets more and more anxious to get home as it nears the earth. In the Renaissance the Aristotelians said that a pendulum oscillates because it too wants to get home but takes an erratic course to do so (Kuhn, 1962). In the nineteenth century it was said that morphine makes people sleepy because it contains a "dormative principle." Freud postulated an "ego" and an "id." Now his followers say that the ego gets sick or strong, controls behavior, and makes decisions. If no physicalistic subject can be found as the source or prime mover, the rule of thumb is this: *make up one.*

Commonly the unseen essence, cause or originator of an event is seen as an amorphous substance. Phlogiston and the celestial ether are examples from the graveyard of science past. More recently the causative subject is seen as a force within the thing or person. Gravity, instinct, libido, drive, motive, and emotion are contemporary examples. *We so deeply believe in the heuristic forces of contemporary theory that we tend to forget that they are conceptions and nothing more.* We attribute them so much reality that we build a conceptual geography to provide them an imaginary place of residence. We place evil forces below and good one's above such as hell and heaven. Accordingly we located emotions below the diaphragm in the Middle Ages, below the neck in the Renaissance, and nowadays we locate emotions in the *hypo*thalamus.

In sum, an Aristotelian view concentrates upon a subject. If none can be discovered, one is postulated anyway or some conception of force or substance is given the status of a causative subject. This process of conception is often called "reification."

Collectively reduction and reification lead to an automatic supposition, i.e., *phenomena have a cause that is to be found within a subject.* It is not presumed that phenomena have multiple causes that can be found in, of, around, through, and between subjects.

Expressional and response models are typical Aristotelianisms. Communication is viewed and explained in reference to a single person who is (1) subject and initiator of the process or (2) object and respondent to the process. These versions reflect the classical alternatives of Aristotelianism. Either a phenomenon has its source *within a selected subject or* it has an external source *from some other body, person, or reification.*

Notice that an interactional model is slightly more complex. It countenances two or more bodies or organisms that give source or cause *to each other's behavior.* Historically this version of Aristotelianism stems from Newton's extension to a view of mutual force. This version is less reductive but it retains the Aristotelianism of causative and emergent sources. In interactionalism the investigator looks at one person *at a time*, from speaker to speaker as each one "takes turns."

Real Truth

The third "R" of Aristotelianism is the belief in real truth. Of all possible causes and sources one is the real, deep, or true cause. All other possibilities are accordingly labeled unreal, superficial, or false. Of all possible tactics of exploration one constitutes *the* method of science. Accordingly all other methods are "unscientific." One of all possible explanations is true and the others are therefore untrue. The notion of a real truth leads to the formation of doctrines that we cherished without question. On this account millions of people have been put to death, or relegated to the fringes of science.

Fortunately the doctrines of science do not now bring us to the sword but the collective steps of Aristotelianism leave us with some very unfortunate problems. Within any school of thought, for instance, a very crazy logic comes to prevail. The postulates of the school include some notion of heuristic force that a founder has conceived as a means of explanation. The followers attribute this explanatory notion that status of a natural reality. They come to believe that this notion is a force that exists in the body and emerges to cause things. They are now in the silly position of believing that some academic notion causes the phenomenon it is supposed to explain. To many instincts, motives and gravity are the realities of our destiny.

The process of Aristotelianism also leads science as a whole to a hodgepodge of confused and conflicting dogmas. Consider how this occurs. The process of reduction leads to a long list of component elements. A theorist selects one of these, gives it a central and causative role, and then a whole doctrinal school develops around this notion. But a host of alternatives have thus been ignored. Soon a second theorist seizes upon another one and a second doctrinal school emerges. Then a third item is picked up as a subject of focus and explanation and so on. In a few decades there are as many doctrines as there are cults in the Protestant religion.

Kuhn (1962) points out that old paradigms are replaced by new ones in the physical sciences. This replacement occurs whenever an existing paradigm has proliferated into a host of subdoctrinal interpretations and its inadequacy has become apparent. We are not so lucky in the sciences of man. Old paradigms do not disappear. They are cherished eternally in some circles and new ones are just added to the stew pot. This is the state we are in now in trying to understand communication. Multiple sciences, which appear in multiple doctrinal versions, have contributed their usual Aristotelianisms. Advocates of each one still believe that their version will ultimately prevail by dint of proof or persuasion and bring us to the real truth.

PART II. A VIEW OF STRUCTURE AND PROCESS

In this part of the paper I will discuss the emergence of an alternate epistemology in science and its application to the study of communication.

The Emergence of an Alternative View

If we accept these criticisms we must search for an alternative way of conceiving our experience. The alternative must avoid at least some of the shortcomings of Aristotelianism. We can reduce our observations of a complex phenomenon but the elements must be of a phenomenological type or we cannot regain a synthesis. We cannot be satisfied to classify or categorize or list them if we are to see how they are interrelated to form a whole. And we cannot decide that one element is important and ignore the other ones if we are to hold an adequate perspective. In short we can do science by employing reductions but we can not quit work until we have reassembled a picture of elements in a gestalten.

With these points in mind we could invent an alternative epistemology—one that could take us in an integrative direction. Before we invent one we could look to Eastern philosophy or to anthropological accounts of alternative realities in neolithic man. But we need not invent one or go this far afield.

Actually there is a pervasive epistemology in Western thought that does not have the characteristics of Aristotelianism. This alternative is at least as ancient as Aristotle's work and much older than Aristotelianism, which did not emerge until centuries after Aristotle's death. This alternative way of conceiving our universe was employed in the Greek drama. It was sketched by Galen (see Lewin, 1931). It was well developed by Shakespeare in the view of people acting in a web of unfolding events. It was applied long ago in astronomy and architecture, and Western people have long employed it in drama, music, games, and rituals. Yet this epistemology has not been acceptably applied in most sciences and academic affairs until the last century.

Darwin's concept of evolution employs a view of processes through time. So do many views of history and the evolution of social systems that appeared late in the nineteenth century. A spatial view of fields was added late in the nineteenth century, but a view of events *in space and time* did not come into its own until the turn of the century. Such a view was in the air at that time. It appeared in the continental drift theory, in quantum theory, in the concept of culture, in gestalt concepts of perception, in Freud's concept of the structure of dream processes, and in other views of that period.

So a change of epistemology was "in the air" about 1900. It was Einstein who most dramatically made use of it and solved the old Newtonian dilemmas of ether and force-at-a-distance by looking at astronomical phenomena in an non-Aristotelian way. He did not take a sun-centered view of the universe but focused instead upon space as a field. Instead of employing a dichotomy between matter and force, Einstein employed a relativistic concept of relations and described energy as a function of mass and speed. He ignored the heuristic concept of ether altogether. He repudiated the idea of thing-force causation and *employed an epistemology of field order in which physicalistic bodies held place.* Later on a theory of the evolution of the universe was developed.

About 1940 a further stage of the field- or event-centered revolution began to take place. Mechanisms of equilibrium in a system were elucidated in cybernetics. The notion that a single cause operates linearly from past to present was repudiated first for a concept of retroaction and later for a further view of multiple simultaneous causation (Marayuma, 1963). The field idea of processes in equilibrium was further developed and applied to the biological sciences by Bertalanffy (1960) in a variant of this epistemology that he called "general systems theory." Physiology was revolutionized in the 1950s by this shift in epistemology (Pribram, 1971). A view *of patterns of* behavior as culture emerged in anthropology (Benedict, 1946; Mead, 1964). Concepts of networks developed in sociology (Cherry, 1961). Biologists became interested in the social relations of animals, and ethology developed. In this science patterns of social behavior were described in spatial terms as territories (Lorenz, 1952; McBride, 1964).

Epistemologically speaking these developments are homologous. *The focus is upon events* rather than upon bodies or people. Events are conceived as *relations of movements, changes or behaviors* in dynamic equilibrium for a time but subject to reorganization in larger contexts. The events are not viewed as having *a* cause that is found within some central body or thing. Instead each behavior of the field or system "causes" the others.

The system is a field of mutually related actions. No thing or person causes it and no heuristic forces need be imagined to account for it. It has no main body or force and its elements are of a single phenomenological type. They are perceivable actions and each is examined in relation to the others rather than being examined in relation to some theory about them.

The Evolution of Structural Views of Communication

There were several reductive spin-offs of this revolutionary series that had implications for the study of communication. In the 1920s structural linguistics began to develop. In this off-shoot the pattern of sounds in language was studied (Sapir, 1921). Lewin's field theory also emerged (Lewin, 1951). Concepts of networks (Cherry, 1961) gave us a view of networks or channels of communication. Information theory (Shannon and Weaver, 1949) described transmission in communication. This offshoot was adopted in the social psychologies and elaborated as interactionalism. The social psychology of human relationships, group and family psychotherapies, and other social-level approaches emerged in the systems era but these tended to return to a Newtonian model.

In their early days field and systems applications has a serious deficit. They were systems or field views in some measure but they were highly abstract (except for structural linguistics). The relations in a communicative field were represented simply by lines on a diagram as in network theories or by simple causative arrows as in early concepts of interaction. Or the relations and processes of communication were simply named with abstracted notions such as transmission or information. But an important realization developed in the 1950s. Nothing was transmitted in face-to-face relations, the *process of communication occurred through the mutual* use of *coded behaviors*. Participants use patterns of sound and movement that have customary meaning in a particular tradition. With this realization the study of communication could focus upon observable phenomena, i.e., upon the pattern or structure of audible and seeable behavior.

Another realization developed. Participants do not only employ a common behavioral code in communication but they also follow a score or script or program. With this realization an ancient version of a non-Aristotelian epistemology could be utilized. In one way communicational events are like the play, the concert, or the game.

In the last generation a great deal of research has been carried out on nonlanguage codes and agendas. At first this approach had no generally acceptable name. I use the term "behavioral systems approach" (Scheflen, 1973) but this term never caught on. In recent years the term "structural" has come into more common usage.

The term structure refers to the composition or organization of elements of behavior in a pattern or field. But there are a number of versions of the structural approach to behavior. Levi-Strauss (1963) focuses upon the structure of myths and beliefs in a culture. In some sociological versions, maps are developed of channels of connection in an organization or community. Goffman (1961, 1963) abstracts the rules that people employ in communicational activities. Ethnomethodologists employ a similar orientation but focus upon the sequencing of linguistic participation (Mehan and Wood, 1975). In social psychology interactionalists now conceive that an agenda governs the taking turns in communication (Ducan, 1972). Some of us have broadened the methodology of structural linguistics and described the organization of nonlanguage behavior in communicational events. This method is variously known as linguistic-kinesic analysis or "context analysis" (Birdwhistell, 1970; McQuown et al., 1971; Scheflen, 1973, 1974).

The Structural Paradigm and Its Operations

In Kuhn's terms (1962) the structural approach could be regarded as a paradigm, i.e., a body of theory and a set of operations that enable this theory. The theory holds that societies have evolved customary codes of behavior and programs of procedure that are enacted in particular situations. The members of a society modify instinctual behaviors and learn these patterns of behavior and pass them on in cultural transmission. They enact parts in these customary events in order to maintain or alter the ecological systems of their existence.

The methodology of the structural paradigm is focused upon describing the behavioral organization of customary events and the contexts in which these events are enacted. In structural approaches a context is more than a physical environment. It is a larger system of events and places. I should say more about the operations of search and research in structural studies for these are not like those of clinical inference or of statistical-experimental science. They reflect instead a non-Aristotelian epistemology.

The first goal of a structural research is to map the behavioral occurrences of some communicational event in space and time. By this means the structuralist reports *what* happens in the realm of perceivable activity. Questions of function, purpose, and evolution are left to a later time or sometimes they are not answered at all.

The structuralist uses a number of tactics in this effort; audiovisual recordings, measurements, photographs, and space-time diagrams, for instance. He may also use experiments, statistics, metaphors, and persuasion. But this secondary group of tactics must not take the place of systematic observation and description.

The structuralist operates in a world of perceivables, so he or she does not need to measure consensus about inferences like the psychologist does. When the operational field of a science is made up of observables, these can be described rather than inferred. So the structuralist does research somewhat like the astronomer and the ethologist.

A distinction of great importance is implied here. Cognitive and metabolic processes mediate communicative behavior, but *one does not have to describe these mediational processes in order to describe communicational event*. Events of communication occur at the social level. The media is audible and visible. When physiological events or metabolic states are manifest in skin, pupils, bodily weight, or other indicators, they are perceivable and communicative and hence they are described in reporting the structure. If thoughts are verbalized or acted upon they too become communicative. In this case such activities are included in a structural analysis. Otherwise the structuralists sticks to the level of manifest behavior in social process.

Our main problem in making a structural description of behavioral integration is our Aristotelian preoccupation with inferring traits and motives. We are addicted to judgments and inferences about participants. We observe an event and *say* that we "saw," resistance, motives, instincts, closeness, disaffiliation, poor communication, and so forth. What in fact we *saw* were patterned movements and nonmovements and what we *heard* were patterned sounds and silences.

We may not be able to observe some contexts of an event directly. We may find representations of them in what the participants say, in the shape and decor of the place, and in the dress and insignia that are worn. We may have to take a focus at some higher level of integration to observe contexts directly. We may have to observe surrounding events, for instance, and learn what has happened before an occurrence and what follows it. We can interview participants or other informants to learn at least what people think the contexts are like.

There is a pressing issue I have so far ignored. How does one define AN event? Where does an occurrence leave off and its context begin? How do we separate an event from a next one and how do we distinguish an event from a constituent subevent?

In general the structuralist finds that events have discernable boundaries. These are not physicalistic boundaries. They are spaces and gaps in the action that are marked as well by special forms of behavior that signal extent and duration. Furthermore, a traditional event has a characteristic gestalt in space and a characteristic sequence in time. So anyone who is familiar with it can tell where it stops and when it is over. Still further a customary event occurs in some customary territorial site and some particular sort of temporal slot. These features of a behavior have been described by a number of structuralists (Z. Harris, 1951; M. Harris, 1964; Birdwhistell, 1970; Scheflen, 1973, 1974).

These generalizations about the boundaries of an event seem to apply at all levels of complexity from events as short as a syntactic sentence to those as long as a festival. Accordingly the structuralist can identify an event at various levels of complexity. *More complex events constitute the contexts of events that occur within them.*

When a particular kind of communicational event has been described in detail, one must collect a larger sample of comparable events. Since events have a customary form in a particular tradition, many similar repetitions can be found. The sample is controlled, then for place and conditions and for the class and ethnicity of its participants.

Once a sample of like events has been studied, the structuralist can compare examples. Each will have some features in common and each will show some variations. Suppose one chooses to abstract all similarities first. They are rarely difficult to find. In instance after instance much the same facial sets, postures, topics, and placements may appear in quite the same order. In this way one can define the usual or customary shape of a particular type of event and one can generalize about the contexts in which this type of event tends to be reenacted.

When one had identified the regularities in a class of customary events, it is more possible to make sense of the variations. These too can be described, noting in each case what context the variation occurred and what the participants did about it.

There are a variety of uses one can make of careful mappings of the integration of actions in an event. First, one can abstract the characteristics, formats, or rules of this class of event in a particular tradition. Then comparisons can be made between its form in other traditions or between this sort of event and another sort. Second, one can derive the function or meaning of an event by showing just what contexts elicit its occurrence and what difference the occurrence makes. In fact, such questions can be asked about any particular occurrence within an event. In this way we can determine the significance of a particular facial display, gesture, posture, sequence of touch, or linguistic statement. But notice how meaning is defined in a structural approach. It is defined by what it "does," so to speak, in social and communicational processes. What a behavior means psychologically can be quite another thing as I will explain later on in this paper.

A structural study of events will leave many questions unanswered. It will not tell us about cognition, physiology, or metabolism. It will not tell us much about the life-long personality traits of participants either. It is not primarily a science of people but rather *it is a science of events*. But once we know about the structure of human events we can learn much about its participants. We also have another basis for making inferences about unseen physiological processes and mechanisms.

PART III. ORGANISMIC PROCESSES IN COMMUNICATIONAL FIELDS

Obviously it takes people to do communication. Abstract maps of the shape of communicational events tell us what is expected but they do not depict communication itself. We should bridge the gap between a science of events and the sciences of people and intraorganismic processes.

Individual and Cultural Differences in Communicative Behavior

It is apparent that all people do not act alike in communicational activities. In fact no two people carry out even the most ritualized event in quite the same manner and style. On this account we can observe the participation of various kinds of people in an event of known structure and make inferences about the people. We can infer their styles, their affective states, their exercise of options, their proclivity to conform or deviate, and so on. We can gain another dimension on these matters by interviewing the participants or by showing them film recordings of their own behavior and inquiring systematically about *their* interpretations.

By such measures we can gain information about the relation of performance to mood, personality, age, status, gender, and so on. Individual psychology can thus be placed in a perspective of action-in-context. But performances do not vary on the basis of personality, role, and organismic state alone. Events vary by region, occupational group, class, and ethnicity. So the type of participation and the type of event provides us as well with a record of social memberships and cultural backgrounds.

If we are willing to deal with this degree of complexity, we can systematically study participation in relation to individual and categorical differences. However, we cannot follow the reductionistic practices of some theorists of communication and claim that differences in participation can be explained by psychological theories alone. Nor can we hold that communicational behavior is the same the world over and therefore say it is genetically determined. Some elements of communicative behavior are morphologically similar in much of our species but the *organization* of behaviors in events differs from one tradition to another.

Metabehavior and Change

There is another major concern in the sciences of human experience that goes beyond the issue of individual, categorical, and cultural differences. So far I have written as though people passively enact the programs of their background in a ritualistic way. People may act ritualistically in ceremonies and in some situations in everyday life; but it is evident to us from common experience that this is by no means always or even usually the case. The fact is that people alter, modify, clarify, manipulate, and adapt their participation in customary events. They even contrive and innovate new ones.

Thus a theory of communication must countenance changes too. In order to do so we can make use of a distinction that was originally offered to us by Bateson (1955). He pointed out that people provide signals *about* the ongoing processes in which they were involved. They smile to indicate teasing, for instance, and distinguish it from naked aggression. This behavior alone can alter the course of an event. There are many other behaviors of this kind. People can employ flirtation routines to gain the floor in a discussion. They can display dominance to alter an argument. They can stop the stream of activities and request, suggest, or mandate a change in the agenda. And they can effectively boycott an activity or stage a movement for change.

Bateson used the term "metacommunication" to describe this sort of behavior. It is behavior *about* what is happening. We know that people also have feelings, beliefs, and attitudes about the events they engage in. Many of these are thought about and experienced emotionally while a person participates in an event. Some of them are stated, and many are reflected in facial displays and movement qualities.

When they are visibly or audibly manifest they are communicative—or metacommunicative by Bateson's definition. *They are signals and cues as* well as expressions and reactions and they can modify, govern, or even terminate a communicational event.

In short, people do not only act in communication according to a traditional format. They act about, toward, and in defiance to such programs. We can write about the psychology of communication in these terms. *BUT we cannot systematically say what is metacommunicative unless and until we have done the structural work of learning the usual and routine shape of particular events in a tradition.*

So far I have made room in a structural perspective for two of the important concerns of psychology. Here is another: We can also deal systematically with deviations and pathologies of behavior when we have shown what is expected and usual in a particular kind of event. There is yet another consideration. Since people can behave predictably in an event, they must hold cognitive images of that event and have cognitive plans for enacting their particular contribution by neuromuscular action (Pribram, 1971). When we have described such patterns of action we can make inferences about patterns of cognition too. Certainly cognition is not usually made up of lists of variables or statistical tables.

But cognition must be infinitely more complicated than this. If people can be observed to act metacommunicationally, e.g., to show disapproval or approval, then we must postulate levels of metacognition too. These crudely correspond to the values and attitudes of the participants. But there must be more complex levels of metacognition. There must be images of alternative ways to participate and of alternative programs of action for the other participants as well. And there must be metalevels, too, at which people know how to construct new "grammers" of action and context. We have but vague ideas about these multiple orders of cognitive and metacognitive process. But we may soon develop them if we will take time first to observe and describe what activities people and other animals are capable of performing in a context.

Communicative Fields and Neural Organization

There is another aspect of suborganismic behavior that we must consider. We must ask about the *functional* organization of the human nervous system. And we must learn to do this in neural terms rather than only using abstractions about cognition.

We could approach this question by first taking a field view of communicational processes. Imagine how broad such a picture would have to be. Events are enacted simultaneously in millions of places and these occur around-the-clock in some time zone or another. In fact, the whole globe is now bathed in continuous broadcasts via transcontinental media. So communication is an endless, ubiquitous process. Every human being is continuously behaving in ways that are at least potentially communicative even though at certain times a person is alone. Even in sleep postural shifts and bodily movements continue. Communicational activity is nearly as universal as an electromagnetic field.

With this motor activity, neural processing is occurring in each human organism. Perceived events are decoded and compared with stored images in a way we do not understand. The integrates of these neural processes are continuously being encoded or transformed back again to neuromuscular patterns of activity. In short, *communicative codes and neural codes must be homologous and transforms are continuously made between these isomorphic forms of the code.* Communicative (motor) codes and neural codes are different forms of the same patterning and the process continuously occurs in, through, among, and around all human organisms.

From the standpoint of the field, people and groups are biased homeostats. We tolerate *a range of* variability and change. At one limit of this range we are conservative. We resist change and maintain the communicational status quo. At the other limit we support or induce change and thus maintain a dynamic equilibrium in human affairs that is hopefully adaptive.

Humans do not live in communicative fields alone; we also live in systems of reproduction by codes that are in some ways similar to those of communicational activity. We also live in fields of terrestrial-metabolic processes. Our activity in these fields is also coordinated by neural mechanisms. In one of these fields organisms are reproduced; in another, organisms develop and stay alive, and in the third they become persons and maintain relation to physical environments and to each other.

There are multiple modalities of behavior (one of which is language) by which people maintain relations in the communicative field. Hence the study of communication should include all of these, and embrace all of the behaviors by which people form, maintain, and alter relationships (Birdwhistell, 1970). This does include tennis and warfare. In fact it includes almost all behavior. Therefore the term "communication" *does not refer to a type of behavior.* It refers to a perspective from that we can visualize *conjoint or shared* organizations of behavior.

References

Bateson, G. The message, "this is play." In B. Schaffner (Ed.)., *Group process. Volume II.* Madison, N. J.: Madison Printing Co., 1955.

Benedict, R. *Patterns of culture.* New York. Mentor Books, 1946.

Bertalanffy, L. Von. *Problems of life.* New York: Harper Brothers, 1960.

Birdwhistell, R. L. *Kinesics and context.* Philadelphia: University of Pennsylvania Press, 1970.

Cherry, C. *On human communication.* New York: Science Editiors, Inc., 1961.

Duncan, S. Some signals and rules for taking speaking turns in conversations. *Journal of Personal and Social Psychology,* 1972, *23,* 283-292.

Goffman, E. *Encounters.* Indianapolis: Bobbs-Merrill, 1961.

Goffman, E. *Behavior in public places.* Glencoe: The Free Press, 1963.

Harris, Z. *Methods in structural linguistics.* Chicago: University of Chicago Press, 1951.

Harris, M. *The nature of cultural things.* New York: Random House, 1964.

Kuhn, T. S. *The structure of scientific revolutions.* Chicago: University of Chicago Press, 1962.

Levi-Strauss, C. *Structural anthropology*. C. Jackson (Trans.). New York: Basic Books, 1963.

Lewin, K. The conflict between Aristotelean and Galilean modes of thought in contemporary psychology. *Journal of Genetic Psychology*, 1931, *5*, 141-177.

Lewin, K. *Field theory in social science*. D. Cartwright (Ed.). New York: Harper Brothers, 1951.

Lorenz, K. *King Solomon's ring*. New York: Thomas Y. Crowell Co., 1952.

Marayama, M. The second cybernetic: Deviation-amplifying mutual causal processes. *American Scientist* (June), 1963, *51*, 164-180.

McBride, G. *A general theory of social organization and behavior*. St. Lucia: University of Greensland Press, 1964.

McQuown, N. A. *et al*. *The natural history of the interview microfilm collection of manuscripts in cultural anthropology*. Series XV 95, 96, 97, & 98. University of Chicago, Chicago Library, 1971.

Mead, M. *Continuities in cultural evaluation*, New Haven & London: Yale University Press, 1964.

Mehan, H., & Wood, H. *The reality of ethnomethodology*. New York: Wiley & Sons, 1975.

Pribram, K. H. *Languages of the brain*. Englewood Cliffs, N. J.: Prentice-Hall, 1971.

Sapir, E. *Language*. London: Harcourt Brace, 1921.

Scheflen, A. E. *Communicational structure*. (Rev. Ed.) Bloomington, Indiana, Indiana University Press, 1973.

Scheflen, A. E. *How behavior means*. Garden City, N. Y.: Anchor Press/Doubleday, 1974.

Shannon, C. E., & Weaver, W. *The mathematical theory of communication*. Urbana, Illinois: University of Illinois Press, 1949.

UNIVERSALS IN HUMAN EXPRESSIVE BEHAVIOR

I. Eibl-Eibesfeldt

Forschungsstelle für Humanethologie
Max-Planck Institute, Germany

I. CULTURAL DIVERSITY VERSUS BIOLOGICAL UNITY

Cultural diversity is a fascinating fact, so fascinating indeed, that man often seems to be inclined to believe that his behavior is shaped by culture alone, that it is molded by his social environment that passes on the traditions. Man learns his behavior is a widely accepted thesis; and everyday life seems to justify such statements. But if everything that determines our conduct could be learned as cultural relativism assumed to be the case, then problems would arise as far as humanity is concerned. What about our ethic norms? Are they solely made up by culture, each culture defining as good what contributes to its survival as Skinner (1971), for example, holds to be true? if so, we would be in a mess indeed, since what contributes to the survival of one culture does not necessarily contribute to the survival of another culture. And indeed, cultures developed cultural norms of conduct that imposed ruthless pressure on other cultures and even led to their extinction. This seems to prove the relativity of human norms of behavior. But at a second, more careful look, we shall discover that such cultural norms often are superimposed on phylogenetically evolved biological norms that are shared by all man as a common inheritance. Take the command "thou shall not kill" for an example. Biological man universally seems to have strong inhibitions to kill or maltreat a conspecific. He is programmed to react to certain pity releasing signals of submission like pouting, crying, or infantile appeals. However, nonetheless, he kills. Cultural man has superimposed on his biological filter of norms a cultural one demanding to kill the enemies of his group. He defines his people at the same time as the only real people, differentiating his group from all the others and treating them as if they were not real man.

Obeying his cultural norms he can kill, but in doing so, a conflict of norms occurs, since even though the biological filter of norms is superimposed by a cultural one, it is nonetheless in existence and responding to the cues to which it is tuned. Man might not be bothered by distant killing of a conspecific, e.g., by bombing their cities; in personal encounter, however, a feeling of guilt is experienced when men kill each other. Already Sigmund Freud (1950) pointed to this interesting fact. He found out that warriors who had killed are in many cultures considered as impure and therefore have to obey rituals of purification that Freud interpreted as an expression of bad consciousness: "Wir schliessen aus all diesen Vorschriften, dass im Benehmen gegen Feinde noch andere als bloss feindselige Regungen zum Ausdruck kommen. Wir erblicken in ihnen Äusserungen der Reue, des bösen Gewissens, ihn ums Leben gebracht zu haben. Es will uns scheinen, als wäre auch in diesen Wilden das Gebot lebendig: Du sollst nicht töten!" (Freud 1912, quotation from the newprint edition 1974 Vol. IX p. 330).

In recent years, human ethologists have again and again emphasized the biological unity of man as contrasted to the cultural diversity; a unity on which our hopes for a better future can be based (Eibl-Eibesfeldt, 1973a, 1975a).

The biological unity of man is most clearly visible when we start to examine man's expressive behavior. It is a striking experience, indeed, to come in contact with people of another culture who have not had any contact with the outer world so far, and to realize how easy it is to communicate on the basis of nonverbal expressive behavior. What are the cues, what are the universal patterns that allow man to overcome the barriers of communication that cultures erect?

II. UNIVERSALS IN HUMAN BEHAVIOR

Charles Darwin pointed to the fact that man is equipped with a repertory of expressive movements that need not be learned. Anthropologists, for a while, were reluctant to accept this. La Barre for example wrote in 1947: "The anthropologist is wary of those who speak of an 'instinctive' gesture on the part of a human being" (p.49). He consolidates this statement by pointing out cultural variables that have to be accepted and, finally, even includes laughing and smiling in this list. "Smiling, indeed," he writes, "I have found, may almost be mapped after the fashion of any other culture trait; and laughter is in some senses a geographic variable." On a map of the Southwest Pacific one could perhaps even draw lines between areas of 'Papuan hilarity' and others where a Cobuan Melanesian dourness reigned. In Africa, Gorer, (1947) noted that laughter is used by the negro to express surprise, wonder, embarrassment, and even discomfiture; it is not necessarily or even often a sign of amusement; the significance given to black laughter is due to a mistake of supposing that similar symbols have identical meanings. Thus it is that even if the physiological behavior be present, its cultural and emotional functions may differ. Indeed, even within the same culture, the laughter of adolescent girls and the laughter of corporation presidents can be functionally different things . . ." (p. 52). La Barre finally writes: "There is no natural language of emotional gesture" (p. 55).

To date I have been unable to locate data apart from these anecdotal remarks to back this statement. La Barre does not provide a correlational analysis of Papuan or Melanesian laughter. He evidently did not collect data, but provides a personal subjective impression. Similarly the generations of Birdwhistell (1963, 1967), according to whom there are no universals in the expressive behavior of humans, lack supporting evidence.

La Barre (1947) associates the different meanings that an expressive behavior can have uncritically with different cultures and does not ask the question whether or not a similar spectrum of meanings might be found in other cultures. Nor does he search for a possible common denomination.

In recent years interest in patterns of human communication was revived, modern techniques of filming allowed documentation and analyses and a wealth of information was gathered.

III. INBORN MOTOR PATTERNS OF EXPRESSION

In order to find out whether there are any inborn motor patterns of expression in man, I first turned to the study of those born deaf and blind who provided a clear-cut deprivation experiment of nature. Should these children that grew up in eternal darkness and silence exhibit the same facial expressions as people without such a handicap, it would constitute a proof. And indeed, the documentation revealed that the basic-patterns of facial expressions were present. The deaf and blind smile, laugh, cry, and show the expressions of anger and fear, to mention a few examples (Eibl-Eibesfeldt, 1973a, 1974a). Figure 1A shows a deaf and blind girl smiling and Fig. 1B shows the same girl crying.

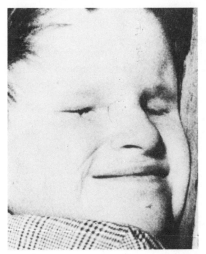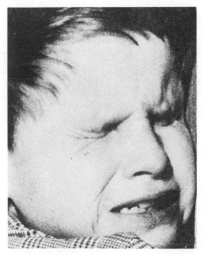

Fig. 1.   Deaf and blind born girl smiling and crying. (Photograph by the author.)

The argument that there is only a limited number of muscles available for producing facial expressions and that the probability of inventing similar expressions
therefore should be high, does not stand examination. There are at least 23 facial
muscles, most of them occurring in pairs. If we allow each of these 23 muscles to
assume only two stages of contraction, we have already 253 possible combinations.
Theoretically the possible combinations are almost unlimited. A smile therefore
does not occur by chance. Once in a discussion the argument was promoted that
the born deaf and blind might orient themselves by touch and thus learn the adequate way of behavior. It would be hard to believe that they could catch all the
cues, involved for example, in an anger-syndrome. Furthermore, we are in a position
to reject this hypothesis on the basis of the data. I examined born deaf and blind
thalidomide children who had no arms and who therefore were unable to touch
their mother's face, but nonetheless exhibited the typical facial expressions of man.
There remains only the slight probability that the mothers shaped the babies' responses by reacting adequately to their expressions. For such reinforcement, however, the patterns must be present and recognizable at first. A step-by-step shaping
unintended by the caretaker is highly improbable or would at least demand that the
baby is in a particular way tuned to pick the adequate cues that again would saddle
us with an inborn disposition.

The information derived from the study of the born deaf and blind is of great
theoretical interest, but limited however, since many of our social behavior patterns
are released by auditory and visual cues. Since these channels are blocked in them,
we have to explore other ways if we want to find out whether more complicated
patterns of social interactions belong to our phylogenetically acquired behavioral
program. We investigated this question by the study of the born blind and by cross
cultural comparison, including the study of the ontogenetic development.

By speaking to the born blind, we can release quite complex behavior patterns,
e.g., the pattern of coyness. We just need to pass a compliment to a young girl to
get blushing, lowering of the head, turning away in short cut-off behaviors in
alternation to patterns of approach by turning against the speaker, looking into
his direction and by smiling. A born blind boy hid his face behind his hands when
slightly embarrassed.

IV. THE CROSS-CULTURAL COMPARISON

A. Homologous Motor Patterns

The cross-cultural comparison is based on film documentation. Until recently,
ethnological documentation focused on aspects of material, cultural, and performances like dance and rituals. How people weave mats, how they form pots, or how
they build a hut, activities like these have been thoroughly documented. If one
however would like to see how people in different cultures greet each other, how

they hug their children, how they flirt or quarrel, then we will search for systematic collection of unstaged documents in vain.

We therefore started a cross-cultural documentation program filming people without their knowing it by means of mirror lenses (for details see Eibl-Eibesfeldt 1973a, 1975b). During the last ten years we focused on rapidly vanishing cultures that still followed their original way of life, choosing those that represented for different stages of cultural evolution. In regular intervals we visited the Kalahari Bushmen (!Ko, G/wi, !Kung) who live as hunters and gatherers, the Yanomami (Upper Orinoco) who are incipient horticulturists, the Eipo, Biami, and other neolithic horticulturists of New Guinea, the Himba (Kaokoveld, Southwest Africa) representing pastoralists, the Balinese representing rice farmers, and many other groups. We collected films of unstaged social interactions mainly. Every scene is accompanied by a protocol that states the context in which the pattern occurred (what released it), what followed it, and what had happened before to allow a correlational analysis at a later time. We furthermore avoid selectivity as much as possible by filming whenever an interaction is expected to occur, e.g., when people move or turn towards each other, not knowing in advance whether the interaction will be of friendly or aggressive type. The uncut original is archived. Film publications are made from duplicates. They are archived in our institute (Humanethologisches Filmarchiv der Max-Planck-Gesellschaft/Archive of Human Ethology, 8131 Seewiesen and the publication accompanying the films appear in the Journal *Homo* (Eibl-Eibesfeldt 1976).

The cross-cultural studies revealed that indeed, a great number of motor patterns occur universally in the same context. Certainly, not all of these need to be considered as inborn to man. Similar experiences in early life of the child may shape a behavior in different cultures along similar lines. Should it be true, for example, that the headshake signalling "no" derives from the child's turning of the head when refusing the breast after satiation as Darwin assumed, then this could well explain why headshaking occurs in so many different cultures as a signal for "no." We furthermore have to take the possibility into account that inborn learning dispositions may provide a bias for learning along similar lines in different cultures, a number of facts that we will discuss points to the existence of such dispositions.

There is certainly a great number of cross-cultural similarity to be explained by a shared function. There are not too many ways to push or kick an opponent, and if, therefore, similarities are encountered cross culturally, we would not uncritically assume that a shared biological inheritance exists. Even though it might be, I thought, for example, that hiding the face in a state of embarrassment is learned. Children hide themselves behind their hands and assume, since they do not see, that they are not seen at the same time. It seemed plausible that children in other cultures experience the same, which would explain the universality of the patterns. Since I filmed the pattern of hiding the face with a born blind boy, I am not sure anymore, whether it is indeed learned in the proposed way. Besides, in such dubious cases, there are many behavior patterns whose particular patterns or forms are not dictated by function. That smiling expresses friendly intent, crying and weeping, sorrow, and laughing, a particular form of aggression, is based on a convention. And it seems to be a phylogenetic grown convention, as indicated by the fact that they are passed on with apparent little change in contrast to undoubtedly culturally grown conventions that undergo rapid changes, that we need only to think of language. In New Guinea several hundred languages are spoken. One does not need too many generations to create new languages. It is the conformity in details that strikes the observer. I like to point the eyebrow flash as one particular example. I found that in a great diversity of cultures the following patterns of greeting occur: following a short uplifting of the head (headtoss) the brows are rapidly raised and held for about 1/6th of a second in raised position. This is followed by a nod and accompanied by a smile that may precede the eyebrow flash. I have discussed the original occurrence and functions of the patterns in more detail elsewhere (Eibl-Eibesfeldt, 1975b). I surmised that the expression was derived from an expression of surprise indicating friendly surprise by an accompanying smile and thus readiness for contact. We observe it while greeting, flirting, and thanking to emphasize agreement and in other situations expressing contact readiness. There are other lines of ritualization to be observed where eyebrow raising combined with a threat stare indicates contempt. In this case the eyebrows remain raised during the encounter.

Cultural differences affect the readiness by which an eyebrow flash is signalled. Polynesians easily give eyebrow flashes. They also greet the stranger by eyebrow flash and they accompany a "factual yes" with this signal. The Japanese, however, repress it during encounters with adults. It is considered as improper. Small children, however, are freely addressed in this way. We seem to hold the intermediate position. We use the signal while flirting, when greeting very good friends, and finally when emphasizing our agreement.

It is certainly the motor pattern "eyebrow flash" that ethologists consider as a "Erbkoordination" or "innate motor pattern." The term "fixed action pattern" is also used but it suggests a rigidity that is not given, a point discussed elsewhere in more detail together with the so often discussed term "innate" or "inherited" (Lorenz, 1965; Eibl-Eibesfeldt, 1973a, 1975b). The eyebrow flash regularly occurs in concurrence with the other innate motor patterns as smiling, head toss, and probably nodding and appears as a part of the given program.

Another behavior pattern that occurs as a universal sign of affection is the kiss. In all cultures I have studied so far, I found that mothers hug and kiss their little children, in Papuas as well as in Australian aborigines, Japanese, Balinese, Bushmen, Himba, Yanomami, and many others more. The cultural differences observed affect the use of this pattern in adult communication. In some cultures it seems to be tabooed, at least in public. The pattern derives from mouth to mouth feeding and links to homologous behaviors of nonhuman primates.

But let us turn to more complicated patterns. It was argued that mammalian behavior shows so much variability that one could hardly speak of any fixed patterns (Schenkel, 1947). Lorenz (1953) answered by showing that the intention movement of anger and fear in the dog results in a number of different expressions if we allow them to combine in various intensities of the different intention movements. In a similar way many of the human expressive patterns that at first glance seem so variable can be reduced to a number of "invariables" that super-impose or occur in alternation. Let's take the pattern of coyness as an example. A coy girl may look at a person, then lower the lid and turn the head away and after gaze aversion, return the gaze either by looking from the corner of the eyes, the head still turned away or by turns back to a full face-to-face orientation. See for example the pattern of coyness in a Zimba girl (Kaokoveld Southwest Africa) in Fig. 2a-i, released by the author with a compliment: "you are beautiful, I like you." A girl may in the same situation smile and at the same time activate the antagonistic muscles, suppressing the smile that results in what might be called a coy smile. She may hide her mouth behind her hand to hide the expression or may hide herself behind a friend or any object at hand and even clasp the object as if seeking protection. She may give a friendly eyebrow flash but at the same time

Fig. 2. The ambivalence of approach and withdrawal in a young Zimba girl in response to a friendly remark by a male subject. Eye contact is followed by gaze avoidance and reestablishment of eye contact. Smiling, a signal of contact readiness is suppressed. There is a clear fluctuation between the two tendencies. (From a 16-mm film by the author.)

avoid the eye contact by lowering the lid. She may look at you, but turn the chest away showing her shoulder. And she may even show some patterns of aggression like stumping the feet, hitting a nearby friend jokingly, laughing and biting her own fingers or nails or her lips. In short, it is evident that two systems are aroused at the same time, a friendly approach system and the agonistic system that controls the reactions of aggression and flight. The motor patterns of aggression and flight on the one hand are combined with the patterns of approach and of expressions of social contact readiness. They can be combined simultaneously or in alternation. And since many different patterns of both systems can be combined, a great variety of expressions occurs.

We have no difficulties to interpret and classify the pattern even when we encounter the situation in a completely different culture. This fits the findings of Ekman, Friesen, and Ellesworth (1972) who present people of literate and illiterate cultures, photographs and videotape recordings of staged expressions. The subjects recognized the expression of another culture with a high degree of accuracy.

The ambivalence expressed in the behavior toward his fellowman does manifest itself very early in life as stranger awareness which may express itself in varying degrees ranging from slight withdrawal responses to strong fear reactions. These being in conflict with responses of friendly contact seeking. Stranger awareness matures in children of all cultures and regardless whether the child has collected any aversive experiences with strangers. It is good demonstration of an innate maturational process during which the child gets responsive to fear-arousing signals of his fellow man. Personal acquaintance helps to buffer this fear-arousing effect. Amongst others the eyes are preceived with ambivalence, as is demonstrated by the patterns of gaze avoidance particularly during encounters with strangers. (For a detailed discussion and references see Eibl-Eibesfeldt, in press, a).

B. Cultural Convention and Inborn Motor Patterns

Movements accompanying "yes" and "no" are sometimes puzzling. It is well known that cultural variation exists but headshaking certainly is the most widespread motor sign accompanying a no. I filmed it among others in several Papuan tribes, the Yanomami Indians, the Kalahari Bushmen, and the Himba. The pattern occurs worldwide in a scatter distribution; but certainly it is not the only way to express a no. The Greek and many other people of the Mediterranean and Near East express a no by jerking their head back, closing their eyelids, often turning the head sideways and sometimes by lifting one or both hands in a gesture of refusal. This pattern can be observed in many other cultures as an expression of annoyance, e.g., when we are insulted by a proposal and thus refuse with strong emotional involvement, we demonstrate the same pattern. As a "factual no," however, its use is quite restricted.

The Ayoreo Indians of Paraguay have still another way of expressing no. They wrinkle their nose as if some pungent smell is encountered, close their eyes, and often push their lips forward in a pouting way. As a factul no the pattern is again quite restricted, but if we observe peoples' reaction to offensive smells, we find universal eyeclosing and nosewrinkling. The pattern derives from an attempt to block off the annoying stimuli.

The Eipo of New Guinea use two motor patterns to express no. The factual no is a headshake but if they refuse in a social encounter, then they push their lips forward—they pout. And pouting again is a universal pattern that people show when they are insulted and when they cut the contact off.

In other words, no certainly can be expressed in different ways but several patterns are adapted to be used, since they are already expressing a no, either in a social context or by refusing to accept a stimulus or simply by shaking something off.[1] The latter has the least emotional loading and thus offers itself more easily to express a factual no than others that could be interpreted as an insult. But sometimes cultures pick those patterns up by convention. The motor patterns in such cases are universal, which, however get their specific meaning as a cultural adaptation.

C. Analogies in Principle

Quite a number of behavior patterns prove similar on cross-cultural comparison although the similarity is not so much in form but in principle. Quite a number of these similarities are brought about by inbuilt biases on the receptor side, constituting a part of humans' phylogenetic adaptation. Animals as well as man are not only outfitted with motor patterns, they are also equipped with detector devices tuned at certain stimuli or stimuli situations. These often act as signals and release certain behaviors, it has, so to speak, an inborn knowledge. The receptor device by which reactions are released is called the "innate releasing mechanism." Numerous investigations have demonstrated the existence and explored the function of such innate releasing mechanisms. Ball and Tronick (1971) performed experiments with babies. Already a baby 15 days old responds to a symmetrically expanding dark spot projected at a screen with avoidance reaction and an increase of the pulse rate. They interpret the visual image as an object approaching in collision course although they never experienced such a situation before. An asymmetric spot does not release such an avoidance reaction. This and similar experiments prove the existence of inborn data processing mechanisms.

Some of our data processing mechanisms are tuned to signals coming from others. Babies, e.g., are characterized by a number of features that we perceive as cute. Some concern characteristic relationships, e.g., a large head in relation to the body, relatively short extremities, a protruding front in relation to a small face, and relatively large eyes. Furthermore, the cheeks seem to be signals. It is fairly easy to

---

[1] The explanation given by Darwin cannot be supported so far. It seems that the pattern derives from shaking something off, a motor pattern widespread in mammals and birds.

produce decoys that are cute, and by exaggerating, one characteristic feature is enough to produce the effect as can be seen by numerous cartoons, e.g., from the Disney productions where cute animals are produced by exaggerating the head size in relation to the body size. The baby features are universally the same and so is the response to the cute features that inhibit aggression. It is therefore not particularly surprising that a child participates in numerous rituals of encounter, when peaceful intent is demonstrated. When Yanomami Indians are invited to a feast they take women and children along. When entering the village the visiting warriors first dance in a warlike display, prancing and showing off with bow and arrow. This aggressive display is counteracted and neutralized in antithesis by a child dancing with the man and waving green palm leaves (see Fig. 3). In our culture visitors of states are greeted by shooting salutes (aggressive display) and in antithesis by children passing a bouquet of flowers. Advertisement, that is aggressive by imposing upon the television viewer, often is interspersed by friendly cartoons depicting children or cut animals.

In many nonhuman primates peculiar phallic displays have been described that serve the function of aggressive threat. When a group of vervet monkeys forges on the ground, some males sit guard with their back to the group exposing their brilliantly colored genitals (red penis, blue scrotum). When conspecifics of another group approach, an erection occurs. This phallic threat has the function of spacing and it is derived from a mounting threat. Mounting indicates dominance in many mammals.

Fig. 3. Greeting display of a Yanomami: The visitor dances with aggressive display in front of his hosts. His behavior serves to preclude any attempts of domination by his partners. In antithesis a friendly appeal is presented via the accompanying child, who dances and waves green palm fronds. (Photography by the author.)

Man now certainly does not sit guard in this way. But he produces figurines serving as scare devils to protect his house and fields. They demonstrate facial expression of threat and phallic display. Such figurines are known from all over the world and so are phallic displays in aggressive encounters. The details of the pattern, however, vary. We know such figurines from Europe, tropical Asia, New Guinea, South Africa, and other places. Such figurines often are used as amulets, e.g., in Japan. They are supposed to protect the person.

Direct phallic threats occur during aggressive displays. They can be performed as mounting threat, just by certain gestures or even by a verbal threat. The male Eipo (Indonesian New Guinea), if startled, klick with the nail of their thumb repeatedly against their phallocrypt, thus drawing attention to their phallic display organ. Probably in situations of surprise one does not really know whether anything dangerous may happen and to saveguard oneself, the apotropaic display is shown. It includes also verbal utterances. The Eipo use sacred words that are taboo in everyday life. We follow a similar principle when calling the names of saints in situations of surprise or in the more profane situation of cursing.

Another interesting male display involves the emphasizing of the shoulders. Yanomami emphasize them by feather decorations, Japanese and Europeans by cloth. Broad shoulders are a beauty–ideal in man. If we look at the hairline on man's back, we will find that in contrast to the great apes the human hairline runs in an upward direction in such a way that a tuft on the shoulders is formed by individuals that have strong hair growth. We may assume that this tuft was even more marked in our hairy ancestors and that it served to enlarge the outline of the body. It must have been an adaptation to the upright gait, since it is missing in great apes. It is our hypothesis that a preference probably based on an innate releasing mechanism survived the reduction of the originally displayed organ and shaped the cultural invention of display organs. In a similar way, steatopygia emphasizes woman's buttocks. In some races it serves as a secondary sex characteristic of the woman and is appreciated as a sign of beauty. It is lacking in many other races. The fact, however, that the fashion in one way or the other still emphasizes the region by adding tufts, cushions, and the like, may indicate that the signal was formerly more widespread.

We can certainly assume that given biases in our perception will shape the cultural elaboration of signals. Koenig's (1975) recent monograph on the use of eyespot patterns in apotropaic designs provides a wealth of evidences to illustrate this fact.

The woman's breast is another signal used in apotropaic displays. Eipo women grasp, when surprised, their breasts from below with both hands, lift them in an offering way and sometimes squeeze milk. I found descriptions of the same pattern and paintings and carvings depicting the pattern from other parts of Melanesia, Polynesia, Australia, Europe and South America. Here, of course, a learning interpretation would provide the simplest explanation. Everywhere the breast is offered to a baby and certainly serves as a token of appeasement.

D. Verbal Clichees and Strategies of Social Interaction

The vocabulary and the grammar that people use when speaking is certainly a product of cultural evolution. But what people speak in a given situation seems to be the same in principle. Since this field has been little explored, I want to draw attention to this fact. When people greet each other, they exchange also a few words. The opening statement expresses concern: "How are you?" is a common phrase. It may also present a symbolic gift, e.g., by wishing sômething good ("Good morning"). The interaction is often continued by a dialog that really does not contain factual information. One person may do a statement like "fine weather today" whereupon the other may continue with another banality "But we could use some rain for the crops" and the other again may signal agreement "Yes, indeed, we could." It is not the factual information exchanged that is important. Both know already at the beginning that it is a nice day. But what is signalled is the information that the channels for communication are open and that both agree with each other. The interaction may finally end with another good wish on parting, again with a symbolic (verbal) gift.

Man verbalizes much of his instinctive behavior. Gift exchange is a universal pattern. It links analogous patterns in animals and it is probably based on inborn dispositions. But man can present gifts by verbal wishing and promising. He can mourn to express concern, but he can also do it verbally. Man can use verbal threats instead of fighting an opponent. Considering the importance ritualizations play in the course of evolution, e.g., replacing damaging fights by ritual, we have to consider the possibility that this acted as one important selection pressure in the evolution of language.

How a man is addressed in anger, how he is addressed by a loving one, what he utters when surprised, seem to be in principle universally the same. Parental appeals ("My baby", my little bird") play an important role in bonding, dehumanization ("You pig") in spacing, to provide just an example.

Our cross-cultural documentation revealed a number of universal strategies of social interactions. The strategies by which people put themselves in the focus of attention, the means by which a friendly encounter is initiated, the strategies of agonistic buffering or the etiquette which one must obey too in order to be given —to mention some examples—was found to be universally the same in principle. In fact, when small children perform these behaviors by nonverbal behaviors, the strategies look alike across the cultures. Variability results from man's ability to substitute a variety of behavior patterns as functional equivalents within a given framework of rules, characteristic for the particular strategy. Thus in a greeting encounter appeasement and bonding can be performed in a variety of ways and also the display which regularly goes with it. The antithetic combination of display with patterns of appeasement and bonding remains as a characteristic of the event, regardless of whether the display is performed by shouting "salut," performing a display dance, or firmly pressing our opponents hand. Similarly we can appease in a great number of ways, for example, via a child but smiling, bow-ing, laying the armor to the ground and taking off the gloves before reaching out for a handshake, are functional equivalents. We found that many of the diverse cultural rituals, for example, those of gift exchange, are cultural differentions of such basic strategies (Eibl-Eibesfeldt, in press, a, b; Hesschen, Schiefenhövel, and Eibl-Eibesfeldt, in press). Of particular interest in this context is man's ability to verbalize these strategies in totality. The rules according to which the event is structured remains nonetheless alike, regardless of whether the interaction is verbalized or performed through nonverbal acts. This discovery bridges the gap between nonverbal and verbal behavior and opens the way for the exploration of a universal grammar of social behavior covering both the verbal and nonverbal. A new field of "etholinguistics" opens up (Eibl-Eibesfeldt in press, a, b).

E. Cultural and Biological Ritualization

Cultural and biological ritualization follow a similar course since the operating selection pressures are in principle the same. Signals and ritualization concerns the evolution of signals; they have to be conspicuous and must convey unmistakably the meaning to the specific addressee. Movement patterns, during the course of their evolution into signals, get simplified, and at the same time, changes in amplitude of movement occur (mimic exaggeration). The performance is emphasized by rhythmic petition. The courtship ritual "Tanim Het" that we filmed and described elsewhere (Eibl-Eibesfeldt, 1974b) provides a good example. Sometimes movements freeze into postures (e.g., of threat). Biological and cultural rituals often start from similar preadaptations. Analogous patterns develop, therefore, independently. The way weapons are presented to demonstrate peaceful intent is similar in both man and animals. Boobies and other birds, e.g., demonstrate by sky pointing. The beak is turned away from the opponent toward the sky, clearly indicating that the weapon will not be used. When we present the gun in a greeting ritual, we follow the same principle. Presenting food to a companion serves as a function of bonding in man and in animals alike, and rituals of food and gift exchange develop in analogy. Many more examples of analogous developments in cultural and biological rituals could be added (examples in Eibl-Eibesfeldt, 1973a, 1975a). There are laws derived from functions that govern both developments.

F. The Positive Aspects of the Common Inheritance in Man

Ethologists have been attacked for pointing to biological determinants of behavior. I therefore want to emphasize once more the positive aspect of a common inheritance. This inheritance provides a base for common understanding and concern. Would it not be so, cultures would indeed behave like different species and it would be very difficult to surmount the communicational barriers that cultures erect. Ethnocentrism would flourish without any moral inhibition. That mankind still considers himself as belonging to one family, despite cultural diversity, is based on biological inheritance. Not that biologists do not see and appreciate the beauty of cultural and racial diversity, but in order to enjoy them, we should foster the feeling of unity in diversity and take advantage of our inherited programs in order to take the sting from ethnocentrism.

References

Ball, W., & Tronick, W. Infant responses to impending collision: Optical and real. *Science*, 1971, *171*, 818-820.

Birdwhistell, R. L. The kinesis level in the investigation of emotions. In P. H. Knapp (Ed.), *Expression of the emotions in man*. New York: International Universities Press, 1963.

Birdwhistell, R. L. Communication without words. In P. Alexandre (Ed.), *L'aventure humaine*. Paris: Societe d'Etudes Litteraires et Artistiques, 1967.

Eibl-Eibesfeldt, I. *Der vorprogrammierte mensch. Das ererbte als bestimmender faktor im menschlichen verhalten*. Vienna: Molden, 1973a.

Eibl-Eibesfeldt, I. Deaf and blind born girl (Germany)–Expressive behavior. *Homo*, 1973b, *24*, 39-47.

Eibl-Eibesfeldt, I. The expressive behavior of the deaf and blind born. In M. von Cranach & I. Vine (Eds.), *Social communication and movement: Studies of interaction and expression in man and chimpanzee*. London: Academic Press, 1974a.

Eibl-Eibesfeldt, I. Medlpa (Mbovamb)-Neuguinea-Werberitual (amb Kanant) Medlpa-Court dance. *Homo*, 1974b, *25*, 274-284.

Eibl-Eibesfeldt, I. *Krieg und frieden aus der sicht der verhaltensforschung*. Munich: Piper, 1975a.

Eibl-Eibesfeldt, I. *Ethology. The biology of behavior*. New York: Holt, Rinehart, & Winston, 1975b.

Eibl-Eibesfeldt, I. *Menschenforschung auf Neuen Wegen*. Munich: Modlen Verlag, 1976.

Eibl-Eibesfeldt, I. Ritual and ritualization from a biological perspective. Symposium organized by the Werner Reimers Foundation in Bad Homburg, October 25-29, 1977. In M. von Cranach et al. (Eds.), *Human ethology, claims and limits of a new discipline*, in press (a).

Eibl-Eibesfeldt, I. Human ethology—Concepts and implications for the sciences of man. *The Behavioral and Brain Sciences*. in press (b).

Ekman, P., Friesen, W., & Ellesworth, P. *Emotion in the human face: Guidelines for research and integration of findings*. New York: Pergamon, 1972.

Freud, S. *Totem und Tabu Teil II: Das Tabu und die Ambivalenz der Gefühlsregungen*. Imago 1, 213-227 und 301-333. Newprint by S. Fischer (Publ.) Freud Studienausgabe Vol. IX, Conditio Humana 1974, 311-363.

Freud, S. *Gesammelte werke*, London: Image Publication, 1950.

Heeschen, V., Schiefenhövel, W., & Eibl-Eibesfeldt, I. Requesting, giving, and taking: The relationship between verbal and nonverbal behavior in the speech community of the Eipo, Irian Jaya (West-New Guinea). In M. Ritchie Key (Ed.), *Verbal and nonverbal communication*. The Hague: Mouton, in press.

Koenig, O. *Urmotiv auge. Neuentdeckte grundzüge menschlichen verhaltens*. Munich: Piper, 1975.

La Barre, W. The cultural basis of emotion and gestures. *Journal of Personality*, 1947, *16*, 49-68.

Lorenz, K. Die entwicklung der vergleichenden verhaltensforschung in den letzten 12 jahren. *Zoologischer Anzeiger. Supplementum*, 1953, *16*, 36-58.

Lorenz, K. *Evolution and modification of behavior*. Chicago: University of Chicago Press, 1965.

Schenkel, R. Ausdrucks–Studien an Wölfen. *Behaviour*, 1947, *1*, 81-129.

Skinner, B. F. *Beyond freedom and dignity*. New York: Knopf, 1971.

FACIAL EXPRESSION, EMOTION, AND MOTIVATION[*]

Carroll E. Izard

University of Delaware

The purpose of this paper is to demonstrate relationships between nonverbal communication, particularly facial expression, and emotions and then to show relationships between emotion and motivation and behavior. There are two kinds of evidence that link facial expression and emotion. The first type of data comes from cross-cultural studies of facial expressions and their interpretation. Evidence for the universality of facial expressions supports the notion that they have an evolutionary biological basis and makes it reasonable to infer that they play some role in motivating adaptive actions. The second type of evidence comes from psychophysiological studies of emotion-related imagery, emotion experience, and facial expression. These studies demonstrate a relationship between emotion-specific cognitive processes and corresponding emotion-specific expressions.

A. FACIAL EXPRESSION AND EMOTION

People in general agree that emotion and facial expression are associated, but scientists are not in complete agreement about the nature of this relationship. Some theorists maintain that facial expression is a component of naturally occurring emotion. Others prefer to study facial expression or facial movements as units of behavior without making any assumptions about underlying emotion experiences.

Neither of these approaches assumes that there is always a one-to-one correspondence between a particular facial pattern and a particular emotion. An expression can be made voluntarily without a corresponding underlying emotion experience. In fact, one expression can be made in an attempt to hide the true inner experience. Although I assume that facial patterning is an integral part of naturally occurring emotion, the principal concern of this paper, I recognize that even innate expressions may have some overlapping or similar components.

[*]Part of the material for this chapter was adapted from: Izard, Carroll E. *Human emotions.* New York: Plenum, 1977.

31

1. The Universality of Facial Expression

The early work of Darwin (1872, 1877) and the more recent work of Eibl-Eibesfeldt (1971), Ekman, Friesen, and Ellsworth (1972), Hass (1970), and Izard (1971) has shown that certain emotions, referred to in this paper as fundamental emotions, have the same expressions and experiential qualities in widely different cultures from virtually every continent of the globe, including isolated preliterate cultures having had virtually no contact with Western civilization. The data from these investigations provide a sound basis for inferring that the fundamental emotions are subserved by innate neural programs. However, the fact that there are genetically based mechanisms for the fundamental emotions does not mean that no aspect of an emotion can be modified through experience. In most advanced cultures people learn to inhibit or modify the innate emotion expressions. While the innate expression of anger involves baring of the teeth as in preparation for biting, many people clinch their teeth and compress their lips as though to soften or disguise the expression. People of different social backgrounds and different cultures may learn quite different facial movements for modifying innate expressions. In addition to learning modifications of emotion expressions, sociocultural influences and individual experiences play an important role in determining what will trigger an emotion and what a person will do as a result of emotion.

As used in this paper the terms "innate" and "learned" do not imply an absolute dichotomy. In the wake of the long standing controversy over the nature of intelligence or IQ, Murphy (1958) remarked that "nothing is innate, nothing is acquired." Most behavioral scientists tend to agree with Murphy in the sense that virtually any response or behavior pattern requires some practice or experience. Innate emotion expressions come as close as anything to being an exception to Murphy's rule. For example, the prototypic distress expression (crying) appears at birth. The work of Dumas (1932, 1948), Fulcher (1942), Goodenough (1932), Thompson (1941), and Eibl-Eibesfeldt (1971) indicate that congenitally blind children express emotion in the same way as seeing children, although the expressions of the born-blind tend to deteriorate in quality with increasing age. The decrease in the quality of the expressions of the blind may be mainly a result of disuse, since changes in the expressive movements around the eyes are the most profound.

Cross-cultural studies of the interpretation or significance of facial expression and studies with the born-blind clearly points to a relationship between a particular expression and a specific emotion experience. For example both literate and preliterate people describe the inner experience of joy and sadness or anger and fear in the same way. Further, the cross-cultural data indicate that people in widely differing sociocultural settings tend to describe similar action consequences for the various emotion. It is easy to infer that the link between facial expression, emotion, and certain action or action tendencies is the inner emotion experience and its motivational properties.

2. Psychophysiological Studies of Facial Expression and Emotion

The second type of data that link particular facial expressions to corresponding specific emotion experiences consist of electromyographic studies of the facial muscles of expression during periods of self-generated emotion imagery and emotion experience. The EMG studies were based in part on early experiments by Izard (1972), which showed a relationship between emotion-specific imagery and self-reported emotion experience. In a typical study of this type, the experimenter requests a group of subjects to imagine a situation that makes them feel distressed or sad. They are encouraged to recall or imagine a sad situation and to visualize it as clearly as possible. After a few moments of such imaginative-cognitive processes, the experimenter asks the subjects to describe their inner experiences on an instrument like the Differential Emotions Scale, which represents the fundamental emotions with adjectival subscales. This procedure results in a reliable pattern of self-reported emotions. Essentially similar emotion profiles have been obtained from independent groups. Schwartz, Fair, Salt, Mandel, and Klerman (1976) asked normal and depressed individuals to self-generate happy, sad, and angry thoughts and feelings, and the thoughts and feelings associated with a typical day of their life. Using surface electrodes they recorded the EMG activity of the frontalis, corrugator, depressor anguli oris, and masseter muscles of the face. As in their earlier study this experiment showed clearly different profiles of facial muscle activity in the happy, sad, and angry conditions.

In the experimental conditions the profiles of the normal and depressed patients were rather similar in form. For example, in the happy condition the depressed patients showed considerably less change in the corrugator muscle and somewhat greater change in this muscle in the angry condition. The EMG profiles as a group distinguished between the normal and depressive individuals. The depressives showed an attenuated pattern in the image-happy condition. Further, the profiles for the two groups while imaging a typical day were strikingly different. The profile for the typical day in normals is rather similar to that of the profile for the happy condition, while the profile for the depressed patients visualizing a typical day looks like a mix of the sadness (distress) and anger profiles. The finding of a distress-anger pattern in the life of the depressed individual is consistent with both psychoanalytic theory (Abraham, 1968; Freud, 1968) and differential emotions theory (Izard, 1972).

A similar experiment was conducted by Rusalova, Izard, and Simonov (1975) with professional actors and actresses who were trained in the method of Stanislovsky. Their rigorous four-year training program in theatrical institutes emphasized the creation of genuine emotion as appropriate to the character and the situation.

The experimenters chose professional actors and actresses trained in the method of Stanislovsky because they knew both from theater folklore and from previous research (Simonov, 1970) that these people could create emotion in the laboratory. At least, the previous research showed that their imaging of emotion situations resulted in changes in the traditional emotion indicators (EEG, heart rate, respiration, GSR). In the first condition of the present study, subjects were told to experience the emotion and express it naturally. In the second condition subjects were asked to reproduce the same emotion states but in a situation, where they could reveal their feelings because of some personal or social reasons. The task was not to camouflage genuine feelings by facial expression of other emotion (e.g., joy instead of sadness) but to try to look impassive in a state of strong emotion. In the third condition the subjects were asked to show the facial expressions of the same emotion states without actually feeling any emotion.

Subjects started to self-generate each emotion after the signal "start" and tried to preserve the emotion state for 30 sec, when the experimenter gave the signal to "stop." Throughout the experiment subjects sat silently on a chair in a special chamber. They were told not to move their hands, legs, or body. Facial expressions were registered on videotape with simultaneous measurement of heart rate, and EMG of four facial muscles: frontalis, corrugator, masseter, and depressor anguli oris. On the average, the self-generated emotion states increased heart rate, activity of facial muscles, and emotion experiences as measured by the Differential Emotions Scale (Izard, 1972).

The greatest change in heart rate was registered in condition one when subjects experienced the emotion and expressed it freely and naturally. The lowest heart rate was recorded in the third condition during voluntary expression of an absent emotion. Difference between average heart rate in these two conditions were significant ($p < .01$). But even in the third condition heart rate generally increased against the background. Some subjects reported that they could not avoid emotion experience while reproducing facial expressions of this or that emotion.

Electrical activity of facial muscles markedly increased in the first and third conditions. Attempts to impede facial expressions during genuine emotion experience showed generally low activity of facial muscles, but in some subjects EMG activity markedly increased. Differences in facial muscle activity between three conditions were statistically significant ($p < .01$).

The EMG changes were generally consistant with those found by Schwartz, Davidson, Maer, and Bromfield (1973). In state of joy the highest degree of activity was recorded in the depressor anguli oris (smile), in fear the frontalis, in anger the masseter, and in sadness the corrugator.

B. EMOTIONS AS MOTIVATION FOR INDIVIDUAL ACTION

I assume that the emotions constitute the primary motivational system for human being. The underlying theory for this position, differential emotions theory or the theory of differentiated affects, has been presented in detail elsewhere

(Izard, 1971, 1972, 1975; Tomkins, 1962, 1963). Early statements of this position (e.g., Izard & Tomkins, 1966) were considered by some to represent an extremist view (Sarason, 1967). Actually a similar view of the importance of the emotions in behavior and human life had been stated earlier by a leading personality theorist (Leeper, 1948) and by a prominent learning theorist (Mowrer, 1960). Mowrer stated that "the emotions play a central role, indeed an indispensable role, in those changes in behavior or performance which are said to represent 'learning' " (Mowrer, 1960, p. 307). Mowrer went on to decry the widespread tendency in Western civilization to look upon the emotions with distrust and contempt and to elevate the intellect (reason, logic) above them. "If the present analysis is sound, the emotions are of quite extraordinary importance in the total economy of living organisms and do not at all deserve being put into opposition with 'intelligence.' The emotions are, it seems, themselves a high order of intelligence" (Mowrer, 1960, p.308). Mowrer, Tomkins, and the author, though differing in some particulars of theory, agree that it is experiential affect or as Mowrer terms it, the inner subjective field, that provides the ongoing motivational state that modifies, controls, and directs behavior moment by moment. A growing number of theorists and investigators have contributed to our understanding of the motivational and adaptive significance of differentiated affects.

1. Cognitive Transformations Versus Affect Induction in Delay of Gratification

Mischel (1974), although working within the framework of a cognitive theory of motivation, has conducted a series of studies that have definite implications for the thesis that emotion motivates thought and action. The series of experiments examined the effects of different types of imagery and ideation on willingness or ability of nursery school children to delay gratification. The procedural element common to these experiments consisted of showing the subject (age range 3 - 6) two food rewards (e.g., pretzel, marshmallow) and determining which the child most preferred. Prior to leaving the child alone in the experimental room with the reward the experimenter says to the child: "If you wait until I come back you can eat this one, " pointing to the chosen object, "but if you don't want to wait until I come back you can ring this bell and bring me back anytime you want, but if you do so you can only have this one" (pointing to the unchosen object).

Under these conditions Mischel and his students (e.g., Mischel & Ebbesen, 1970; Mischel, Ebbesen, & Zeiss, 1972; Mischel & Moore, 1973; Mischel & Baker, in press) report that the length of time the child will wait in order to obtain the most preferred food reward (length of delay of gratification) is a function of the cognitive processes in which the child engages. However, they found that the children would wait much longer when instructed to think "fun things" than when instructed to think about the food rewards. In elaborating the concept of ideation-as-cause, Mischel noted that any cognitive representation of the rewards that emphasized their motivational (consummatory, arousal) qualities, generates "excessive frustration" and reduces the ability of young children to delay gratification (in this case eating a preferred food reward). On the other hand, he argued that ideation about the nonconsummatory or less arousing qualities of the food rewards facilitates delay of gratification. With this argument Mischel, without explicitly acknowledging it, has admitted affect into his conception of the causal chain. He is saying in effect that if the cognition results in affective arousal or emotion, the results are quite different than if it does not.

It is reasonable to assume that cognitively (think-fun) or behaviorally (toy-play, used in another experiment) induced interest and enjoyment facilitated goal-directed behavior as measured in terms of delay of gratification. While cognitively induced distress or distress-hunger drive interactions (think-sad and think-reward conditions) reduced the children's ability to wait for a preferred food reward. Interest, joy, and distress can inhibit and otherwise alter drive states. Interest-excitement can cause one to entirely forget about lunch or other consummatory activities. We have also indicated that distress is often accompanied, especially in children, by a need for reassurance and comfort. Thus it is quite consistent with differential emotions theory that Mischel's think-fun (induced interest and joy) should facilitate delay of food gratification, while cognitively induced distress or distress-hunger drive interaction (think-sad, think-reward conditions) would fail to delay gratification.

2. Cognitively Induced Distress, Altruism, Self-gratification, and Conscience Development

The differential emotions theory interpretations of Mischel's findings is supported by three other experiments using quite different dependent variables—altruistic activity, self-gratification, and resistance to temptation. In the first of these experiments, Underwood, Moore, and Rosenhan (1973) instructed one group of children to think of things that made them happy, another to think of things that made them sad, and gave another group to cognitive instructions. After the cognitive manipulation was finished, the children (tested individually) were asked to help themselves to pennies from a container within their field of vision, but were also told that if they wished they could leave some pennies for the children who would not have time to participate in the experiment. Cognitively induced joy made children significantly more altruistic (left more pennies for nonparticipants) than did either the cognitively induced distress (think-sad condition) or the no-instruction condition. Further, the children who experienced distress or sadness were significantly less altruistic than the control subjects.

In the second experiment (Underwood, et at., 1973), the experimenters used the same manipulations but measured as the dependent variable only self-gratification (amount of money taken by each child during the experimenter's 60 sec absence from the room). That is, the children were not restricted as in the earlier experiment by the instruction that they might want to leave some pennies for nonparticipants. For male children the cognitively induced positive affect resulted in significantly more self-gratification than did the negative affect or the control condition, the latter two not having differential affects. For female subjects, both the joy and the distress produced significantly more self-gratification than the control condition, but they did not differ significantly in the two affected conditions. The investigators concluded that it was the emotion or affective experiences that determined the observed spectrum of effects. The differential effects of the two emotion experiences in male and female children require further study.

In an experiment with 7- and 8-year-old children, Fry (1975) found that a positive affect (think-happy) condition resulted in greater resistance to temptation than did either a negative affect (think-sad) condition or a neutral condition. The children in the think-sad condition showed significantly less resistance to temptation than did those in the natural condition. Fry attributed the experimental effects to the imagery-induced affective (joyful, sad) states and pointed up the implications of this conclusion for child-rearing practices. He considered it reasonable to infer the conditions that make for joyful or happy experiences increase ability to resist temptation while distressful experiences have the opposite effect.

C. EMOTION EXPRESSION AS MOTIVATION
IN SOCIAL INTERACTION

Long before infants can speak a single word, their facial expressions convey messages that are crucial in binding mother and infant in an affectional relationship and in the maintenance of the infant's well-being. These messages have vital importance not only because they are the infant's chief means of communication, but also because what they communicate is highly important. They indicate the emotional state of infants. Their facial expressions tell us whether they are happy or sad, angry or frightened, surprised or shy. If we could not "read" infants' faces, we could not understand their most important communication. We could not empathize with them or show them sympathy.

1. The Face as a Social Stimulus

The literature on the role of the face in the infant and child's social development has been reviewed by Charlesworth and Kreutzer (1973) and Vine (1973). Numerous studies show that the human face is an extraordinary social stimulus. Although there are inconsistencies in the findings on the face as a visual stimulus in infancy, some of these undoubtedly result from problems of measurement. A list of some of the more important findings will illustrate the significance of the face in early social development.

The infant will focus his eyes on the eyes of an attending person in a true mutual gaze by the age of three weeks (Wolff, 1963). The face (or a facial schema) is preferred by the neonate to various stimuli (Fantz, 1963; Stechler, 1964), and the more realistic the face the greater the visual fixation time of the infant (Frantz, 1973, 1966). The face in comparison with several other stimuli (photographs of nursing bottle and panda bear, checkerboard, bull's-eye target) resulted in more visual attention and motor quieting (including decreased heart rate) in six-month old infants (Kagan & Lewis, 1965; McCall & Kagan, 1967).

2. Smiling, Laughing, and Social Interactions

The weight of the evidence on facial expression indicates that the smile is an innate expression, preprogrammed in the human infant to elicit and assure a strong bond with the mother and to facilitate positive social interactions with other human beings. A morphological facsimile appears in the first hours of life and a genuine social smile enlivens the face as early as the sixth week postpartum. The fact that the infant smiles indiscriminately at all human faces from approximately three to five months of age probably testifies to the importance of smile-elicited affectionate behavior for the infant's welfare and healthy development. The effect of mutual smiling on the mother-infant relationship and infant development probably shows more clearly than any other situation the importance of emotion and emotion expression as motivational variables in human affairs.

Sroufe and Wunsch (1972) have conducted extensive research on the ontogenesis of laughing. Building on the work of Washburn (1929) and following suggestions of Spencer (1855), Darwin (1872), Bergson (1911), and Hebb (1949), they developed a heterogeneous set of stimuli and proceeded to conduct a number of systematic studies on large samples of infants.

These investigators' extensive studies of the development of laughter provide further support for the hypothesis that emotion is motivational and plays a role in guiding behavior. "We have observed repeatedly that when an infant cries he pulls back in the high-chair and turns from the stimulus, whereas when laughter occurs the baby maintains an orientation towards the agent, reaches for the object, and seeks to reproduce the situation" (Sroufe & Wunsch, 1972, p.1341). If the motivation for the behavior described here was solely a function of information processing or other cognitive activity, then the resulting positive or negative emotion would seem to be superfluous. However, the emotion is clearly related to the direction and intensity of the behavior of the infant. Further, as already suggested in the discussion of the smiling response, the infant's laughter (positive emotion expression) tends to elicit (motivate) joy and joy-related responses from the mother or caregiver and hence to deepen social ties and attachment.

In discussing the functions of laughter, Rothbart (1973) pointed out that if arousal due to incongruous or strange stimuli always elicited negative response (distress, fear), the infant would very likely be comforted by the caregiver and removed from the disturbing stimulus. However, when the infant responds to such stimuli with laughter, the mother or caregiver is inclined to reproduce the disturb-

ing stimulus, giving the infant the opportunity to experience and explore the situation. She also suggested that early laughter games may foster two kinds of learning:
(a) the development of general expectations and (b) the social experience of learning that one's actions (in this case expressive behavior) influence activities of other
people. The observations of other theorists and investigators, together with those
of Rothbart, make a good case for the adaptive value of laughing.

Rothbart correctly pointed out that it is the infant or child who initiates the
behavior sequence involved in mother-infant interactions surrounding distress and
laughter. The child's crying in distress initiates the mother's efforts to comfort and
care for the child, and in the laughter game, although the mother may present the
initial stimulus for arousal, if the child does not laugh the sequence is terminated
and the game does not begin.

3. Emotion Communication and Mother-Infant Attachment

Mother-infant attachment has been considered by many scientists as the foundation of social life, and the systems of behavior that constitute attachment are
usually considered to be closely related to the emotions (Bowlby, 1969).

Attachment can be described as a set of emotion ties that create a strong bond
between two individuals. In infancy the establishment and maintenance of these
ties depend in large measure on emotion communication via the facial-visual system.
The vocal expression of emotions (cooing, babbling, crying, screaming) also plays a
significant part in this special interpersonal relationship. The third important factor
in developing and maintaining attachment is the sense of touch and the exercise of
this sensory modality by body contact.

The emotion communication theory of social attachment does not rule out the
role of learning, but the type of learning that is important may better be explained
on the basis of exercise of innate tendencies and in terms of perceptual development, which go hand in hand as the infant grows. This crucial exercise of functions
is like learning in that growth and development of the relevant perceptual skills
requires practice that results from "stimulation"—facial-visual, vocal-aural, and
tactile interaction with the mother or principal caregiver. Further, through a learning process like classical conditioning, the infant may learn to respond to certain
idiosyncracies in the mother's emotion signalling and consequently develop some
idiosyncracies of its own.

The emotion communication theory is not necessarily inconsistent with
Bowlby's (1969) notion that much of the behavior in mother-infant attachment is
instinctive. He used the term instinctive, like contemporary ethologists (e.g., Hinde,
1959), to refer to a biological character that is environmentally stable—one that
is little influenced during the course of its development by variations of the environment. On the basis of the robust evidence for their universality, the facial
expressions of fundamental emotions meet all the criteria of biological characters
that are environmentally stable. Thus Bowlby's notion that the mother-infant
attachment is based largely on instinctive behavior is consistent with the emotion

communication theory of attachment. The latter holds that the infant's emotion communication system is based in large part on expressive responses whose morphology was determined through evolutionary-genetic processes.

With the emergence of language and the rapid increase in cognitive and social skills, involuntary (reflexive, spontaneous) emotion expression is no longer the only type of facial patterning that influences the mother-infant relationship. Probably as early as the last half of the second year of life the child is capable of two broad classes of facial expression. Any given emotion has an expression that occurs naturally or instinctively as a part of the normal emotion process. The same emotion can be expressed willfully or voluntarily as in the case in which one wants to convey to another that one feels a certain emotion. Voluntary expressions may be considered as a social skill and people (from infancy to old age) vary widely in the degree to which they develop and use this skill.

Voluntary expression may vary from something like "making faces" to a situation where an individual feels a little of an emotion but wants to show much more of it. In still other instances an individual may want to feel an emotion and may use the facial expression to facilitate the experience. While little is known about the relationship between ability to express emotions voluntarily and other personality characteristics, it appears to be a fruitful area for investigation.

4. Expression Motivated Behavior in Older Children and Adults

In an ingenious study with four to seven-year old children, Nevrovich (1974) used a variety of manipulations to induce distress or concern for others and measure the subsequent effects on altruistic activity. In each condition she had a group of four- to-five-year-old children and a group of five- to six-year-old children. In condition one a child was brought into the experimental room and shown a disorderly array of toys. The child was asked to put the toys in order "so your friends can play with them later; if you do not put the toys in order your friends will not be able to play with them and they will be sad." At the end of 20 min the child was asked whether they wanted to continue working on ordering the toys or go for a walk, a diversion uniformly perceived as interesting and enjoyable by Russian children. In this condition only four out of twelve of the four- to five-year-old children elected to remain in the room and finish the task of placing the toys in proper order. Six out of twelve of the five- to six-year-olds elected to remain and complete the task for the sake of their friends. In the second condition the children were given the same verbal instructions, but in addition they were shown pictures of children with sad faces looking at the toys in disarray, unable to play with them. In this condition seven out of twelve of the four- to five-year olds elected to forego the walk and remained to complete the task of ordering the toys; eleven out of twelve of the five- to six-year-olds did the same. In the third condition, in which the children were shown photographs of a child who was both sad and sick and unable to play with the toys because they were in disarray, even more of the children elected to forego the walk and complete the task.

Nevrovitch interpreted the improvement in task performance as a function of distress experience induced in the subjects by a combination of verbal instructions and photographs of other children showing distress that would be relieved by the subject's task-oriented activities.

In a study by Savitsky, Izard, Kotsch, and Christy (1974), male college students (N = 96) were treated either in a neutral or insulting manner and then given an opportunity to deliver electric shock to the insulter (confederate victim), who responded to the shock with a facial expression of anger, fear, joy, or neutrality. The insult had no effect, but the victim's facial expressions were clearly perceived by the subjects and two of them significantly influenced the amount of shock delivered to the victim by the subjects. The expression of enjoyment (smile) increased aggression while that of anger decreased aggression. The effect of the distress expression on a critical decision process had been studied systematically by Savitsky and Sim (1974). They showed judges a series of standardized one-minute videotape segments of individuals playing the role of juvenile offenders and expressing either distress, anger, joy, or no emotion in an interview with a person in the role of a social worker. The supposed offenders had all committed offenses that were prejudged to be equal in seriousness. The subjects' task was to decide what punishment they would recommend for the offenders. Savitsky and Sim found that significantly less punishment was recommended for the persons whose faces expressed distress while being interviewed than was the case for those who expressed either anger or joy.

5. Cross-Cultural Differences in Attitudes Toward Emotion: The Example of Shame

Although there is some evidence (Blurton-Jones & Konner, 1973) that sex-linked genes may influence the tendency to experience shame, the individual's social milieu and culture constitute other important determinants of the shame threshold. Each culture and subculture transmits certain norms or rules, the violation of which may lead to shame. Some findings from cross-cultural research on attitudes toward shame illustrate differences between cultures that probably originate from cultural differences in child rearing practices and peer interactions that constitute the socialization process. The data to be discussed were obtained by administration of the *Emotion Attitude Questionnaire* (Izard, 1971) to groups of American, English, German, Swedish, French, Swiss, Greek, and Japanese college students. The seven cultural samples varied in size from 41 to 153. Prior to the administration of the *Emotion Attitude Questionaire* (EAQ), the students had taken the *Emotion Recognition Test* and thus were familiar with photographs representing each of the fundamental emotions and with the names and definitions of the emotions.

EAQ question 1 asked: "Which emotion do you understand best?" Considering the average percentages of subjects from all cultures selecting each emotion, joy, as expected, was chosen more frequently than any other emotion, and not surprisingly shame was chosen less frequently than any other emotion. There are several reasons for the generally low frequency with which individuals indicated that shame was the best understood emotion. The shame face tends to hide itself and the experience of shame elicits a tendency toward concealment and isolation. It is a threat to the self-concept (or ego) to be seen with a look of shame on the face, particularly during adolescent years when the self- and body-image are relatively more vulnerable (at least in most cultures). In the socialization process children are taught to hide their shame. These factors lead to a great reluctance to admit to the experience of shame, much less to reflect upon it and try to understand it. In addition to these forces, the experience of shame tends to hamper logical thought and frequently there is little meaningful cognitive content accompanying the shame experience. This too makes it difficult for us to reflect upon and analyze and understand the shame experience. In comparing the responses across cultures, it was found that more Greeks than any other cultural sample indicated that they understood shame better than any other emotion. For Greek men, there were 29% who indicated that shame was the best understood emotion, and this figure is two standard deviations larger than the mean frequency for all cultures. There is no specific evidence as to why the Greeks deviated in this way. It is generally agreed by psychological and anthropological observers that the Greeks are relatively high on sociability and emotion expressiveness, especially Greek males. Perhaps the Greeks have a somewhat greater tolerance for the shame experience and are able to look at it more objectively.

The second EAQ question was "Which emotion do you understand the least?" In answering this question far more Japanese than any other cultural group selected the emotion of shame. The percentage for Japanese males was 68%, two standard deviations higher than the average frequency for the eight cultures considered together. The next highest frequency, that of Swedish males, was 40%. There is strong evidence that shame is a highly important emotion in the Japanese culture (Benedict, 1946), especially in the Japanese culture prior to the influx of Western influence. An act bringing shame upon the self, or more importantly, upon one's family and the Japanese society was perhaps the highest of crimes. In these earlier times shame must have been considered a highly intolerable emotion. Our data suggest that a strong negative attitude toward shame continues to prevail in Japan.

The third question of the EAQ asked: "Which emotion do you dread the most?" Here again the responses of the Japanese are quite distinct from all of the Western cultures, including the Greeks. Seventy-two percent of the Japanese males and 69% of the females indicated that contempt was the most dreaded of all the emotions. Both these figures are more than two standard deviations greater than the average frequency for the eight cultural samples combined. The data from the previous EAQ questions, as well as the interpretation of the Japanese psychologist who collaborated in this research, indicated that the Japanese students interpreted this question to mean "what emotion expression from other people do you dread the most?" The use of the look of contempt to elicit shame is well-known in Eastern and Western cultures, but apparently the look of contempt is generally considered an adequate cause for shame by virtually all of the Japanese. Thus for the Japanese, being looked upon with contempt is equivalent to being found in a shameful condition or situation.

There are many more cultural differences in the experiencing and expression of shame than we have touched upon here. It is reasonable to assume that the differences discussed in the foregoing paragraphs reflect real differences in shame thresholds and in the antecedents and consequences of the shame experience and shame expression. Although the data did not always justify clear explanations of the observed cross-cultural and sex-cultural differences, they did clearly demonstrate that these differences exist.

D. EMOTION COMMUNICATION, PSYCHOLOGICAL ADJUSTMENT, AND PSYCHOTHERAPY

The systematic use of nonverbal emotion signals in psychodiagnosis and psychotherapy has a meager history, but work in this promising area is increasing. This section of the paper will consider some studies that show the fruitfulness of studying nonverbal emotion signals as a means of understanding people and helping them therapeutically.

1. Emotion Perception and Emotion Expressions in Psychological Assessment

In an early study of person perception, Izard (1959) showed that paranoid schizophrenics attributed negative emotions to facial photographs more frequently than did normal subjects. Schizophrenics also showed much more ambivalence in making preference ratings of the faces. In a later study Savitsky and Izard (1970) showed that children make comparisons between persons on the basis of their facial expressions as early as four years of age.

In a study by Dougherty, Bartlett, and Izard (1974), the Izard photographs of facial expressions that were cross-culturally standardized to represent eight fundamental emotion categories were given to comparable normal and schizophrenic samples in the United States and France. Each group was asked to label the expressions in free-response style (EL) and later to categorize each picture into one of the eight emotion categories (ER). ER scores were about the same for the American and French samples, with both normal groups having significantly higher average scores than the two schizophrenic groups. Cross-cultural differences were found only when a separate series of complex facial expressions was used. Schizophrenic subjects had the greatest difficulty in responding appropriately to pictures depicting disgust-contempt and shame, and they exhibited a large positive response bias to the enjoyment category. The results for EL were not as decisive, but they were generally similar to those for ER. It is interesting to note that Tomkins (1963) has theorized that shame and contempt are highly important in the emotion dynamics of paranoid schizophrenics. The results of the present study lend some support to Tomkins' analysis.

Heimann (1967) studied facial motion in patients with psychopathological conditions. His technique consisted of making a moving picture of the subject, without the latter's knowledge, during an interview. Every tenth frame (picture) was then projected on a calibrated glass screen. The static parts of the face (root of the nose, inner corners of the eyes, and chin or incisors) served as reference points for two orthogonal axes. These furnished a means for measuring the movements of the movable parts of the face. The medial part of the eyebrows and the corners of the mouth were used as marker points for the most important movable parts of the face. The vertical and horizontal movements of each of the marker points were measured numerous times. He worked with two different indexes of facial motion. The first is a symmetry coefficient, which is an index of the relative left-right synchronization of facial movements. The lower the symmetry coefficient, the less symmetrical and less synchronized are the movements of the face. The second index relates to overall movement or motion and summarizes the mimic activity of marker points during a time sample. In a number of different samples Heimann found that schizophrenic patients showed considerable deviation from normals on his indexes of mimic activity or facial motion. The symmetry coefficient of schizophrenics was considerably smaller than that for normals. Even when left-right facial movements of schizophrenics were synchronous, one part tended to show larger movements than the other.

Gilbert (1969) reported a study that focused on the relationship between the young child's awareness of affect or emotion concepts and the relationship of such awareness to adjustment and performance. The 102 children, ages 4-6, were given six verbal and performance tasks, including sorting of facial expressions. According to the teachers' ratings, children who were more aware of their emotions were also more likely to express a range of emotions, to be emphatic, imaginative, and happy. Children with high scores on the emotion tests tended to be rated by teachers as having signs of ego strength and independence.

2. Emotion Expression and Physiological Arousal

A number of studies (Prideaux, 1922; Landis, 1932; Jones, 1935; Block, 1957; Learmonth, Ackerly, & Kaplan, 1959; Buck, Savin, Miller, & Caul, 1969; Lanzetta & Kleck, 1970) have found an inverse relationship between physiological (internal) arousal and overt expression under various stimulus conditions. That is, the more people show their emotion facially and in emotion-related gestures and actions, the less they experience internal arousal. Buck et al., 1969) presented their subjects with a series of slides that had been prerated on a pleasantness-unpleasantness continuum and measured their heart rate and skin resistance as they viewed the slides. Judges were asked to indicate whether the expressor was viewing a pleasant or unpleasant slide. The experimenters found that females were better negative expressors (senders) than males, and consistent with earlier studies they found a correlation between facial expressiveness and physiological responsiveness (skin resistance and heart rate).

In their study of the personality characteristics of "internalizers" and "externalizers," Buck *et al.* (1969) showed that internalizers were more introverted and had lower self-esteem than externalizers. Internalizers were also more impersonal in their vocal descriptions of their emotions. One finding that stands in apparent contradiction to the others showed that internalizers had higher scores on sensitization on the Byrne (1961) repression-sensitization scale. The puzzle here is that previous studies have described sensitizers as individuals who express their emotions freely rather than denying them. Further research will be required to elucidate the meaning of this finding.

Buck *et al.* (1969) offered a possible explanation of the oft repeated finding of a negative relationship between physiological responding (internal arousal) and overt expression. They suggested that experiences associated with learning to inhibit overt expression tend to be stressful and threatening and that the stress, and not the inhibition per se, produces the increased physiological responding.

Kleck *et al.* (1976) and Lanzetta, Cartwright-Smith, and Kleck (1976) have found situations in which the inverse relationship between external and internal expression does not hold. They found that individuals who thought they were being observed while receiving painful electric shock decreased both their external (facial) expression and their internal expression (heart rate) significantly more than individuals who thought they were not observed by fellow students.

Studies of expressiveness should probably allow for the possibility that voluntariness and involuntariness of expression, though commonly accepted as categorically different in terms of conscious control, actually vary on a continuum of awareness. Further, suppression of enhancement of voluntary external expression may be congruent or incongruent with one's conscious wishes or goals. Some voluntary (or partially voluntary) expressions, such as those that occur when one wants to show sympathy or control an undesired emotion may effectively regulate internal expression so that it varies directly with external expression.

3. Principles of Emotion Control and Psychotherapy

Most people have some ideas about how to manage emotions, and they try to implement these ideas in daily life. One of the more common notions is that one can control a particular emotion by assuming the expressive posture and frame of mind of a counteremotion. Early and recent scientific opinion support this notion.

> The free expression by outward signs of an emotion intensifies it. On the other hand, the repression, as far as possible, of all outward signs, softens our emotions (Darwin, 1872, p.22).

> Refuse to express a passion and it dies. . . . If we wish to conquer undesirable emotional tendencies in ourselves, we must assiduously, and in the

first instance coldbloodedly, go through the outward movements of those contrary dispositions which we prefer to cultivate (James, 1890, p. 463).

The educational and therapeutic value of the control of the expressive movements (including that of the tone of the skeletal muscles) lies in the fact that they may be used to trigger or to inhibit the emotions by the employment of relatively simple physiological procedures (Gellhorn, 1964, p. 467).

Man's emotions, though restrained and inhibited, are nonetheless sending impulses or preimpulses to his body, which he generally suppresses. Suppressed or not, emotions are sending messages which are intended to be acted upon. Emotions are messages to the body to be responded to as action or behavior. . . . Psychomotor (exercise) attempts to give all physiological and emotional messages to the body the restraint-free use of the body in a sort of "bill of rights" for the internal needs (Pesso, 1969, p.77).

Thus folklore and scientific opinion say that the person who looks, acts, and thinks happy will be happy and the person who looks, acts, and thinks sad will be sad. The experiments of Izard (1972), Schwartz *et al.* (1973, 1974), Rusalova *et al.* (1975), Moore *et al.* (1973), Underwood *et al.* (1973), and Fry (1975) show that cognition or imagery relating to a certain emotion state tends to be followed by conscious or felt emotion and by thought and action relevant to that emotion.

Some principles and techniques of emotion regulation and psychotherapy have been detailed elsewhere (Izard, 1971, Chapter 15), so only a brief summary will be presented here. Theoretically, any component of emotion or any personality subsystem that interacts with emotion is potentially a vehicle for controlling or regulating emotion. Indeed, in our present stage of developing a science of the emotions, it will probably be wise to consider all such possibilities for facilitating emotion regulation. Emotion expressive role-playing combined with appropriate cognitive processes should facilitate activation of desired emotions and inhibit undesired ones. One emotion can be used to activate, amplify, or attenuate another. For example, a little anger may assuage unbearable fear.

Two principles of emotion regulation pertaining to normal healthy development and effective personality functioning may be conceived as principles of emotion control. First is the principle or assumption that each experience of emotion has an inherently adaptive aspect. For this principle to work well, the individual has to execute the adaptive function or action called for by the inherent adaptiveness of the emotion. Second is the related principle of emotion control via integration of emotion, cognition, and motor activity into appropriate and effective person-environment or interpersonal interaction.

These two principles may be better conceived as principles of emotion utilization. They are principles that normal personalities can use to increase spontaneity and effectiveness. In addition to their use in facilitating effective functioning in normals, they are probably most applicable with mild to moderate adjustment problems. Ideally, all therapeutic programs would make some use of these principles.

References

Abraham, K. Notes on the pscyo-analytical investigation and treatment of manic-depressive insanity and allied conditions. In W. Gaylin (Ed.), *The meaning of despair: Psychoanalytic contributions to the understanding of depression.* New York: Science House, 1968.

Ainsworth, M. D. *Infancy in Uganda: Infant care and the growth of love.* Baltimore: John Hopkins Press, 1967.

Benedict, R. *The chrysanthemum and the sword.* Boston: Houghton-Mifflin, 1946.

Bergson, H. L. *Laughter: An essay on the meaning of the comic.* (translated by Cloudesley Brereton). New York: MacMillan, 1911.

Block, J. Studies in the phenomenology of emotions. *Journal of Abnormal and Social Psychology,* 1957, *54,* 358-363.

Blurton-Jones, N. G., & Konner, M. J. Sex differences in behavior of London and Bushman children. In R. P. Michael and J. H. Crook (Eds.), *Comparative ecology and behavior of primates.* London: Academic Press, 1973.

Bowlby, J. *Attachment and loss, Vol I. Attachment.* New York: Basic Books, 1969.

Buck, R., Savin, V. J., Miller, R. E., & Caul, W. F. Nonverbal communication of affect in humans. *Proceedings of the 77th Annual Convention of the American Psychological Association,* 1969, *4,* 367-368.

Byrne, D. Interpersonal attraction and attitude similarity. *Journal of Abnormal and Social Psychology,* 1961, *62,* 713-715.

Charlesworth, W. R., & Kreutzer, M. D. Facial expressions of infants and children. In Paul Ekman (Ed.), *Darwin and facial expression: A century of research in review.* New York: Academic Press, 1973.

Darwin, C. R. *The expression of emotions in man and animals.* London: John Murray, 1872.

Darwin, C. R. A biographical sketch of an infant. *Mind,* 1877, *2,* 285-294.

Dougherty, F. E., Bartlett, E. S., & Izard, C. E. Responses of schizophrenics to expressions of the fundamental emotions. *Journal of Clinical Psychology,* 1974, *30,* 243-246.

Dumas, G. La mimque des aveugles. *Bulletin de L'Academie de Medecine.* Paris, 1932, *107,* 607-610.

Dumas, G. La vie affective. Paris, Presses Universitaires de France, 1948.

Eibl-Eibesfeldt, I. *Love and hate: On the natural history of behavior patterns.* New York: Holt, Rinehart, and Winston, 1971.

Eibl-Eibesfeldt, I. Similarities and differences between cultures in expressive movements. In R. A. Hinde (Ed.), *Nonverbal communication.* Cambridge, Mass. Cambridge University Press, 1972, pp. 20-33.

Ekman, P., Friesen, W. V., & Ellsworth, P. *Emotion in the human face: Guidelines for research and an integration of findings.* New York: Pergamon Press, 1972.

Fantz, R. L. Pattern vision in unborn infants. *Science,* 1963, *140,* 296-297.

Fantz, R. L. Visual perception from birth as shown by pattern selectivity. In L. J. Stone & L. B. Murphy (Eds.), *The competent infant: Research and commentary.* New York: Basic Books, 1973.

Fantz, R. L. Pattern discrimination and selective attention as determinants of perceptual development from birth. In Aline H. Kidd and J. L. Rivoire (Eds.), *Perceptual development in children.* New York: International Universities Press, 1966, 143-173.

Frued, S. Mourning and melancholia. In W. Gaylin (Ed.), *The meaning of despair: Psychoanalytic contributions to the understanding of depression.* New York: Science House, 1968.

Fry, P. S. Affect and resistant to temptation. *Development Psychology,* 1975, *11,* 466-472.

Fulcher, J. S. Voluntary facial expression in blind and seeing children. *Archives of Psychology,* 1042, *38,* 1-49.

Gellhorn, E. Motion and emotion: The role of proprioception in the physiology and pathology of the emotions. *Psychological Review,* 1964, *71*(6), 457-472.

Gilbert, D. C. The young child's awareness of affect. *Child Development,* 1969, *40*(2), 629-640.

Goodenough, F. L. Expressions of emotions in blind-deaf child. *Journal of Abnormal and Social Psychology,* 1932, *27,* 328-333.

Hass, H. *The human animal: The mystery of man's behavior.* New York: Putnam's Sons, 1970.

Hebb, D. O. *The organization of behavior: A neuropsychological theory.* New York: Wiley, 1949.

Heimann, H. Die qualitative analyze mimischer bewegungen und ihre anwendungsmoglichkeiten. Bericht uber den 22. Kongress der deutschen Gesellschaft fur psychologie, Gottingen, 1967.

Hinde, R. A. Unitary drives. *Animal Behavior,* 1959, *7,* 130-141.

Izard, C. E. Paranoid schizophrenic and normal subjects perceptions of photographs of human faces. *Journal of Consulting Psychology,* 1959, *23*(2), 119-124.

Izard, C. E. *The face of emotion.* New York: Appleton-Century-Crofts, 1971.

Izard, C. E. *Patterns of emotions: A new analysis of anxiety and depression.* New York: Academic Press, 1972.

Izard, C. E. Patterns of emotions and emotion communication in hostility and aggression. In P. Pliner, L. Kramer, and T. Alloway (Eds.), *Nonverbal communication of aggression.* New York: Plenum Press, 1975.

Izard, C. E., & Tomkins, S. S. Affect and behavior: Anxiety as a negative affect. In C. D. Spielberger (Ed.), *Anxiety and behavior.* New York: Academic Press, 1966, pp. 810125.

James, W. *The principles of psychology.* New York: Holt, 1890.

Jersild, A. T., & Holmes, F. B. Children's faces. *Child development monograph,* No. 20. New York: Teachers College, Columbia University, 1935.

Jones, H. E. The galvanic skin reflex as related to overt emotional expression. *American Journal of Psychology,* 1935, *47,* 241-251.

Kagan, J., & Lewis, M. Studies of attention in the human infant. *Merrill-Palmer Quarterly,* 1965, *11,* 95-127.

Kleck, R. E., Vaughan, R., Colby, C., Cartwright-Smith, J. E., Vaughan, K., & Lanzetta, J. T. Effects of being observed on expressive, subjective, and physiological responses to painful stimuli. *Journal of Personality and Social Psychology,* 1976, *34*(6), 1211-1218.

Koestler, A. *The act of creation.* London: Huchinson, 1964.

Landis, C. An attempt to measure emotional traits in juvenile delinquency. In K. S. Lashley (Ed.), *Studies in the dynamics of behavior.* Chicago: University of Chicago Press, 1932.

Lanzetta, J. T., & Kleck, R. E. Encoding and decoding of nonverbal affect in humans. *Journal of Personality and Social Psychology,* 1970, *16,* 12-19.

Lanzetta, J. T., Cartwright-Smith, J. E., & Kleck, R. E. Effects of nonverbal dissimulation on emotional experience and autonomic arousal. *Journal of Personality and Social Psychology,* 1976, *33,* 354-370.

Learmonth, G. J., Ackerly, W., & Kaplan, M. Relationships between palmar skin potential during stress and personality variables. *Psychosomatic Medicine,* 1959, *21,* 150-157.

Leeper, R. W. A motivational theory of emotion to replace "emotion as disorganized response." *Psychological Review,* 1948, *55,* 5-21.

McCall, R. B., & Kagan, J. Attention in the infant: Effects of complexity, contour, perimeter, and familiarity. *Child Development,* 1967, *38,* 939-952.

Mischel, W. Cognitive appraisals and transformations in self-control. In B. Weiner (Ed.), *Cognitive views of human motivation.* New York: Academic Press, 1974.

Mischel, W., & Baker, N. Cognitive transformations of reward objects through instructions. *Journal of Personality and Social Psychology,* in press.

Mischel, W., & Ebbesen, E. B. Attention in delay of gratification. *Journal of Personality and Social Psychology,* 1970, *16,* 329-337.

Mischel, W., & Moore, B. Effects of attention to symbolically presented rewards upon self-control. *Journal of Personality and Social Psychology,* 1973, *28,* 172-179.

Mischel, W., Ebbesen, E. B., & Zeiss, A. Cognitive and attentional mechanisms in delay of gratification. *Journal of Personality and Social Psychology,* 1972, *21,* 204-218.

Moore, B. S., Underwood, B., & Rosenhan, D. L. Affect and altruism. *Developmental Psychology,* 1973, *8,* 99-104.

Mowrer, O. H. *Learning theory and behavior*. New York: John Wiley, 1960.

Murphy, G. *Human potentialities*. New York: Basic Books, 1958.

Nevrovich, A. Personal communication, Institute of Preschool Education, Moscow, USSR, 1974.

Osgood, C. E., Suci, G. J., & Tannenbaum, P. H. *The measurement of meaning*. Urbana: University of Illinois Press, 1957.

Pesso, A. *Movement in psychotherapy*. New York: New York University Press, 1969.

Prideaux, E. Expression of the emotions in cases of mental disorders. *British Journal of Medical Psychology*, 1922, *2*, 45.

Rothbart, M. K. Laughter in young children. *Psychological Bulletin*, 1973, *80*, 247-256.

Rusalova, M. N., Izard, C. E., & Simonov, P. V. Comparative analysis of mimical and autonomic components of man's emotional state. *Aviation, Space, and Environmental Medicine*, 1975; *46*, 1132-1134.

Sarason, I. G. Anxious words. *Contemporary Psychology: A Journal of Reviews*, 1967, *12*, 601-602.

Savitsky, J. C., & Izard, C. E. Developmental changes in the use of emotion cues in a concept formation task. *Developmental Psychology*, 1970, *3*(3), 350-357.

Savitsky, J. C., & Sim, M. Trading emotions. Equity theory of reward and punishment. *Journal of Communication*, 1974, *24*, 140-146.

Savitsky, J. E., Izard, C. E., Kotsch, W. E., & Christy, L. Aggressor's response to the victim's facial expression of emotion. *Journal of Research in Personality*, 1974, *7*, 346-357.

Schwartz, G. E., Davidson, R. J., Maer, F., & Bromfield, E. *Patterns of hemispheric dominance in musical, emotional, verbal, and spatial tasks*. Paper read at the meetings of the Society for Psychophysiological Research. Galveston, Texas, 1973.

Schwartz, G. E., Fair, P. L., Greenberg, P. S., Mandel, M. R., & Klerman, J. L. Facial expression and depression: An electromyographic study. *Psychosomatic Medicine*, 1974, *36*, 458.

Schwartz, G. E., Fair, P. L., Salt, L., Mandel, M. R., & Klerman, J. L. Facial muscle patterning to affective imagery in depressed and nondepressed subjects. *Science*, 1976, *192*, 489-491.

Simonov, P. V. Teoriya otpasheniya i psikofizyologiya emotsii. Moscow: *Izdatellstvo Hauka*, 1970.

Spencer, H. *The principles of psychology*. Vol. *I*. New York: Appleton, 1896. (1st ed. 1855.)

Sroufe, L. A., & Wunsch, J. R. The development of laughter in the first year of life. *Child Development*, 1972, *43*, 1326-1344.

Stechler, G. Newborn attention as affected by medication during labor. *Science*, 1964, *144*, 315-317.

Thompson, J. Development of facial expression of emotion in blind and seeing children. *Archives of Psychology*, 1941, *37*, 1-47.

Tomkins, S. S. *Affect, imagery, consciousness*. Vol. *I*. *The positive affects*. New York: Springer, 1962.

Tomkins, S. S. *Affect, imagery, consciousness*. Vol. *II*. *The negative affects*. New York: Springer, 1963.

Underwood, B., Moore, B. S., & Rosenhan, D. L. Affect and self-gratification. *Developmental Psychology*, 1973, *8*(2), 209-214.

Vine, I. The role of facial-visual signalling in early social development. In M. Von Cranach & I. Vine (Eds.), *Social communication and movement*. New York: Academic Press, 1973.

Washburn, R. W. A study of the smiling and laughing of infants in the first year of life. *Genetic Psychology Monographs*, 1929, *6*, 397-537.

Wolff, P. H. Observations on the early development of smiling. In B. M. Foss (Ed.), *Determinants of infant behavior. II*. New York: Wiley, 1963, pp. 113-134.

THE STATE OF THE ART:
Past and Present Trends in Body Movement Research

Martha Davis

The Institute for Nonverbal Communication Research
New York, New York

A HISTORICAL PERSPECTIVE

This book is a manifestation of the "movement movement," a reflection of the enormous growth in nonverbal communication[1] research in recent years. In the past five years alone more books have been published on body language than in the preceding 95. It is an idea that has found its time. But there is a considerable history of research on nonverbal behavior and it bears examination (Davis, 1972). The current wealth of studies and publications can give the impression that an "America" of nonverbal communication (NVC) has just been discovered; in fact much of it has been ventured into; it is the extent of the exploration that is new today.

In 1872 Darwin published a work on bodily expression of emotions in man and animals for which he had collected material for over 30 years. It might well have been a part of his *Origin of the Species* except that by the time he had accumulated observations of facial expressions, gestures, postures of his own children, mental patients, peoples around the world, animals, and he himself, he had enough to fill a book of its own. The patterns of expressive movement he observed were for Darwin no less stable and subject to laws of selection and evolution than anatomical structures. Darwin literally laid out a field and provided it with an important theoretical substrate.

After Darwin the field fragmented according to academic discipline and research trends of the times (see Table I). Apparently developing one line of Darwin's obser-

---

[1]I will use the following terms interchangeably throughout this paper: body movement, movement behavior, body language, nonverbal communication, nonverbal behavior, NVC, expressive movement, and kinesics. There are drawbacks to all of these terms, both aesthetic and theoretical. For purposes of this article I prefer the widest definitions to encompass research dealing with the anthropology or psychology of movement done at different periods and by widely divergent behavioral researchers.

TABLE I: Historical Perspective of Movement Research[a]

	Pre-1900	1900-1930	1930s	1940s	1950s	1960s
Developmental patterns	Darwin		Gesell ——→ Halverson Washburn Buhler	McGraw Spitz ——→	Mittelmann	Kestenberg
Expression of emotion	Darwin	James-Lange Landis Ruckmick	Jenness Goodenough		Schlosberg Frijda Bull	Ekman and Friesen
Personality-psychodiagnosis	Darwin Bleuler	Ferenczi	Allport and Vernon Reich ——————————→	W. Wolff C. Wolff	Lowen ——————→	Christiansen North Davis
Psychological interpretation of actions		Freud	Krout		Deutsch	Mahl
Cultural comparisons	Darwin			La Barre Efron	Birdwhistell ——→ Kurath Hewes ——————→	Hall Ekman Eibl-Eibesfel Lomax, Bartenieff and Paula‍
Interaction and Communication					Birdwhistell——→	Scheflen Condon Duncan Argyle Kendon Loeb Mehrabian Exline
Ethology	Darwin	von Frisch ———————————————————————→ Yerkes ——————→ Lorenz —————→	Carpenter	Tinbergen——————→ Armstrong	Hediger Morris———	Andrew Schaller Hinde Bowlig Van Hooff Marler

[a] Adapted from Davis, 1975, p. 27. N. B. These are key or representative authors, not of cours‍ complete listing.

vations, German and American psychologists became very interested in the potential of facial expression for revealing inner psychological states and feelings. The 1920s and 1930s saw a wealth of studies on how consistently people interpret facial expressions, whether blind-deaf children have normal facial expression, how knowledge of the context in which the expression occurs influences its recognition, etc. (cf. Landis, 1929; Ruckmick, 1921; Jenness, 1932; Goodenough, 1932). The study of facial expressions and their interpretation virtually died out by the 1940s. In later years it has been resumed by a few research psychologists (notably Frijda, 1953; Schlosberg, 1954; and now Ekman, Sorenson, & Friesen, 1969) who have done more sophisticated analyses that support the hypothesis that there are facial expressions that are consistently associated with specific "primary" emotions.

As Table I indicates there are areas of interest that remain largely separate over time. For example, the study of movement patterns in development has a history of its own. Most notable is the period in which Gesell and his associates mapped out normal stages of posture, locomotion, and prehension development in infants. They were interested in motor development as a reflection of normal maturation and raised questions as to the relationship between motor skills, intelligence, and normal development in general. They were the first to do minute frame-by-frame analyses of films of movement patterns (cf. Halverson, 1931). Some child psychologists attended to nonverbal behavior of children at play or with their mothers, but intensive study of social behavior and nonverbal interaction of children had to wait until the 1960s. A few psychoanalytically oriented child-development specialists have examined the importance of body language in early character formation (cf. Spitz, 1946; Mittelmann, 1954). The work of Kestenberg (1971) and her associates in the past decade greatly elaborated on this line of investigation.

Darwin assumed, as did early psychiatrists developing diagnostic criteria, that distortions in bodily expression accompany psychiatric disturbances. A few psychoanalysts contributed papers on motor disturbances associated with severe neuroses (e.g., Ferenczi, 1921). But the relationship between movement styles and personality seems limited in the 1930s and 1940s to two early and quite separate works—Allport and Vernon's experimental study of individual consistency in motor styles and Reich's clinical assessment of the relationship of body movement and muscle tension patterns to psychological defenses and "character armor." Allport and Vernon (1933) produced the first experimental evidence that individuals have characteristic ways of moving, consistent patterns of tempo, pressure, spatial stress, etc., across diverse motor tasks, and these movement patterns appear congruent with personality features. Reich provides in-depth psychoanalysis of one's style of walking, talking, gesticulating, etc., and its role in psychological defense mechanisms. Although Lowen and others influenced by Reich have continued this work, the subject of understanding personality through nonverbal behavior remains a research focus of relatively few researchers (e.g., Davis, 1975; North, 1971). Related to this intrapsychic focus, however, are the psychoanalytic studies of specific actions, e.g., Freud's interpretations of chance acts, Deutsch's observations of positions and limb actions of analytic patients, and Mahl's analyses of mannerisms and actions of individuals being interviewed. Historically one finds a thread of interest in what specific actions mean or symbolize, what they indicate about the mover's unconscious conflicts and feelings (cf. Krout, 1935; Deutsch, 1952; Mahl, 1968).

Table I illustrates that in the 1950s a new research trend emerges, initiated by Ray L. Birdwhistell. Abandoning the theoretical position that body motion primarily reflects inner states and intrapsychic processes, Birdwhistell has argued that it is one "channel" of communication, culturally derived and serving group organization, social role delineations, and cultural identity. The value of this shift in focus can be seen in the extraordinary analysis of group interaction that Scheflen reports, patterns between people of reciprocal interactions as regular as a computer program (Scheflen, 1965). Much current body motion research involves the study of communication and the sociology of nonverbal behavior, e.g., behavior in public places, greeting rituals, teacher-student interactions, etc., and today the ethologists, who have their own history of body motion literature (cf. von Frisch, 1967; Lorenz, 1966; Tinbergen, 1953; Morris, 1956), are quite at home with anthropologists, linguists, and sociologists interested in nonverbal communication. In some ways the body movement patterns of primates appear similar to that of humans, at least when one looks at at phenomena such as dominance hierarchies, greeting and affiliative behaviors, and patterns of group cohesion.

Finally there is the emergence of cross-cultural studies of movement. Darwin asked a number of missionaries in various parts of the world to answer a questionnaire for him on how people in other cultures expressed various emotions. Anthropologists have frequently noted the dance patterns of diverse cultures. But a concentrated focus on nonverbal behavior in everyday life cross-culturally is still quite rare. Of note here are Efron's (1941) comparison of Jewish and Italian gesticulating, Hewes (1955) comparison of sitting and standing postures around the world, and the "choreometrics" study of dance and work movement styles around the world (Lomax, Bartenieff, & Paulay, 1968).

Historically one sees a pattern from psychophysical-affective aspects of body motion to personality to interpersonal and cultural referents of movement in the scan of what is primarily attended to in any one period of time. Not coincidentally, what was long called "expressive movement" becomes commonly referred to as "nonverbal communication." And perhaps it is not a coincidence that whereas early writers focused on facial expression and muscle tension out of interest in emotion and anxiety, later writers interested in personality focused on movement style and characteristic postures, and current communications researchers may attend to group formation, proximity, eye contact, spatial relationships, and the like.

In many ways the "movement movement" appears to reflect and be a part of several current trends in behavioral research. One is the current stress on interpersonal and cultural determinants of social behavior. Another is an affinity with a kind of "neobehaviorism." Movement research is essentially the study of overt behavior and so lends itself to certain behavioristic orientations. Also it seems to be part of a renewed investment in naturalistic observation that becomes a common ground for researchers of very diverse disciplines and theoretical orientations. Above all, the movement movement reflects a renaissance in direct behavioral observation. Attempts at theoretical integration are still rather rare and tentative. While the nature-nurture debate may be found in the writings of Ekman and Friesen and Birdwhistell, and Birdwhistell himself is in his writing far more of a theoretician than a reporter of observations and findings, still the vitality of the movement research appears to be in the wealth of new observations. Finally, of course, there is the current "nonverbal" climate in psychotherapy and the shift of attention to body motion in the "new therapies" that encourage and draw on the NVC research.

One indication of the rather disorganized state of the movement research art is the chaotic welter of terms scattered throughout the literature. Every researcher seems to adopt his own terms, often without clearly defining what exactly he is referring to. Sometimes the terms are simple everyday action words such as "crossed her legs" or "smiled." Sometimes the terminology is adapted from another discipline such as linguistics (e.g., "kinemorphic construction") or computer technology (e.g., "monitors" or "regulatory behaviors"). In other cases the terms are interpretive ones (e.g., "sad face" or "receptive postures").

In recent years attention has turned to movement or dance notation systems as a source for systematic terminology. Some have utilized these as a critical part of their research (cf. Bartenieff & Davis, 1965; Lomax, Bartenieff, & Paulay, 1968). Others have considered them and apparently rejected them. However, there is very little debate on the subject in the literature.

For a final look at past research, I would like to utilize the movement notation systems as a source for a systematic terminology. Suppose one "translates" diverse movement studies into a common set of terms (Davis, 1975). That is, suppose one peruses the movement notation systems for concepts or terms embedded in them and then abstracts a lexicon for movement.[2] For example:

Rotation: turning on the axis of the limb or part that is moving
Floor Plans: general clustering and movement path of a group
Path Type or trace form: the character of the lines in space drawn by the tip of
                                     the moving part, such as straight or curved

With what becomes a long list of carefully defined terms, one can examine various descriptions of movement behavior and translate them into the standardized movement language like so (movement terms are in brackets):

The two soldiers stood in parallel [same bilateral position], legs akimbo with an intrafemoral index of 45 degrees [range, thighs rotated outward]. In unison [group synchrony], each raised his right upper arm to about an

[2] In the present exercise I used Labanotation (Hutchinson, 1970), Effort-shaped analysis (Dell, 1970), and Eshkol-Wachmann notation (Eshkol and Wachmann, 1958).

80 degree angle with his body and, with the lower arm at approximately a 100 degree angle [right-left distinction, range] . . . .

(Birdwhistell, 1970, p. 176)

His rhetorical gestures exhibited many of the tendencies found in the gestural behavior of ghetto Jews [recurring characteristics] : confined sweep [range] , "baton"–and "pointer"–type motions with hand [spatial path, upper limbs] . . . .

(Efron, 1941, p. 133)

In the study referred to, I examined 17 major pieces of research this way, including works by Ekman and Friesen (1969), Kestenberg *et al.* (1971), Efron (1941), Reich (1949), Scheflen (1965), and Birdwhistell (1970). Simply checking on a grid with the movement terms listed vertically and the research works horizontally, it is possible to determine who attends to what aspects of movement for a given description or study. For example (and not surprisingly) researchers concerned with social interaction concentrate on "group" terms such as synchrony between movers or group formation, while those focusing on personality and temperament accounted for most entries under "force" and "weight." What emerges from this analysis is the realization that

(1)   different researchers focus on different aspects of movement, each with his or her own "gestalt" of terms;
(2)   different aspects of movement appear to correlate with different psychological and cultural phenomena.

For example, two very different studies may talk about "body attitude" or "posture," but on close examination it is clear that they analyze it in very different ways. In the choreometrics project of Lomax, Bartenieff, and Paulay (1968), "body attitude" is defined in terms of spatial stress and trunk articulation (fixed, one-unit or two-unit twists and bends). These are sufficient to help distinguish large cultural groups. In contrast Lowen (1958) describes various "chronic postures" characteristic of different neurotic styles. To do so he focuses on areas of muscle tension and flaccidity, overall alignment, weight placement, and frozen defensive postures. Such examples abound. Studies vary enormously in terms of the degree of detail, kind, and relative constancy of the movement features. Considered as a whole they do not contradict each other at the level of straight description, rather they complement each other. Theoretically this suggests that (a) some current conflicts may be baseless because A is talking about apples and B is referring to oranges, and (b) there is something in the nature and complexity of movement that it simultaneously reflects very diverse aspects of behavior from cultural differences to social roles to individual differences and affect.

This descriptive analysis leads to a consideration of the nature of the movement dimension. Somehow, implicitly or unconsciously very diverse researchers seem to be saying that there are consistent relationships between certain dimensions of movement and certain levels of behavior; that one should cut out that range of terms and parameters which best yields information about that which one is interested in (Figure I). So if one wants to study social organization and interaction, focus on formation, synchrony, complementarity of positions, proximity, etc. (cf. Scheflen, 1972; and Kendon and Ferber, 1973). But if you are interested in affect look at "configurations" such as the set of muscle tensions in the trunk or the expression of the face and/or attend to the intensity and rhythms of muscle tension at a given moment (cf. Darwin, 1965). For aspects of movement related to personality, the literature suggests concentrating on the recurrent, persistent aspects of postural tension, spatial and rhythmic preferences analyzed in fine detail (cf. North, 1971), while cultural movement style draws on spatial and intensity patterns broadly defined (cf. Efron, 1941).

CURRENT RESEARCH DEVELOPMENTS

The previous historical overview brings us up to the 1970s. But what of the current research scene? What trends can be seen? Who is doing nonverbal communication research, where, and in what subjects? To explore the current situation in a general way, I have examined printouts provided by the Smithsonian Science Information Exchange (SSIE)[3] and issues of the Nonverbal Components of Communication (Paralanguage, Kinesics, Proxemics) Newsletter.[4] The SSIE printouts (26 reports from the 1973 edition and 47 different studies from the 1975 edition) cover funded research from mid-1971 to mid-1976. These are reports of research in progress, its location, funding, duration, and design. The NVC Newsletter is a less formal report of who is doing what and where. The eight issues I surveyed span a time period from mid-1973 to November 1975 (131 separate listings noted). In many ways these two sources compliment each other. The SSIE printout cites research that is primarily government-funded and includes many large grants mainly in psychology, education, and psychiatry. It has very few entries in anthropology. The NVC newsletter primarily chronicles work going on in universities and colleges by graduate students and professors in anthropology, communications, and linguistics departments. The SSIE deals with research in the United States, while by mid-1974 the NVC newletter was going to about 28 countries and has contributions from all over the world. Both sources appear to rely on contributions of information from the researchers, a factor that may skew them considerably. It is of course difficult to say how representative the two sources are taken together. References to animal behavior research are not well represented at all. Altogether there are about 270 different researchers and 204 separate studies cited in these sources.

[3] Research Date Package #D107: Nonverbal Communication, Smithsonian Science Information Exchange, 1730 M St. N. W., Washington, D. C.

[4] Edited by Mary Ritchie Key, Program in Linguistics, Univ. of California at Irvine, Irvine, California, 92664. After being discontinued in 1975, this newsletter has been reissued by Rosalyn Lindner, ed. Department of Geography/Sociology State University College at Buffalo, 1300 Elmwood Ave., Buffalo, New York.

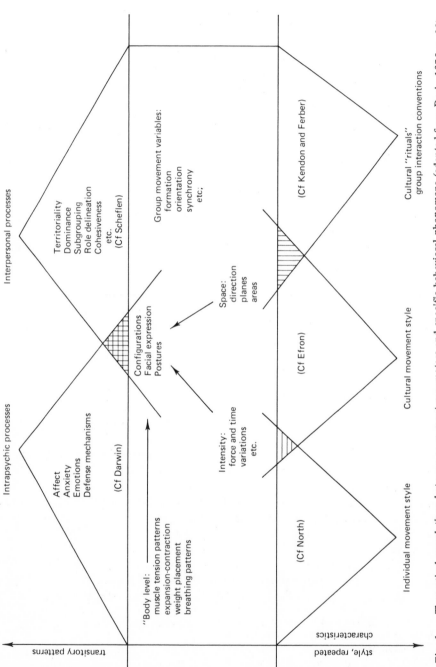

Fig. 1. Theoretical correlations between movement parameters and specific behavioral phenomena (adapted from Davis, 1975, p. 98).

(N. B. I have examined only those entries dealing to some degree with body language and have excluded references dealing *solely* with linguistic or paralanguage study.) It seems fair to estimate that the actual number of individuals who are actively engaged in the study of body language is close to three times this number. And this is not to mention the number of psychotherapists and teachers for whom the understanding of body language is an integral part of their work. Consider, for example, that the American Dance Therapy Association has a membership of over 600. But with due respect for the limitations of this sample, it does give an interesting picture of the current state of the art.

Overall, the subject appears to most involve those in anthropology, sociology, communications, and linguistics. In this sense it still reflects the interpersonal-cultural focus heralded by Birdwhistell in the early 1950s. Considering the SSIE source separately for a moment, there is a noticeable increase in funded research by psychologists and psychiatrists. From 1973 to 1975 the number of funded studies identified as within psychology or psychiatry more than doubles. An interesting new topic to emerge in the SSIE reports is the examination of NVC in medical settings, both in terms of doctor and/or nurse with patient interaction or the body language of patients with specific medical disorders. There are also the beginnings of support for the effects of drugs and alcohol on nonverbal communication. Another high priority new topic in the SSIE reports is NVC relative to classroom interaction and teacher effectiveness. A new focus on the development of kinesics from infancy into latency age is in evidence in both sources, but there is a notable lack of attention to adolescents in the research. Within the studies on development of gesticulation in childhood, there is reference to intellectual maturation, but the possibilities for research into NVC and cognition in general are not being realized as yet.

Another major development documented by both sources is the increase in parent-child NVC studies, particularly mother-infant interaction in the home. There is also considerable financial support for interaction analyses such as the rules for "turn-taking" in dyadic interaction. While there is very little cross-cultural research cited in SSIE except Ekman's cross-cultural affect display research, there is notable interest in social interactions involving ethnic groups such as in black-white encounters.

Subjects cited in the NVC newsletter are of course far more diverse. They range from greeting behavior in West Africa to turn-taking cues in American sign language; from sex differences in smiling to anxiety and gaze aversion; from the kinesics of bilingual children to Mexican father-son nonverbal communication. Most notable of course is the concentration of communication and "linguistic" aspects of nonverbal behavior such as its "syntax." Along with this appears a renaissance of attention to deaf sign language and formal sign languages of diverse cultures. There is indication in the NVC newsletter of increasing attention to sex differences in NVC but this is not so evident in the SSIE reports.

As has been mentioned, NVC research is being done all over the world. Sometimes it appears to be unfunded work done alone by a graduate student; sometimes it is well-funded research on various aspects of NVC done by a multidisciplinary team of senior researchers, fellows, and graduate students. University of California at Irvine, University of California at Los Angeles, and Penn State U. are often cited as having NVC research by various individuals. The places having the largest inter-disciplinary research projects seem to be Paul Ekman's Laboratory for the Study of Human Interaction and Conflict in San Francisco, Norbert Freedman's Clinical Behavior Research Unit at Downstate Medical Center in Brooklyn, a multidisciplinary group at the University of Delaware headed by Ralph Exline, and one at the University of Chicago represented by Starkey Duncan, Jr. These support NVC research in a diverse number of subjects. Perhaps the single most ambitious study of one topic and context is the study of nurse-doctor-patient interaction at Ohio State University School of Nursing directed by Jean Daubenmire.

Funding sources and amounts are rarely cited in the NVC newsletter but are usually listed in SSIE. The following observations about funding patterns are from the SSIE and so are skewed by its particular range of disciplines and subjects. It is notable that from mid-1971/1972 to mid 1975/1976 the average amount of the NVC grants peaks in the 1974/1975 period and there are indications funds begin to decrease after that. The total amount of reported funds for research in which NVC is a major part over this five-year period is about $1,200,000. An additional $600,000 for grants that note NVC brings the total to $1,800,000. Conjecturing further as to unreported funds, a reasonable estimate would seem about 3½ million in federal and foundation support for NVC research in the United States by mid-1976 with the possibility that it has already peaked. Of course, as can be seen in the NVC newsletter, the universities are at least indirectly supporting via salaries and fellowships a tremendous amount of NVC research that is being done by their professors and students.

The major source of funds within the SSIE printouts is the National Institutes of Mental Health (26 out of 73 reports) with a growing number from other branches of Health, Education, and Welfare (HEW) such as divisions within the Office of Education. The National Science Foundation Division of Social Sciences appears relatively uninterested in NVC (one in the 1973 report and four in the 1975 report). The Veterans Administration shows a noticeable interest by 1975 (one in 1973 report and 10 in 1975); otherwise, one finds a scatter of one or two projects over such sources as the Department of Defense, the Carnegie Foundation, and a few state governments.

Descriptions of the research itself are not often found in the NVC newsletter; and in the SSIE reports they are not uniform. Certain trends, however, can be detected. As might be expected in research that is largely government funded, priority is given to studies with strict experimental design or rigorous correlational measures. Naturalistic observation or the kind of systems analysis advocated by Birdwhistell and Scheflen is not readily funded according to the SSIE source. There are a few projects largely devoted to literature searches or to development of observation techniques per se.

In summary the overall picture is encouraging for its richness and vitality. To clinicians, educators, and others in service professions wishing to learn something of direct application to their work, the wealth of textbooks and anthologies available and the range of subjects found in sources such as the NVC newsletter is encouraging. For those interested in NVC research, the growing community of NVC devotees largely identified now through Mary Richie Key's efforts is encouraging, while the limitations of funds to certain topics and research methods of current interest to the government funding sources is sobering.

CLINICAL AND TEACHING IMPLICATIONS

Given the chaotic, undeveloped although vital state of the art, what can those in the helping professions do, who want information of practical value in their work? Given that little is experimentally established and a lot is conjecture, how can a psychotherapist or teacher make responsible use of NVC research? As a movement researcher who is also a practicing clinical psychologist, I offer the following suggestions.

(1)   Train your eye and your kinesthetic sense. Formal training in observation of body language is hard to come by. Notably there are two institutes in New York where one can take seminars in analysis of body movement: The Institute for Nonverbal Communication Research and the Laban Institute of Movement Studies, but you can do a lot on your own. For example, you might obtain a film or video-tape of an individual or group in the context of interest to you. Preferably the film or tape will show the person(s) from head to toe all the time. Cameraman editing often distorts and breaks up the nonverbal behavior. Remember that you lose detail in a longer shot. Ideally three or four cameras running simultaneously would give a full, well-detailed picture, but barring that unheard-of luxury, select a film or videotape that gives you the most complete view of what you want to study. An exercise you might find very helpful is to take a five-minute segment of your film or tape (cf. Richards, 1973), turn off the sound, play it once and then stop. In your own words write down what you saw. Then repeat the segment, stop, and again write what you saw in your "log." Do this ten time trying to keep as open as possible in your perceptions and in how your describe what you remember. You may interpret, describe minute details of action, make drawings, give literary associations, cite visceral reactions, do the movements yourself and describe how they feel, focus on one mover, or between movers, but try to do it each time forgetting what you wrote before. When you are done you can then scan what you have recorded. You probably will notice new details each time, your perception unfolding and developing as you go. Remember there is no one right way to observe, and for a teacher or clinician increased perception of nonverbal communication may be valuable in itself.

(2)   Appreciate the complexity and relativity of nonverbal communication. NVC is complex behaviorally as was discussed in the first section. There are hun-

dreds of details one can focus on. At any one time it reflects diverse psychological and cultural phenomena. NVC is also relative—it varies according to context, time, and participants. It is part of a total communication system. When you are in a situation such as a classroom or a therapy session, it is difficult to see how you and the others are moving together. But remember there are profound interactional effects. For example teachers may have more eye contact with students they regard as brighter or more competent (Kalish, 1971). Patients and therapists create interaction sequences together. These are not understandable as simple action-reaction sequences or in terms of who is doing what to whom; these are shared mutual dances. But they often recur and so you may in time get a sense of what "dances" you are involved in even as you do them.

(3)   Be respectful yet circumspect about your interpretations of body movement. Facile or premature interpretations may close you to what is going on or they may really be uninformed. The young woman with her arms and legs tightly folded in a psychotherapy session is expressing uptightness maybe and a sex- and age-appropriate position definitely. However, appreciate that impressions, interpretations, subjective reactions organize your perceptions and give order and sense to so much detail; they should not be dismissed. When you do interpret, ask yourself what about the nonverbal behavior suggested the interpretation. There are some suggestions in the literature as to how to interpret specific nonverbal patterns. For example the size and degree of tilt of a positions degree of smiling, and length eye contact is maintained appear to reflect the status relationship (cf. Mehrabian, 1972). That is, an interviewer will probably sit with more expansive, off-center positions, smile less, and hold his gaze longer than his interviewee. Or for another example, "chronic" or persistent facial expressions and body postures appear related to important affective components of personality (cf. Reich, 1949), as in the perfect verticality, slightly raised eyebrows, and delicate gestures of a perfectionistic person. But remember most of this is either clinical impression or is based on pilot research. Also your context may be unstudied or not matched by existing research, so such possibilities must be considered with a healthy reservation.

(4)   Consider how you want to use your perceptions. Clinically it is probably better to use your perceptions of NVC in a general way, i.e., to share your clinical impression of what is occurring with the client rather than to point out specific movements he or she made that tend to produce a great deal of not-very-useful self-consciousness. I think it is more helpful to say "you seem angry as you talk about that" than to say "I notice that you crumpled and tore up your kleenex just now." If you do explicitly discuss NVC, it is probably best to focus on persistent patterns because clients seem to connect or resonate with nonverbal patterns they have "lived with." In my experience the one time such explicit reference is clinically very good is when the therapist accurately perceives and describes a personal manner or persistent interaction that the client has long experienced but usually felt was trivial or not perceived by others. Here video playback may be very helpful for both to look at. Some clients do seem very relieved and animated when

a detail of their nonverbal manner is explicitly discussed and they may have a series of associations as to what it means to them that may surprise the therapist in their richness and animation. Of course when the therapist's observation is experienced as perjorative or caricaturing, it is not helpful.

You may also find body movement very helpful in the struggle to select what is most important or cogent to focus on at the time. There are so many dimensions therapist and client may attend to, and the problem of what is most relevant and at issue at the moment is an important one. I think that while movement behavior does not tell all the truth, it does not lie, and what you may perceive at the NVC level is usually one cogent dimension to pursue.

(5) Make use of the literature by visualizing it. If you are listening to a researcher or reading a report on NVC, ask what exactly in NVC are they talking about. Can I visualize the behavior? Can they give concete examples? If you cannot see it at least in your mind's eye, it will be very difficult to apply to your own experience. Best of all request film, videotape, or live demonstration of the research observations. Hopefully in the next five years there will be teaching tapes and films that will facilitate practical application of a subject that is best comprehended through nonverbal means.

References

Allport, G. W., & Vernon, P. E. *Studies in expressive movement.* New York: The Macmillan Company, 1933.

Andrew, R. J. The origin and evolution of the calls and facial expressions of the primates. *Behavior,* 1963, *20,* 1-109.

Argyle, M. Nonverbal communication in human social interaction. In R. Hinde (Ed.), *Nonverbal communication.* London: Royal Society and Cambridge University Press, 1972.

Armstrong, E. A. *Bird display and behavior: An introduction to the study of bird psychology* (repr. ed.). New York: Dover Publications, 1965.

Bartenieff, I., & Davis, M. *Effort-shape analysis of movement: The unity of expression and function,* Albert Einstein College of Medicine, 1965. Reprinted by Arno Press, 1972, in the series *Body movement: Research perspectives.*

Bartenieff, I,. & Paulay, F. Choremetrics profiles. In A. Lomax (Ed.), *Folk song style and culture.* Washington, D. C.: American Association for the Advancement of Science, Publication No. 88, 1968.

Birdwhistell, R. L. *Kinesics and context.* Philadelphia: University of Pennsylvania Press, 1970.

Bleuler, E. *Dementia praecox or the group of schizophrenias.* New York: International Universities Press, 1950.

Bolwig, N. Facial expression in primates, with remarks on a parallel development in certain carnivores (A preliminary work in progress). *Behavior,* 1963-64, *22,* 167-192.

Buhler, C. The social behavior of children. In C. Murchison (Ed.), *A handbook of child psychology.* Worcester, Massachusetts: Clark University Press, 1933.

Bull, N. *The attitude theory of emotion.* (Originally published, 1951.) New York: Johnson Reprint Corporation, 1968.

Carpenter, C. R. *Naturalistic behavior of nonhuman primates.* University Park: The Pennsylvania State University Press, 1964.

Christiansen, B. *Thus speaks the body: Attempts toward a personology from the point of view of respiration and postures.* Olso, Norway: Institute for Social Research, 1963. (Reprint ed. New York: Arno Press, 1972.)

Condon, W. S., & Ogston, W. D. Sound film analysis of normal and pathological behavior patterns. *Journal of Nervous and Mental Disease,* 1966, *143,* 338-347.

Darwin, C. *The expression of the emotions in man and animals.* Chicago: The University of Chicago Press, 1965. (Originally published, 1872.)

Davis, M. Movement characteristics of hospitalized psychiatric patients. *Proceedings of the Fifth Annual Conference of the American Dance Therapy Association,* 1970, 25-45.

Davis, M. *Understanding body movement: An annotated bibliography.* New York: Arno Press, 1972.

Davis, M. *Towards understanding the intrinsic in body movement.* New York: Arno Press, 1975.

Davis, M. Focusing beyond words: The nonverbal dimension of therapeutic interactions. Videotape produced at Hahnemann Medical College and Hospital, Department of Mental Health Sciences and Communications in Medicine Department, 1976.

Dell, C. *A primer for movement description: Using effort-shape and supplementary concepts.* New York: Dance Notation Bureau, 1970.

Deutsch, F. Analytic posturology. *Psychoanalytic Quarterly,* 1952, *21,* 196-214.

Duncan, S., Jr. Nonverbal communication. *Psychological Bulletin,* 1969, *72,* 118-137.

Duncan, S., Jr. Towards a grammar for floor apportionment: A system approach to face-to-face interaction. *Proceedings of the 2nd Annual Environmental Design Research Association Conference,* 1970, 225-235.

Efron, D. *Gesture and Environment.* New York: King's Crown Press, 1941.

Eibl-Eibesfeldt, I. Transcultural patterns of ritualized contact behavior. In A. J. Esser (Ed.), *Behavior and environment: The use of space by animals and men.* New York: Plenum Publishing Corporation, 1971.

Ekman, P., & Friesen, W. V. Nonverbal behavior in psychotherapy research. In J. M. Shlien (Ed.), *Research in psychotherapy,* Vol. 3. Washington, D. C.: American Psychological Association, 1968.

Ekman, P., & Friesen, W. V. The repertoire of nonverbal behavior: categories, origins, usage and coding. *Semiotica,* 1969, *1,* 49-98.

Ekman, P., Friesen, W. V., & Tomkins, S. S. Facial affect scoring technique: a first validity study. *Semiotica,* 1971, *3,* 37-58.

Ekman, P., Sorensen, E. R., & Friesen, W. V. Pan-cultural elements in facial displays of emotion. *Science,* 1969, *164,* 86-88.

Eshkol, N., & Wachmann, A. *Movement notation.* London: Weidenfeld and Nicholson, 1958.

Exline, R. V. Explorations in the process of person perception: visual interaction in relation to competition, sex, and need for affiliation. *Journal of Personality,* 1963, *31,* 1-20.

Exline, R. V., Gray, D., & Schuette, D. Visual behavior in a dyad as affected by interview content and sex of respondent. *Journal of Personality and Social Psychology,* 1965, *1,* 201-209.

Ferenczi, S. Psycho-analytic observations on tic. *International Journal of Psycho-Analysis,* 1921, *2,* 1-30.

Freud, S. Symptomatic and chance actions. In A. A. Brill (Ed.) *The basic writings of Sigmund Freud.* New York: Random House (Modern Library), 1938.

Frijda, N. H. The understanding of facial expression of emotion. *Acta Psychologica* 1953, *9,* 294-362.

Gessell, A. L., Halverson, H. M., & Armatruda, C. *The first five years of life.* New York: Harper & Row, 1940.

Goodenough, F. L. Expression of the emotions in a blind-deaf child. *Journal of Abnormal and Social Psychology,* 1932, *27,* 328-333.

Hall, E. T. *The hidden dimension.* New York: Doubleday and Co., 1966.

Halverson, H. M. An experimental study of prehension in infants by means of systematic cinema records. *Genetic Psychology Monographs,* 1931, *10,* 107-286.

Hediger, H. *Studies of the psychology and behavior of captive animals in zoos and circuses.* London: Butterworth Scientific Publications, 1955.

Hewes, G. W. World distribution of certain postural habits. *American Anthropologist* 1955, *57,* 231-244.

Hinde, R. A. *Animal behavior: A synthesis of ethology and comparative psychology.* New York: McGraw-Hill Book Co., 1966.

Hutchinson, A. *Labanotation or kinetography laban: The system of analyzing and recording movement.* New York: Theatre Arts Books, 1970.

Jenness, A. The recognition of facial expressions of emotions. *Psychological Bulletin,* 1932, *29,* 324-350.

Kalish, B. A study of nonverbal interaction in the classroom. *American Dance Therapy Association* Monograph No. 2, 1971.

Kendon, A. Some relationships between body motion and speech: An analysis of an example. In A. W. Siegman and B. Pope (Eds.), *Studies in dyadic communication.* Elmsford, New York: Pergamon Press, 1972.

Kendon, A., & Ferber, A. A description of some human greetings. In J. H. Crook & R. P. Michael (eds.), *Comparative ecology and behavior of primates.* New York: Academic Press, 1973.

Kestenberg, J. S. The role of movement patterns in development: 2, flow of tension and effort. *Psychoanalytic Quarterly,* 1965, *34,* 517-563.

Kestenberg, J. S., Marcus, H., Robbins, E., Berlowe, J., & Buelte, A. Development of the young child as expressed through bodily movement. I. *Journal of the American Psychoanalytic Association,* 1971, *19,* 746-764.

Krout, M. H. Autistic gestures: An experimental study in symbolic movement. *Psychological Monographs,* Whole No. 208, 1935, *46,* 1-126.

Kurath, G. P. Panorama of dance ethnology. *Current Anthropology,* 1960, *1,* 233-254.

La Barre, W. The cultural basis of emotions and gestures. *Journal of Personality,* 1947, *16,* 49-68.

Landis, C. The interpretation of facial expression of emotion. *Journal of General Psychology,* 1929, *2,* 59-72.

Lange, C. G., & James, W. *The emotions Vol. 1.* Baltimore: The Williams and Wilkins, Co., 1922.

Loeb, F. F. The microscopic film analysis of the function of a recurrent behavioral pattern in a psychotherapeutic session. *Journal of Nervous and Mental Disease,* 1968, *147,* 605-617.

Lomax, A., Bartenieff, I., & Paulay, F. Dance style and culture. In A. Lomax (Ed.), *Folk song style and culture.* Washington, D. C.: American Association for the Advancement of Science, Publication No. 88, 1968.

Lorenz, K. *On aggression.* New York: Harcourt Brace Jovanovich, 1966.

Lowen, A. *Physical dynamics of character structure.* New York: The Macmillan Company, 1971. (Originally published, 1958).

Lowen, A. *The betrayal of the body.* New York: The Macmillan Co., 1967.

Mahl, G. F. Gestures and body movements in interviews. In J. M. Shlien (Ed.), *Research in Psychotherapy Vol. 3.* Washington D. C.: American Psychological Association, 1968.

Marler, P. Animal communication signals. *Science,* 1967, *157,* 769-774.

McGraw, M. B. *The neuromuscular maturation of the human infant.* New York: Columbia University Press, 1943.

Mehrabian, A. *Nonverbal communication.* Chicago: Aldine-Atterton, 1972.

Mittlemann, B. Motility in infants, children and adults: Patterning and psychodynamics. *Psychoanalytic Study of the Child,* 1954, *9,* 142-177.

Morris, D. The feather postures of birds and the problem of the origin of social signals. *Behavior,* 1956, *9,* 75-113.

North, M. *Personality assessment through movement.* London: Macdonald & Evans, 1971.

Reich, W. *Character-analysis.* New York: Farrar, Straus, & Giroux (The Noonday Press), 1949.

Richards, J. Variations on a theme by Margaret: Improvisational introspection, the process of seeing. Unpublished paper, Hunter College, 1973.

Ruckmick, C. A preliminary study of the emotions. *Psychological Monographs,* 1921, *30,* 30-35.

Schaller, G. B. *The mountain gorilla: Ecology and behavior.* Chicago: University of Chicago Press, 1963.

Scheflen, A. E. The stream and structure of communicational behavior: Context analysis of a psychotherapy session, *Behavioral Studies Monograph No. 1,* Philadelphia: Eastern Pennsylvania Psychiatric Institute, 1965.

Scheflen, A. E., & Scheflen, A. *Body language and social order.* Englewood Cliffs, N. J.: Prentice-Hall, 1972.

Schlosberg, H. Three dimensions of emotion. *Psychological Review,* 1954, *61,* 81-88.

Spitz, R. A., & Wolf, K. M. The smiling response: a contribution to the ontogenesis of social relations. *Genetic Psychology Monographs,* 1946, *34,* 57-125.

Tinbergen, N. *Social behavior in animals: With special reference to vertebrates.* London: Methuen & Co., 1953.

Van Hooff, J. A. R. M. Facial expressions in higher primates. *Symposia of the Zoological Society of London,* 1962, *8,* 97-125.

Von Frisch, K. *The dance language and orientation of bees.* Cambridge, Mass.: Harvard University Press, 1967.

Washburn, R. W. A study of the smiling and laughing of infants in the first year of life. *Genetic Psychology Monographs,* 1929, *6,* 397-537.

Wolff, C. *A psychology of gesture.* London: Metheun & Co., 1945.

Wolff, W. *The expression of personality: Experimental depth psychology.* New York: Harper & Brothers, 1943.

Yerkes, R. M., & Yerkes, A. W. *The great apes: A study of anthropoid life.* New Haven: Yale University Press, 1929.

PART 2: RESEARCH APPLICATIONS

MEASURING SENSITIVITY TO NONVERBAL COMMUNICATION: THE PONS TEST*

Robert Rosenthal
Harvard University
Dane Archer
*University of California,
Santa Cruz*

Judith A. Hall
The Johns Hopkins University
M. Robin DiMatteo
*University of California,
Riverside*

Peter L. Rogers
Harvard University

Our purpose is to present some results of a program of research on the measurement of sensitivity to nonverbal communication. This research program grew out of earlier work on unintended effects of psychological experimenters' expectations on their research subjects' responses and earlier work on unintended effects of teachers' expectations on their pupils' intellectual performance (Rosenthal, 1966, 1974).

Much of the research on interpersonal expectations suggests that the mediation of expectancies depends to an important degree on nonverbal communication. Moreover, there appear to be measurable differences among experimenters, teachers, and people generally, in the clarity of their communication through different nonverbal channels. There also appear to be measurable differences among research subjects, pupils, and people generally, in their ability to understand nonverbal communications transmitted through different nonverbal channels. If we knew a great deal more about differential "sending" and "receiving" abilities, we might be able to learn what kind of person (in terms of sending abilities) can most effectively influence what other kind of person (in terms of receiving abilities). For example, if teachers who best communicate their expectations for children's intellectual performance in the auditory channel were assigned children whose best channel of reception was also auditory, we can predict greater effects of teacher expectation than if those same teachers were assigned children less sensitive to nonverbal communication in the auditory channel.

Ultimately, we shall want accurate measurements of each person's relative ability

*The development of the instrument described and much of the research employing it was supported by the National Science Foundation.

67

to send and to receive information in each of several channels of nonverbal communication. It seems reasonable to suppose that if we have this information for two or more people, we are better able to predict the outcome of their interaction, regardless of whether the focus of the analysis were mediation of interpersonal expectations or some other interpersonal transaction.

As a start toward this goal we have developed an instrument designed to measure differential sensitivity to various channels of nonverbal communication. We shall describe the instrument briefly, report on some preliminary reliabilities and validities (see appendix), and report some early findings. Not included in these findings are results of studies relating performance on the instrument to the mediation of interpersonal expectancy effects. A few such studies have been undertaken but their results have been sufficiently complex that they cannot be reported in the space available. In any case a good many more studies are needed before firm conclusions might be warranted.

The history of nonverbal research, though not very systematic, can at least be divided into two traditions. Since the time that Darwin (1965) drew attention to the expressive functions of facial behavior, most nonverbal researchers have concentrated *either* on the meanings attributable to various nonverbal expressions *or* on people's ability to recognize or express nonverbal cues, whatever their meanings. Researchers in the tradition of assessment of meanings, such as Birdwhistell (1970), Ekman and his collaborators (Ekman, Friesen, & Ellsworth, 1972; Exline, 1972; Hall, 1969; Mehrabian, 1972; and Scheflen, 1972), have asked such questions as "Do certain expressions have the same interpretation in different cultures?", "What is the psychological effect of communicating with someone at a distance of two feet rather than four feet?", and "What does increased eye contact with someone mean for one's feelings about that person?" Such an approach stresses the social meanings of different behaviors, and it has produced the body of research and anecdote that advertising men and market researchers make their livings on.

Incidentally, a number of popular books, like *Body Language* by Fast (1971), and *How to Read a Person Like a Book* by Nierenberg and Calero (1973), also emphasize meanings, although in these cases, mostly for the purpose of manipulating unsuspecting others (Koivumaki, 1975).

The second tradition included, in the early days, Guilford (1929), and Coleman (1949), who asked such questions as "Can people recognize facial displays of emotions?", "Can training improve recognition of emotions?", and "What are the differences in sending or receiving skill between men and women?" All of these questions involve ability or skill, and are less concerned with the meanings of specific cues. Later researchers such as Davitz (1964) (and the authors) have elaborated the measurement question to include the search for correlates of nonverbal ability and the description of individual differences. If a person is "good" or "bad," relatively speaking, at sending or receiving nonverbal cues, what factors may account for it? Of course, this approach requires the development of standardized measuring instruments before the systematic search for correlates can be attempted.

THE PONS TEST

The Profile of Nonverbal Sensitivity Test (PONS) is a 45-min sound black-and-white motion picture consisting of 220 2-sec audio and/or visual nonverbal stimuli (Rosenthal, Hall, DiMatteo, Rogers, & Archer, 1978). Twenty affective situations are represented, all of which are portrayed by a young woman. For each of the 220 times, subjects choose, multiple-choice style, one of two situational labels, one of which correctly describes the situation enacted in the clip and one of which incorrectly describes it. The 220 items consist of a random ordering of these 20 situations *each* represented in 11 different "channels" of nonverbal communication.

The 11 channels can be divided into five "pure" and six "mixed" channels. The three pure video channels are face only, body only (neck to knees), and face plus body, all with no sound. The two pure audio channels (with no video) are called "electronically content-filtered" (Rogers, Scherer, & Rosenthal, 1971) and "randomized-spliced" (Scherer, 1971). These names (abbreviated as CF and RS) refer to two methods of rendering the verbal messages incomprehensible. Electronic content-filtering removes certain critical frequencies from the voice, so the voice sounds muffled—as though coming from inside a closet. Randomized-splicing is a simple technique whereby audiotape is cut into many small pieces, rearranged randomly, and spliced back together again. This technique saves what electronic content-filtering destroys (pitch, intensity) but loses what electronic content-filtering preserves (sequence, rhythm). The six mixed channels consist, simply enough, of all audiovisual combinations of the two audio with the three video channels.

The twenty situations were portrayed as naturalistically as possible by a young woman, not an actress, who "sent" spontaneously, that is, knowing the affect but without prearranged script, to another person who stood just off camera. One hotly contested issue in all research of this kind is the choice between posed and naturally occurring affect. Both methods certainly have their problems, the former because of the danger of introducing overly stylized or stereotyped expressions, the latter because of two things—the extreme impracticability of trying to "catch" real emotions as they occur in people's daily lives, and the difficulty (once the emotion is caught) of identifying it correctly. The approach we used was, we felt, a compromise. Recent research indicates that abilities to send via spontaneous and posed cues are substantially correlated (Zuckerman, Hall, DeFrank, & Rosenthal, 1976).

Our portrayer "sent" in twice as many situations as were actually used in the final form of the test. A panel of judges who knew her (including the portrayer herself and her husband) rated all the audiovisual recordings for authenticity: They were asked, "Is this really how she would enact this situation in real life?" The twenty situations we used were those judged to be the most realistic. The twenty were also categorized (on the basis of the judges' ratings) into four types of emotion, each type created by the crossing of two emotional dimensions: dominance-submission and positivity-negativity. Hence the four types of emotion are positive-submissive, positive-dominant, negative-submissive, and negative-dominant. Five situations fall into each of these categories. Sample situations might be "admiring a baby" (positive-dominant), "being interviewed for a job" (positive-submissive), "being angry at someone for making a mess" (negative-dominant), or "showing someone that one's feelings have been hurt" (negative-submissive). All of the scenes are interpersonal in nature.

In its original length, each situation consisted of several short sentences that lasted 5½ sec, on the average. However, to our surprise, when we pretested subjects using the nonverbal stimuli in their original lengths, subjects were much too accurate, overall, for us to be convinced that the test could discriminate "good" from "poor" nonverbal readers. After experimenting with shortening the length of exposure of the nonverbal stimuli, we arrived at the 2-sec exposure length used in the test. These 2 sec were extracted from the central portion of each scene. Even at 2-sec exposures, subjects were still much more accurate than we would expect by chance (Rosenthal *et al.*, 1978).

RESEARCH RESULTS

Cultural Variation in the Perception of Nonverbal Communication

One of the most debated questions about nonverbal behaviors concerned the degree to which these behaviors are comprehensible across cultures. The essential argument in this field has been between researchers who regard gestures, facial expressions, and other nonverbal behaviors as universal or pancultural [among them Darwin (1965) and Ekman and his colleagues (1972, 1973)], and researchers who claim that these behaviors are culture-specific or culturally relative [among them Birdwhistell (1970) and Hall (1959, 1969)].

Despite (or perhaps because of) differences in the research designs and theories of various researchers, a review of the available literature appears to offer partial support for both the universalist and culture-specific positions. At least some nonverbal stimuli (e.g., the dramatized posed facial photographs of a very few emotions used by Ekman and his colleagues) seem to be recognizable at better than the chance level in several cultures. Conversely, many differences in gestural and kinesic behavior have been found among cultures, and even studies in the universalist tradition have found variance among different cultures in their ability to recognize the same set of nonverbal stimuli.

Almost all empirical research on the universality-specificity question has suffered from the following constraints: (1) the nonverbal behavior studied has almost always been limited to a single channel—with most studies employing still photographs of posed facial expressions; (2) the number of cultural samples studied has been small—with most studies comparing two or three samples and the largest study comparing nine; and (3) no consistent or lawful patterns have been discerned concerning the variation among different cultures in their ability to interpret the same nonverbal materials.

The PONS film overcomes at least some of the shortcomings of earlier research since it presents nonverbal behavior in several channels, and since the items in the film cover a wide range of emótional expressions. The film also includes movement and sequences of continuous nonverbal behavior, and this makes the PONS stimuli more naturalistic than the still photographs used in other studies. The PONS paradigm also has its own limitations, of course, including the presence in the film of only a single encoder.

Cross-cultural testing with the PONS could produce support for one of three general hypotheses concerning cultural variation in the perception of nonverbal communication:

(1) *Cultural specificity,* which predicts that only Americans would do well on the PONS test since the encoder in the film is American;

(2) *Cultural universality,* which predicts that members of all other cultures would do as well as the American samples and as well as one another; and

(3) *Cultural proximity,* an interactionist perspective which predicts great variation among different cultural samples (although all would be expected to do better than chance), and also predicts that this variation would follow a meaningful or lawful pattern.

The cultural proximity hypothesis predicts that samples with greater cultural and linguistic proximity to the U. S. (the culture of the encoder in the PONS film) will do better than samples less similar to the U. S.

As a test of these three general hypotheses, the PONS film was shown to about 2300 people outside the continental U. S. Fifty-eight cross-cultural samples were tested, representing nationals from 20 countries. In addition to the English language answer sheets, the cross-cultural testing used PONS answer sheets translated into Spanish, Hebrew, and German.

The major findings of this cross-cultural program of research were (1) great variation occurred among the 58 samples in their ability to decode the nonverbal behavior in the PONS film (suggesting that the universality hypothesis is not supported); (2) however, even the worst performing samples did better than chance on the test (the possibility of some pancultural nonverbal behaviors, therefore, is not eliminated); and (3) samples culturally and linguistically similar to the U. S., the culture of the PONS encoder, did better on the PONS test (the cultural proximity hypothesis is supported).

In general, the cross-cultural samples did less well on PONS than the American samples. The median PONS score of all 58 cross-cultural samples was 169.09 (76.85% accurate), while the median score of 54 adult U. S. samples was 175.87 (79.94%). Even the English-speaking cross-cultural samples were at a disadvantage compared with the U. S. samples. The median of the 32 English-speaking samples from Britain, Canada, Australia, and New Zealand was 171.94 (78.15%), higher than the cross-cultural average but still lower than the median for the U. S. samples. These differences may indicate that some of the PONS stimuli were culture-specific to the U. S., and that PONS may contain some nonverbal behaviors that reflect an American idiom. This finding may reflect the importance of nonverbal differences in communication even between members of different nations who share the same lexical or written language. For example, people from Britain and the U. S. may have difficulty understanding one another, not because of lexical differences, but because some intentions and meanings may be conveyed in nonverbal channels.

One of the most striking findings was the wide range in performance among the 58 cross-cultural samples. As an illustration of the variance in PONS performance, the mean PONS profiles of four cross-cultural samples, including the highest and lowest scoring, are shown in Fig. 1.

The highest scoring sample was a group of education students at the University of Sydney in Australia, with a mean PONS score of 179.50 (81.59%), and the lowest scoring sample was a group of teachers college students in Port Moresby, New Guinea, with a PONS total of 146.01 (66.36%). Even this lowest scoring sample, however, did better than 110 (50.00%), which is what would be expected by chance alone on a 220-item test with two alternatives for each item. For even this lowest scoring sample, at least some of the nonverbal stimuli in the PONS film, roughly 36 items (146-110), were interpretable across the barriers of culture. While this finding may indicate that there are some pancultural elements of non-verbal communication, it could also be a function of intercultural experience, since the members of this sample had some contact with Australians, Americans, and other foreigners.

Variation among the 58 cross-cultural samples appeared to be nonrandom. Differences in the ability of the 58 samples to decode the PONS film appeared to be a function of their similarity to the U. S., a finding that supports the cultural proximity hypothesis. Two indices of similarity were obtained: (1) ratings by anthropologists and lay persons of how culturally similar the samples and nations were to the U. S., and (2) rankings of the national samples in terms of their linguistic proximity (in the evolutionary descent of languages) to the English spoken by the woman in the PONS film.

The first of these indices of proximity, the ratings of cultural similarity to Americans, were obtained from five groups of raters at various phases in the cross-cultural research. Each group of judges was asked to rate several samples or nations on a scale measuring "cultural similarity to Americans," or to rank them in order of similarity to Americans. For each of the five rating studies (some of the same samples and nations appeared in more than one study), the mean similarity ratings of the samples were correlated with the mean PONS scores of the samples (or the unweighted means of several samples from the same nation). The results showed that correlations between the similarity ratings and PONS scores in the five studies were high: *rho* = .66 (30 samples, $p < .001$); .68 (12 nations, $p < .02$); .74 (20 nations, $p < .001$); .79 (seven samples, $p < .02$); and .83 (12 samples, $p < .003$).

For all five groups of raters, then, the ratings or rankings were significantly related to PONS scores, samples and nations rated as more similar to Americans scored higher on PONS. This finding supports the proximity hypothesis. If the

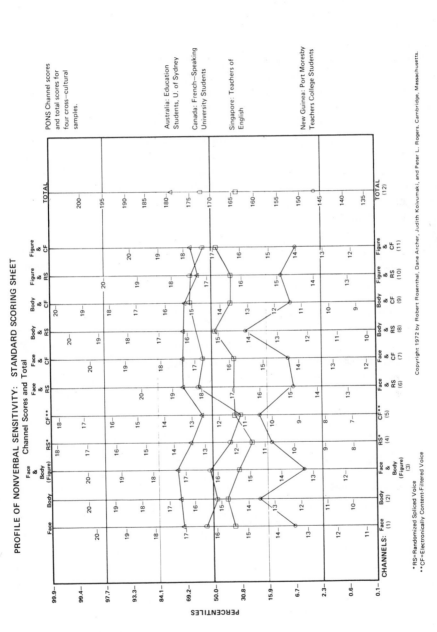

Fig. 1.   PONS channel scores and total scores for four cross-cultural samples. *, randomly spliced voice; **, electronically content-filtered voice.

PONS had featured a Latin American encoder, of course, the proximity hypothesis would predict that samples relatively similar to the culture of the Latin encoder would do better than other samples, including samples from English-speaking countries like the U. S.

The second index of similarity to the PONS encoder's culture was a linguistic ranking of the nations. Four different language groups are represented in the samples, and they can be ranked in order of their genetic proximity (or degree of descent relation from a common parent language) to the English of the PONS encoder. English is a member of the Indo-European language family, as are most (but not all) of the languages in our 58 cross-cultural samples. There are two major branches within this language family, the Centum and Satem branches, and English is a Centum language. There are also subbranches within the Centum branch— the Germanic, Italic, and Hellenic subbranches—and English is a member of the Germanic subbranch. In terms of their linguistic proximity to English, the four language groupings in our 58 cross-cultural samples are (in order of proximity to English): (1) Germanic languages; (2) other (non-Germanic) members of the Centum branch; (3) Satem languages; and (4) non-Indo-European languages.

The four language groups are shown ranked in order of proximity to English in Table 1, along with the languages in each group, the nations in each language, the PONS scores of the nations in each language, and the unweighted mean PONS score of each language grouping.

As Table 1 indicates, language grouping was associated with performance on the PONS test (the correlation between PONS score and proximity to English was +.625, $p < .002$). The highest scoring samples were those with the greatest linguistic proximity to English, and the lowest scoring national samples were those with languages most remote from English. This finding raises the possibility that the similarities among verbal languages may be paralleled by similarities among the non-verbal behaviors of speakers of those languages, i.e., linguistic similarities may have nonverbal analogs. In terms of the history of languages and cultures, it may be that nonverbal behaviors have been socially "inherited" among language groups along with transformations of specific word forms. An example of a word different in related languages but still somewhat recognizable is the word for "name": name (English), Name (German), nom (French), nombre (Spanish), nome (Italian), nome (Portuguese), and onoma (Greek). The results in Table 1 suggest that there may also be nonverbal "vocabularies," which, although altered, are still somewhat recognizable among related language groups. For example, it may be that specific emotional situations have nonverbal concomitants that vary recognizably among cultures with related languages, e.g., the nonverbal expression of the idea of "love" might occur in recognizable permutations like a similar facial expression, a softened voice, lowering of the eyes, etc. It should be mentioned that most of the cross-cultural samples were tested with answer sheets with English language labels, although essentially the same result was obtained for those samples tested with answer sheets in their native language, as Table 1 also indicates.

The relationship between PONS performance and linguistic groupings lends

TABLE 1. Four Language Groups and the PONS Scores of 20 Nations

Language group and type	Languages present in samples	Nations present in each language	PONS scores	Language group PONS mean
1 Germanic (Centum, Indo-European)	English	Canada	172.677	170.935
		New Zealand	171.813	
		Australia	171.677	
		Britain	171.075	
		Ireland	167.431	
	German	Germany	171.666[a]	
	Dutch	Holland	165.250	
	Swedish	Scandinavia	176.500	
2 Italic and Hellenic (Centum, Indo-European)	French	France	172.436	166.256
	Spanish	Spain	164.250	
		Mexico	165.644[a]	
	Italian	Italy	164.208	
	Portuguese	Portugal	159.000	
	Greek	Greece	172.000	
3 Slavic (Satem, Indo-European)	Polish Czecho-Slovak Serbo-Croatian	East Europe	163.500	163.500
4 Non-Indo-European	Chinese	Hong Kong	169.172	159.826
		Singapore	164.101	
	Hebrew	Israel	165.927[a]	
	Turkish	Turkey	144.750	
	New Guinea	New Guinea	155.180	

[a] These samples were tested with PONS answer sheets translated (with back-translation) into their native language.

support to the hypothesis of cultural proximity. Speakers of languages most similar to English did better on the PONS test than speakers of other languages. Again, the proximity hypothesis would expect very different performance rankings if an encoder with another language had been used in the PONS film, e.g., a PONS film with a Portuguese encoder should be more easily decoded by speakers of Italic languages than by speakers of Germanic languages.

As a final effort to explain variation in PONS performance among the 20 national groups studied, three dimensions of the 20 nations were quantified with several indicators for each dimension. These three dimensions were (1) general modernization [steel consumption, motor vehicles per capita (p.c.), physicians p.c.] ; (2) communications development (energy consumption, newsprint consumption, telephones p.c., televisions p.c., radios p.c.); and (3) contact with the U. S. and other foreign societies (ratio of imports from U. S. to total imports, ratio of

U. S. tourists to total tourists, and ratio of foreign letters received to total domestic mail). The 20 nations were ranked on each of the 11 indicators for which data were available. Rankings on some of these indicators were not distinguishable from rankings on similarity to the U. S. For the five communication measures, for example, the U. S. led all other 20 nations in the study, i.e., ranking the 20 nations on these indicators reflected both their relative communication sophistication and also their relative similarity to the U. S.

When the rankings of all 20 nations on these indicators were compared to their rankings on the PONS test, the strongest relationships were with the five communication measures (mean *rho* = .66). The three measures of general modernization were somewhat related to PONS scores (mean *rho* = .54), and the U. S. contact measures were essentially unrelated to PONS performance.

The 20 national samples, of course, included various occupational, educational, and social class backgrounds, and this uncontrolled variance may have attenuated or diminished these correlations. If this is true, the relationship between the indicators and PONS performance should be larger if this variance is controlled. Some of this error variance can be removed if the analysis is repeated for only a subset of our 58 samples. Our cross-cultural samples included samples of English language teachers (who are presumably similar in education, social class, etc.) from 12 nations. If the rank correlations are repeated for only these 12 samples, the relationships increase as predicted. For these 12 samples only, the communications indicators are related to PONS performance with a mean *rho* of .77; the general modernization measures with a mean *rho* of .70; and the U. S. contact measures are still essentially unrelated to PONS.

The results of these indicator analyses place primary importance (of the 11 variables measured) on the level of communications development in a nation—the highest PONS scorers came from nations with sophisticated communications systems. This may indicate a kind of "practice" effect, in that members of nations with developed communications systems have had experience in decoding facial expressions in newspapers and on television, oral paralanguage on the telephone, etc. These experiences may cultivate a generalized decoding skill, and perhaps also an emphasis on the importance of communication in various channels (Rosenthal *et al.,* 1978).

Psychopathology

Our purpose here is to examine the relationship between sensitivity to nonverbal communication and psychopathology, broadly defined. Five samples of neuropsychiatric patients were available for testing with the PONS, all of them hospitalized at the time of testing. Two samples came from different psychiatric hospitals in the Belfast area of Northern Ireland (N = 11 and 15). Two samples came from a single private psychiatric hospital in the Boston area of the U. S. (N = 11 and 9), and one sample came from a psychiatric hospital in the Sydney area of Australia (N = 22). A preliminary analysis of variance showed no significant differences among the five samples in total PONS score, in differential performance in the 11 channels, nor in differential performance in the four quadrants. All five samples were, therefore, combined to form a single sample of neuropsychiatric (NP) patients (N = 68).

Two samples of alcoholic patients were also available for testing with the PONS, all of them enrolled in residential treatment programs of a halfway-house nature. One of the samples was from an urban setting in the Boston area (N = 17), the other from a rural setting in Kansas (N =44). A preliminary analysis of variance showed no significant differences between these two samples in total PONS score, in differential performance in the 11 channels, nor in differential performance in the four quadrants. The two samples were, therefore, combined to form a single sample of alcoholic patients (N = 61).

The PONS performance of the psychiatric patients and alcoholics was then compared with the PONS performance of a large (N = 482) group of nonpsychiatric subjects, all of whom were high school students sampled from the east and west coasts and the midwestern part of the U. S. Figure 2 displays the comparison data on the standard scoring sheet. The performance of the 482 normal subjects conforms very closely to that of the smaller, more preliminary norm group that was the basis for the construction of the standard scoring sheet. The performances of the NP patients and the alcoholics were quite similar to each other but were consistently lower than the performance of the normal subjects. Such a result is consistent with Turner's (1964) finding that psychiatric patients are seriously impaired in decoding nonverbal messages.

By means of the analysis of variance, the patient groups were compared with the normal subjects on the effects on accuracy of adding tone of voice-, body-, and face-derived channels of nonverbal communication. These analyses showed that the addition of tone of voice, body, and face cues, each considered independently of the others, all increase the level of accuracy obtained and to increasing degrees: 1.00σ for audio cues, 1.97σ for body cues, and 3.98σ for face cues. For the PONS test, then, adding body cues adds about twice the information, in σ units, as adding tone of voice cues, and adding face cues adds about twice the information as adding body cues. Finally, the analyses showed that the addition of tone of voice cues, body cues, and face cues is differentially more advantageous to normal subjects than to our patient groups. While all of these effects are modest in magnitude (about one-fifth of a standard deviation) they are remarkable in their consistency. Taken together, they suggest strongly that psychiatric patients and alcoholic patients are less able than normal subjects to profit from the addition of further channels of nonverbal information considered independently of one another.

The works of McGhie (1973) and Meiselman (1973) would suggest further that psychiatric patients should be more impaired when confronted with channels combining audio with video information than on pure channels. We examined this suggestion by obtaining for each of our patients and normals a "pure channel" accuracy score based on single mode channels (CF, RS, face, body, face + body) as

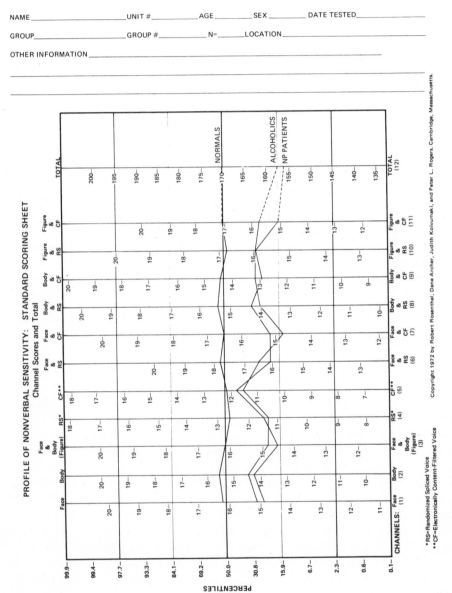

Fig. 2. Comparison of normal, alcoholic, and psychiatric patients.

well as a "mixed channel" accuracy score based on the remaining six channels having both audio and video components. Psychiatric patients were more impaired in their performance relative to normal subjects when confronted with mixed channel information than when confronted with pure channel information though the effect was small in magnitude.

Alcoholic patients were also compared to normal subjects both for their relative performance in audio vs. video channels and for their relative performance in pure vs. mixed channels. In both contrasts, alcoholic patients' performance was in the direction of psychiatric patients' performance (i.e., better performance on audio than video, better performance on pure than on mixed channels) but not significantly so.

It seemed likely in view of the results presented so far that psychiatric patients might be relatively more impaired in handling greater amounts of information regardless of the specific sense modality involved. For the 11 channels of the PONS the definition of information transmitted is the mean accuracy score obtained by a large norm group (N = 482). Those channels in which accuracy is greatest are assumed to be those in which the most information was transmitted. If psychiatric patients were to be most impaired in channels conveying the most information, there should be a sizeable correlation between a channel's information level and the degree to which psychiatric patients would be disadvantaged in performing in that channel relative to the normal subjects. The rank correlation obtained was quite substantial (ρ = .58) suggesting that the more information available in a channel, the less efficiently would psychiatric patients be able to utilize that information. The analogous correlation employing alcoholic rather than psychiatric patients was in the same direction, but substantially smaller in magnitude (ρ = .24).

The finding that patients are less able than normals to profit from the addition of channels of nonverbal communication is consistent with a number of findings reported in the literature of psychopathology. Maher (1966) has summarized the attentional problems often found in schizophrenic patients generally, and Meiselman (1973) has noted that chronic schizophrenics may be especially impaired when required simultaneously to process information from two sense modalities. There are also specific theoretical and empirical formulations that suggest that psychiatric patients may differ from normals in the efficiency with which they can deal with stimuli carried in the auditory and visual channels. McGhie (1973), for example, has suggested that schizophrenics perform relatively more effectively in the auditory than in the visual channel and, in addition, that adding visual information to auditory information may have relatively disruptive effects. Although the authors cited were writing specifically of schizophrenia, or even of restricted subtypes of schizophrenia, their formulations could be tested on our more heterogeneous group of hospitalized psychiatric patients.

Table 2 shows the mean accuracy obtained by the psychiatric patients (N = 68) and the normal subjects (N = 482) for the pure audio channels (content-filtered and random-spliced) and the pure video channels (face, body, face + body). Despite the diagnostically and nationally heterogeneous nature of our patient sample, their

TABLE 2. Mean Accuracy (Percentage) Obtained by Psychiatric
Patients and Normal Subjects in Pure Audio and Pure Video Channels

	Audio	Video	Difference
Psychiatric patients	58.0%	73.0%	15.0%
Normal subjects	62.0	79.7	17.7
Difference	4.0	6.7	2.7[a]

[a] $F = 6.70, p < .01$, effect size = $.21\sigma$.

performance was what McGhie would have predicted for schizophrenic patients.
Their performance was relatively better on the audio than on the video channels
(Rosenthal *et al.*, 1978).

Sex

Past research strongly suggests that females are more accurate at judging the
meanings of nonverbal cues than are males (Hall, 1978). In a review of 52 studies
not using the PONS test in which the direction of the advantage could be determined, 39 (75%) showed female advantage. For 33 of these 52 studies, the magnitude of the effect could be computed from the data provided in the published
reports. For these studies the median difference (d), expressed in standard deviation
units, was .390, computed by subtracting the male mean score from the female
mean score and dividing this difference by the standard deviation of the sample.
Such a statistic is standardized and is hence comparable across studies in which the
range of possible scores varies from study to study (Cohen, 1969; Friedman, 1968).
The studies reviewed here included tasks involving the judgment of cues sent in the
face, body, or voice tone channels, or combinations of these channels. The magnitude of the female advantage did not vary appreciably with either the channel of
sending or the sex of the sender.

In our PONS research, females show an advantage that is somewhat greater in
terms of the standardized difference than that suggested by most of the earlier
studies. This may result from the greater precision with which the PONS test measures nonverbal ability and the fact that d is increased by reducing measurement
error. For 107 PONS samples, representing many ages, nationalities, and occupations, the average standardized difference between the sexes (d) was $.44\sigma$. For the
high school norm group ($N = 480$) and the junior high school norm group ($N = 109$),
the standardized difference was $.48\sigma$. For the grade school samples together (grades
3-6, $N = 200$), the standardized difference was $.52\sigma$.

Figures 3-5 show the profiles for males and females for these three groups. In all
three groups males showed slightly more variability in their scores than did females.

Analyses of grade school, high school, and college samples showed that females
profited more than males from the presence of body cues in the stimuli to be judged.
This effect was apparent among children and adult samples as well. The reason for
this is not clear. Perhaps the body channel has sexual connotations that distract

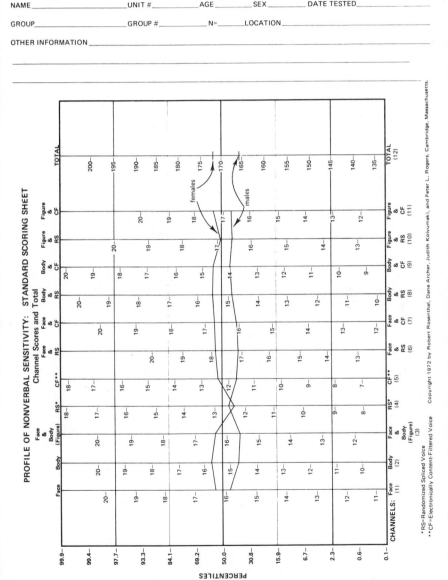

Fig. 3. Eleven-channel profiles and totals, males and females separately, for high school norm group ($N = 480$).

NAME_____UNIT #_____AGE_____SEX_____ DATE TESTED_____ _____

GROUP_____GROUP #_____N=_____LOCATION_____

OTHER INFORMATION_____

_____

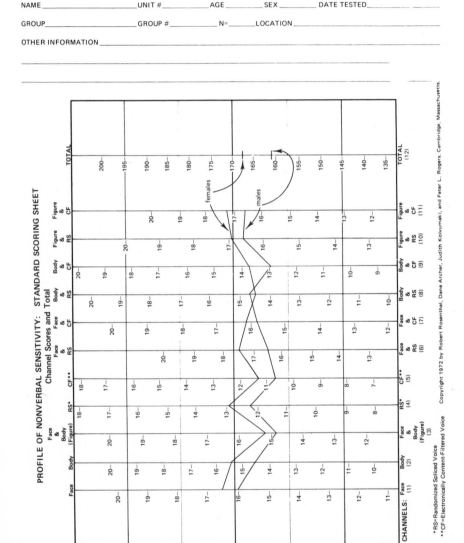

Fig. 4. Eleven-channel profiles and totals for junior high school norm group, sexes separately ($N = 109$).

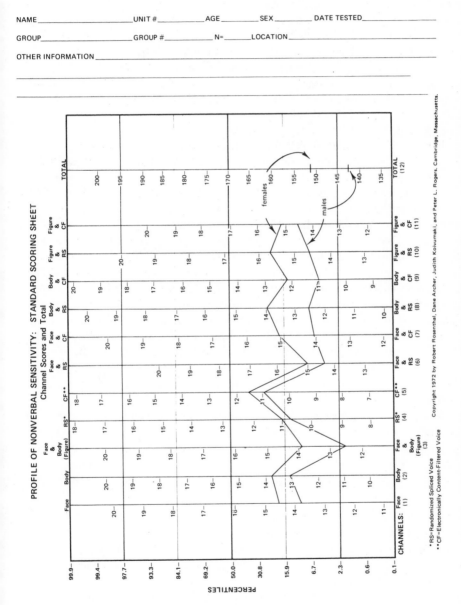

Fig. 5. Eleven-channel profiles and totals for four grade levels of school children (grades 3-6 pooled), sexes separately ($N = 200$).

males from the judging task.

Collapsing the channels in order to examine tone-only skill (RS + CF) versus video-only skill (pure video channels), it becomes apparent that males in the high school norm group performed relatively well on audio and relatively poorly on video, compared with females ($F_{1,5258}$ = 8.86, p < .005). Two three-way interactions of sex with channels were also significant but are difficult to interpret.

For grade school, high school, and college samples, females also performed better than males at judging negative affect. No significant interactions of age with sex have occurred in our research. At all age levels the magnitude of the sex difference is approximately equal. Hence the question of why and when females develop their nonverbal advantage remains open.

In addition to examining PONS performance separately for males and females, we also were able to examine the relationship of PONS ability to other skills and traits separately for the sexes.

For four samples, the degree of relationship between PONS skill and Verbal SAT score was moderate for both sexes, but higher for males. For Math SAT, there was virtually no relationship with PONS skill for females and a moderate relationship for males. These findings, which suggest that analytic skills are less important to females' nonverbal skills than to males', are consistent with the hypothesis that females use a more intuitive approach to making such judgments (Allport, 1924). Males who choose the correct answers on the PONS test may do so in a more analytic, problem-solving way than do females. Further research is needed to clarify exactly how the cognitive processes of the sexes differ on nonverbal accuracy tasks.

The Embedded Figures Test (Witkin, Oltman, Raskin, & Karp, 1971), a test of "field independence" (skill at visual disembedding), was given to three PONS samples. For males there was no relationship to speak of with the PONS, but for females there was a tendency for field independence (good disembedding) to be moderately associated with high PONS skill.

No appreciable differences between the sexes were obtained in the degree of correlation with the following other variables: scales of the California Psychological Inventory; self-reported interpersonal success; and self-reported nonverbal sensitivity.

Age

The development of PONS skill has been examined only cross-sectionally. Children in third grade, the youngest age tested so far, scored above the chance level. Scores improved significantly linearly through grade school, and from grade school through early adulthood. For all PONS samples that had been tested at the time of this analysis (excluding neuropsychiatric and alcoholic samples as well as all samples for which ages were not collected), the correlation between total PONS score and the mean age of the sample was .34 (p < .001). The linear relationship was strongest in the 8-25 age group, after which PONS performance seems to level off.

For children, the PONS answer sheet has been adapted to their level of vocabulary and social maturity. For example, the response alternatives for the scenes dealing with death, divorce, and seduction were changed to describe, respectively, a best friend moving away, a break-up with a boyfriend, and wanting a kiss from a boyfriend. The full PONS test has been administered in all grades down through third grade. In addition, a short battery was developed and used with 275 fourth and fifth graders. This battery consists of the face and body channels from the full PONS test (40 items) and the audio test that uses a child sender (40 items). Internal consistency reliability for the full PONS (for grades three through six) was .86. The reliability of the short battery was lower: .40 for the video test and .55 for the audio test, both corrected for the shorter lengths of the tests.

Analyses of the grade school children by themselves and also of the grade school children along with samples of other age levels indicate that the effects of advancing age are stronger for video than audio accuracy (Fig. 6). Although there are several possible biological, social, or psychometric explanations for this, we feel one of the more interesting and promising hypotheses stems from the work of Bugental and her colleagues (1970). Interpreted broadly, their research suggests that younger children give more weight to audio cues than to visual cues, and that as children grow older they give increasing attention to facial cues. Socialization pressures may account for this. If a person responds to "leaked" or unintentionally sent cues, which may occur more often in the audio mode than in the video mode, and more

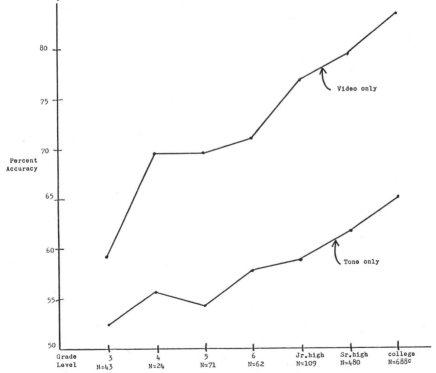

Fig. 6.   Percent accuracy on pure tone and pure video for seven age levels.

in body than in face (Ekman and Friesen, 1969), then that person may pose a threat to the orderliness of social processes—processes in which it is important for people to agree on the meanings of verbal and nonverbal messages that are sent and received. It may be so important for people to respond "at face value" that subtle pressures are effectively brought to bear during a person's early life not to attend too well to the less easily monitored nonverbal channels. Further research is planned to explore this and alternative hypotheses (Rosenthal *et al.*, 1978).

Self-Ratings

In an effort to determine whether an individual can predict his or her degree of nonverbal sensitivity (overall and in specific channels), we have administered a self-rating questionnaire along with the PONS test to 26 of our samples (totaling 627 subjects). On this questionnaire our subjects rated themselves on their warmth, ability to understand people, ability to understand social situations, and ability to "read" nonverbal cues in voice tone, face, and body. The ratings on the first three variables were correlated with total PONS score, and ratings on the latter three variables were correlated with pooled channels [i.e., all tone only items, all face items (with and without tone), and all body items (with and without tone)].

For the most part, self-ratings were poor predictors of PONS scores. Median correlations over all samples on all six variables tended to be close to zero, except that the correlation between predictions of face performance and scores on all face items was a moderately positive +.19. U. S. college students ($N = 53$) and neuropsychiatric patients ($N = 25$) tended to be the best predictors of their performance on the three nonverbal channels, with correlations ranging from +.21 to +.53.

Although individuals seem to be relatively poor predictors of their own nonverbal skill, we have evidence that their spouses are considerably more accurate. In a study of 22 married couples who took the PONS test and completed our questionnaire, we found that correlations of the self-rated nonverbal ability variables with related PONS scores were near zero. However, ratings of a person's nonverbal sensitivity by a *spouse* correlated positively and significantly with most related PONS scores. This trend was not evidenced in a second sample of 11 married couples (older than the first sample). We are planning further investigations of this topic.

Interpersonal Success Variables

Subjects in several samples rated the warmth and honesty of, and satisfaction with their same-sex and opposite-sex peer relationships. They also indicated the number of same-sex and opposite-sex friends they had. In general, both male and female subjects who performed well on the PONS test tended to report warmer, more honest, and more satisfying same-sex peer relationships than did those who received lower scores. In addition, high scoring male high school students (those who accurately perceived the nonverbal cues of the female stimulus person in the movie) tended to report "better" relationships with females than did low scoring male students. Surprisingly, however, both male and female high PONS-scorers reported having fewer same- and opposite-sex friends. It seems, then, that the better nonverbalists tended to form peer relationships of higher (subjective) quality, although they formed fewer of these relationships than did those who lacked nonverbal decoding skill.

We have attempted further to validate the PONS test by considering its ability to predict independent ratings of interpersonal sensitivity. In 22 studies we and our collaborators administered the PONS test to subjects and obtained ratings of their "interpersonal sensitivity" from a person fairly well known to them. An inspection of Table 3 reveals that in 18 out of the 22 studies, the correlations between PONS and judged interpersonal sensitivity were positive. These results contribute further to our developing picture of the validity of the PONS.

Finally, in two different studies, McClelland and Dailey (1973) found that their more effective Foreign Service officers scored as more sensitive to nonverbal communication. McClelland and Dailey did not employ the full PONS to measure sensitivity to nonverbal communication but only the two pure tone channels (CF and RS). In both their studies, the content-filtered speech channel correlated substantially with officer effectiveness (ϕ = .28 and .27) but the random-spliced channel predicted effectiveness in only one of the studies. Although we cannot be sure of any single explanation of these results, Beverly Crane has suggested that Foreign Service officers may often be in the position of listening to native speakers speaking a language the officers know only marginally if at all. Thus, they are frequently in the position of listening to "content-filtered" speech as part of their job. Those more accurate in decoding this type of communication would be in a better position to function effectively, hence the positive correlation between accuracy at CF and job effectiveness (Rosenthal et al., 1978).

Cognitive Correlates

The various measures whose relationship to the PONS we have considered include IQ, scholastic aptitude tests (e.g., SATs), school grades and class rank, scores on tests of verbal ability and English language proficiency, the Bieri test of cognitive complexity, and the Dailey Programmed Cases. In what follows, we hope to address both the convergent and discriminant validity of the PONS test. The demonstration of the former results in confirmation of scores on the PONS by independent measurement procedures while the demonstration of the latter provides justification for viewing the PONS as a novel trait measure.

One of our most important questions regarding cognitive ability correlates of the PONS test has been the degree to which scores on the PONS are correlated with scores on standard IQ tests. If the correlations were very high, the argument could be made that the PONS test measures not nonverbal sensitivity but rather general

TABLE 3. Correlation of Total PONS with Judged Interpersonal or Nonverbal Sensitivity

Study	Students	Raters	N	r	Z
1	Counselors	Supervisors	7	.55	+1.02
2	Undergraduates	Instructor	9	.49	+1.15
3	High School students	Teachers	40	.46	+2.92
4	Student teachers	Supervisors	24	.45	+2.11
5	Dance therapists	Supervisors	15	.34	+1.24
6	Dance therapists	Supervisors	14	.33	+1.06
7	Teachers	Supervisors	39	.32	+1.91
8	Therapists	Peers and supervisors (median)	46	.31	+2.10
9	Student teachers	Supervisors	24	.29	+1.31
10	Student helper role players[a]	Helpees	23	.26	+1.14
11	Clinical psychology graduate students	Supervisors	14	.22	+0.69
12	Clinical psychology graduate students	Supervisors	16	.22	+0.76
13	Ph.D. candidates in clinical psychology	Instructor	6	.20	+0.27
14	M. A. candidates in clinical psychology	Instructor	11	.15	+0.39
15	Nursing school faculty	Peers	58	.11	+0.81
16	Surgeons in training	Peers and supervisors (median)	16	.10	+0.34
17	Internists in training	Peers, supervisors, patients, (median)	39	.06	+0.35
18	Student teachers	Supervisors	86	.01	+0.09
19	Kindergarten teachers	Supervisors	46	.00	+0.00
20	Graduate students	Instructor	8	−.04	−0.08
21	Counselor trainees	Clients	33	−.19	−1.03
22	Various ages	Acquaintance or relative	13	−.35	−1.07
		Σ	587	+4.29	+17.43
		Median		.22	
		Unweighted mean		.20	
		Weighted mean		.16	

$$\text{Combined } Z = \sqrt{\frac{\Sigma Z}{22}} = 3.73$$

Combined $p < .0001$

[a] Employed 40 item face plus body PONS, not full PONS.

intelligence and/or "test-taking ability." If there were, on the other hand, only very low correlations between PONS and standard IQ test scores, the notion that non-verbal sensitivity and intelligence were separate abilities would be supported. We have considered data from four samples in attempting to answer this question.

In two samples of high school students, the median correlations between PONS and intelligence are rather low, the largest being .23. Among the Irish nurses, the PONS-IQ intercorrelations are weakly positive with the range being .13 to .18 with a median of .14.

In the sample of alcoholic patients, the story looks rather different. The most striking difference is in the magnitude of the PONS-intelligence median intercorrelations. These intercorrelations are all at least +.50 with a median of +.52. The strength of this correlation indicates that among these alcoholic patients, there is a moderately strong positive correlation between intelligence and nonverbal sensitivity as measured by the PONS test.

We have seen, then, that there is only a slight relationship between intelligence and nonverbal sensitivity among three out of four of our samples. In accounting for the substantial correlation between PONS and intelligence among alcoholic patients, we suggest that among those subjects diagnosed as pathological, those scoring at the lower ends of the IQ distribution would have difficulty performing in any testing situation (perhaps because of relatively severe psychological, toxicological, or encephalopathological problems). We could expect that those at the higher end of the IQ distribution would be better able to understand the instructions and to concentrate on the test as it is administered. Among "normal" subjects, such as high school students, we propose that nearly all are able to understand the instructions and complete the test. Thus, what is measured by PONS among these latter subjects is nonverbal sensitivity and the question of whether intelligence and PONS ability are relatively orthogonal is given a fairer test. It seems, in our data, that the relative independence of these two abilities has been supported.

Analyses of the relationship between PONS and scores on the Scholatic Aptitude Test tend to tell a story similar to that told by analyses of the IQ-PONS relationship. In general, the median correlations between PONS and SAT scores tend to be low. Across all samples and all PONS measures reported, the median PONS-SAT intercorrelation is +.15. This finding provides further evidence that nonverbal sensitivity as measured by the PONS and general aptitude are relatively independent. This is supported further by the fact that among two samples of college students and one sample of high school students, there is a minimal relationship between PONS and high school rank and grades with the median intercorrelations ranging from −.24 to +.10 with a median of +.02. It seems, then, that academic ability is not related to scores on the PONS test.

Among third and fifth graders, the PONS bears a moderately strong positive relationship to achievement in reading and mathematics, where high achievers score higher on the PONS. Among the subjects this young, however, it might be expected that achievement would be correlated with PONS score because of the positive relationship both variables would be expected to bear to proficiency at reading answers and performing well in a testing situation. Children whose verbal ability was low were probably at a loss in taking the PONS test, while good readers suffered no handicap in reading and understanding the meaning of the alternatives.

We can, thus, account for the discrepancy between older and younger student samples in the magnitude of the relationship between PONS and verbal and mathematical ability. Where these skills may be important in determining a third or fifth graders' ability to take the test successfully, there is no such systematic relationship among high school and college students who have all attained the level of proficiency needed to read the alternatives and choose the appropriate answers.

Among teachers of English in Singapore, substantial positive correlations were found between PONS and three tests of English proficiency. However, when the sample was separated into male and female subsamples, the correlations became slightly stronger for males and nearly disappeared among the females. It seems that, for males, high scores on the test of English Language proficiency are associated with high scores on the PONS test while for females, this relationship does not exist. Since the females in this sample scored significantly higher ($p < .001$) than did males on all three tests of English ability, we suggest that among individuals whose verbal proficiency is high enough to eliminate problems in understanding directions or choosing alternatives on the test, verbal ability and nonverbal sensitivity as measured by PONS are relatively independent. It is only when verbal ability or language proficiency are low that PONS seems to measure verbal as well as nonverbal skill. This notion is supported by the finding reported earlier that a strong relationship between PONS and reading and mathematics ability and achievement was found to exist among third and fifth grade subjects but not among high school and college students.

We consider, finally, two correlates of PONS for which data from only two samples are available. The first correlate, that of "cognitive complexity" was measured by the Bieri test (Bieri, 1955). Cognitive complexity is described as an aspect of an individual's personality that might be expected to influence his ability to discriminate behavioral information. It is an information-processing variable that helps predict how an individual transforms specified behavioral information into social judgment and may be thought of as the capacity to construe social behavior in a multidimensional way. Cognitively complex persons have a more differentiated system of dimensions for perceiving others' behavior than do cognitively simple subjects. While cognitively simple judges respond to the outer, normative quality of another's behavior, complex person-perceivers search for information concerning inner states and are better able to integrate multidimensional information. We might expect, then, that the more complex individuals would be better able to integrate a number of nonverbal cues (perhaps multidimensional in character) to arrive at an accurate perception of the affect conveyed by the stimulus person. For two samples of college students, greater cognitive complexity was associated with higher PONS scores (median $r = .28$).

The method of life-history assessment defines as its primary criterion accuracy in intuitive prediction, which results from a judge's recognition of intelligible interconnections among episodes in a life. This method of assessment presents behavioral events to a judge and measures his ability to predict other behavioral events in the same history. The design is a programmed case and the Dailey Programmed Case method of assessment (Dailey, 1971) was administered to 14 college student subjects along with the PONS test and the correlation with the PONS total was .26 (Rosenthal *et al.,* 1978).

FUTURE RESEARCH RELATED TO PONS

The findings of our research so far have posed many new questions. Each finding seems to suggest new and provocative lines of research with the PONS test. For instance, we have found that the test can be administered in its original form to children as young as 13 and with a larger type and simplified vocabulary to children as young as 8. Below this age, performance on the test may become more and more attributable to verbal rather than to nonverbal skill. We feel it is necessary to develop a version of the PONS where the subject's response does not involve verbal skills. These measures may include observers' judgments of infants' and young children's responses as well as psychophysiological data.

We have tested samples of deaf and blind students on individual channels of the PONS test in order to examine the hypothesis that handicapped persons make up for their disabilities by developing extraordinary nonverbal skills in the channels remaining to them. (The deaf and blind versions of the PONS contain only visual and auditory channels, respectively.) We have, as yet, no adequately matched control groups in order to test this hypothesis. With appropriately designed studies however, we hope to determine whether the handicapped do compensate for their disabilities in certain nonverbal channels and whether the PONS and its related measures can be used as a training instrument for the handicapped. Perhaps, for instance, those deficient or disabled in one channel can be taught more accurately to process nonverbal information in other channels in order to assist their social perception.

We plan to investigate further the relationship between nonverbal sensitivity as measured by PONS and susceptibility to interpersonal expectancy effects. This investigation may include a further study of the relationship between PONS performance and physiological responses (such as alpha rhythm), hypnotic suggestibility, and states of altered consciousness.

In an effort to study the relationship between sending and receiving nonverbal cues, we have designed a rather complex study in which these skills would be observed in on-the-spot sending and receiving. In this design, members of quadrads consisting of two married or dating couples would take turns sending nonverbal messages to each other. The sender's voice could be electronically content-filtered and screens would be employed to create different channels of visual information. In the analysis, same-sex and cross-sex differences in receiving accuracy could be examined as well as spouse-stranger differences. This study will contribute to our understanding of the relationship between sending and receiving, as well as to our understanding of sex differences and acquaintanceship differences in nonverbal accuracy.

Finally, we are developing a training program designed to increase sensitivity to nonverbal cues. The program is designed to give trainees practice in making judgments about nonverbal cues sent in various channels followed by feedback on the accuracy of their judgments. Our initial studies will employ as trainees a variety of mental health professionals and paraprofessionals for whom increases in sensitivity to nonverbal cues should be of special benefit. Subsequent studies will employ teachers and physicians as trainees, people whose work might become more effective with increases in sensitivity to nonverbal communication (Rosenthal *et al.*, 1978).

APPENDIX

Norms and Reliability for the Full PONS Test

Norms

In order for a psychological test to be useful, researchers must assess the level of performance of a standardization sample. If subjects in this standardization sample perform substantially above chance level (50%), as well as substantially below the level of perfect (100%) accuracy, we can entertain the hope that the test may be sufficiently discriminating among subjects. In addition, the mean performance of the standardization sample can be used as a comparison for other group means.

The standardization sample for the PONS test consisted of 480 male and female high school students from one eastern, one midwestern, and one west coast public high school. Their average age was 16.8 yrs. The percentage accuracy scores for this sample appear in Table 4. These percentages are indeed greater than chance level.

The data from 349 students from the midwestern and west coast high schools in this standardization group were collected prior to collecting the data from the students in the east coast school. The means and variances of the scores from this sample on the channels, marginals (pooled channels), quadrants, and total were used to construct the standard scoring sheets that have been used in this paper. The 50 percentile point on each scale represents the mean of our standardization group. Individual performance or mean group accuracy can then be recorded and examined in comparison with standard score on each PONS measure.

A plot of the accuracy score of an individual or group on the standard scoring sheet results in a *profile*.

TABLE 4.   Percentage Accuracy for Standardization Sample $N = 480$

		Video				
		None	Face	Body	Figure	Mean
	None	–	80.76	77.37	80.32	79.48
	RS[a]	62.70	88.35	76.32	83.86	77.81
Tone	CF[b]	60.91	82.40	71.90	85.32	75.13
	Mean	61.80	83.84	75.20	83.16	77.29

[a] RS = randomized spliced voice.
[b] CF = electronically content filtered voice.

Reliability

Reliability refers to the stability or consistency of measurements. A certain degree of score dependability must be demonstrated before the PONS can be considered valuable for use in practical situations. The notion of reliability includes two closely related aspects: internal consistency and stability. If a test is internally consistent, it yields consistent results throughout the test in a single administration. Stability reflects the extent to which the test yields consistent results from testing to testing. High stability means that individuals maintain their rank positions from testing to testing. The degree of reliability of a test (in both senses) is expressed as a reliability coefficient that can range from 0.00 (zero reliability) to +1.00 (perfect reliability).

As measured by two different methods (using our larger standardization sample data), the internal consistency of the PONS test is .86 (KR-20 formula) and .92 [Armor's (1974) theta formula]. Clearly these are substantial. The median correlation (of six samples) of the scores on a first and a second testing was .68. Thus the stability of the PONS test scores over time is adequate though not as high as the internal consistency reliabilities.

Practice effects: Retesting

We wanted to know whether subjects improved their performance on the PONS either during the course of a single testing or by taking the test a second time. For the four samples of subjects consisting of university and high school students who had taken the PONS on two occasions, performance on the first and second halves of the items of the first and second administrations was assessed. Learning was found to occur to a significant extent in going from the first to the second testing ($r = .60$) and also in going from the first half to the second half of each testing though that effect was smaller in magnitude ($r = .23$).

An additional analysis was performed to evaluate the within-test learning of our norm group of 480 high school students. The PONS was divided into five blocks of 44 items, each balanced for representation of the 11 channels and four quadrants. Again learning was found to occur to a significant extent ($r = .34$).

Practice effects: Knowing the sender

One study was done in order to find out what effects on performance result from subjects' having prior acquaintance with the sender. Thirteen people who knew the sender (including her parents, her sister, and sister's husband) and 13 strangers who were of comparable age and socioeconomic status took the PONS test, all in one group. Overall, there was no difference between the two groups in accuracy. However, some interactions were very interesting. Among the friends, females were relatively "too high" and among the strangers, males were relatively "too high" ($F = 5.035$, $df = 1,21$, $p < .04$); in fact, among the strangers the males actually scored higher than the females, which suggests that the group was not representative of the whole population of strangers (as we would have hoped).

Another effect was much more interesting. Disregarding sex, there was an interaction between group and channels, such that the friends tended to be better on pure audio and strangers better (relatively speaking) on pure video ($F = 9.64$, $df = 1,210, p < .002$). We tentatively attributed the greater audio skill on the part of friends to their prior practice on the audio channels that are, objectively, much more difficult than video channels, in other words, on the audio channels there is more room for improvement. Of course this is a very cautious interpretation. However, another study that we did bolsters this hypothesis.

In that study, we developed a way of measuring how often subjects chose to judge each of three different channels, when confronted with various pairs of those three channels. For example, subjects would see a nonverbal stimulus in the face channel and a different nonverbal stiumulus in the body or audio channel, and they then had a choice of which channel to judge. We thereby generated "preference" scores for each subject on face, body, and content-filtered audio. When these "preference" or "differential attention" scores were correlated with PONS scores, it turned out that face preference and body preference postdicted PONS scores on face and body, but audio preference was uncorrelated with PONS audio scores. What is suggested (but not proven, because causation is hard to attribute in correlational analysis) is that paying attention to face and body can improve face and body scores but paying attention to audio does not seem to improve audio scores. The reason this seems to fit with the friends-strangers finding is that it leaves open the possibility that practice rather than attention is a requirement for improved audio accuracy (Rosenthal *et al.*, 1978).

Still Photo PONS

For several practical and theoretical reasons we decided to develop a still photo version of the PONS. From a practical standpoint it would be very desirable to have available a short form of the PONS that required no audio-visual equipment and that could be virtually self-administered. If such a short form of the PONS showed promising correlations with the full PONS, it would enable many more investigators to have access to the instrument with greater convenience and lower cost.

Some of our research with very short exposure times had shown that motion was not required for better than chance accuracy at PONS type tasks in the video channels. Research was therefore planned in which video stimuli were to be presented with and without motion, for varying lengths of time to study the effects on accuracy of adding motion to stimuli varying in exposure lengths. This type of research also required a still photo version of the PONS.

The Still PONS test consists of 60 4 x 5 in. photographs, each taken from one of the 60 scenarios comprising the face, body, and face + body channels in the full PONS test. The order of presentation of the 60 photographs is identical to the order of the 60 corresponding scenes in the full PONS, and the 60 response alternatives are identical to the response alternatives for the corresponding items in the full PONS.

The newly developed Still PONS was administered to 53 high school students in a New England town. Just as was the case for the full PONS, females' performance (77.8%) on the Still PONS was superior to males' performance (74.3%).

Reliability and Factor Structure

The internal consistency reliability of most tests tends to be higher than the retest reliability and that was the case also for the Still PONS. The internal consistency reliability was .76, the retest reliability, .58. Factor analysis suggested five factors. The first of these reflected ability to decode cues sent in the body channel. The next four factors corresponded approximately to each of the four affect quadrants: positive-submissive, positive-dominant, negative-submissive, and negative-dominant. Thus the four affect quadrants developed originally for the movie version of the PONS were relatively well reproduced in the still photo version of the PONS.

Validity

If a single correlation coefficient could be employed to express the concurrent validity of the Still PONS, it would have to be the correlation between the Still PONS and the full 220 item PONS. For our 53 subjects that correlation was +.53 and for the 37 of these subjects who were retested two months later, the correlation was then +.59.

If the Still PONS were measuring very much the same aspect being measured by the full PONS, we would expect that various subsections of the Still PONS should correlate about as highly with the analogous subsections of the full PONS as with each other. The intercorrelations among the face, body, and face + body channels of the Still PONS and full PONS as well as the intercorrelations among the quadrants showed that such was indeed the case.

Further evidence that the subtests of the Still and full PONS were measuring

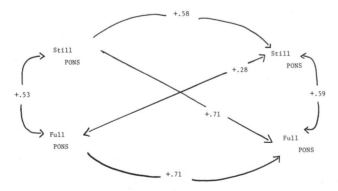

Fig. 7. Cross-lagged correlations of still photo PONS and full PONS (220 items).

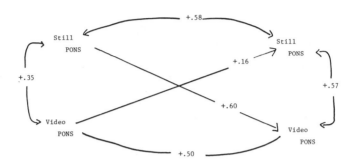

Fig. 8.   Cross-lagged correlations of still photo PONS and full PONS (video only, 60 items).

essentially the same kind of performance came from a consideration of the cross-lagged correlations. Figure 7 shows that the full PONS score on a two-month follow-up testing was as well predicted by the Still PONS taken two months earlier as by the full PONS itself taken two months earlier. Similarly, Fig. 8 shows that the sum of the three video channels of the full PONS was as well predicted by the Still PONS taken two months earlier as by the sum of the three video channels of the full PONS itself taken two months earlier. In short, the Still PONS appears to be measuring just about the same type of skill as that measured by the full PONS and its component parts (Rosenthal *et al.*, 1978).

References

Allport, F. H. *Social psychology*. Boston: Houghton-Mifflin, 1924.

Armor, D. J. Theta reliability and factor scaling. In H. L. Costner (Ed.), *Sociological Methodology, 1973-1974*. San Francisco: Jossey Bass, 1974.

Bieri, J. Cognitive complexity-simplicity and predictive behavior. *Journal of Abnormal and Social Psychology*, 1955, *51*, 263-268.

Birdwhistell, R. L. *Kinesics and context: Essays on body motion communication*. Philadelphia: University of Pennsylvania Press, 1970.

Buck, R. W., Savin, V. J., Miller, R. E., & Caul, W. F. Communication of affect through facial expressions in humans. *Journal of Personality and Social Psychology*, 1972, *23*, 362-371.

Bugental, D. E., Kaswan, J. W., & Love, L. R. Perception of contradictory meanings conveyed by verbal and nonverbal channels. *Journal of Personality and Social Psychology*, 1970, *16*, 647-655.

Bugental, D. E., Kaswan, J. W., Love, L. R., & Fox, M. N. Child versus adult perception of evaluative messages in verbal, vocal, and visual channels. *Developmental Psychology*, 1970, *2*, 367-375.

Cohen, J. *Statistical power analysis for the behavioral sciences*. New York: Academic Press, 1969. Revised, 1977.

Coleman, J. C. Facial expressions of emotion. *Psychological Monographs*, 1949, *63*, (1, whole #296).

Dailey, C. *Assessment of lives*. San Francisco: Jossey Bass, 1971.

Darwin, C. The *Expression of the emotions in man and animals*. Chicago: University of Chicago Press, 1965.

Davitz, J. R. *The communication of emotional meaning*. New York: McGraw-Hill, 1964.

Ekman, P. Universals and cultural differences in facial expressions of emotion. In J. K. Cole (Ed.), *Nebraska symposium on motivation*, Vol. 19. Lincoln, Nebraska: University of Nebraska Press, 1972. Pp. 207-283.

Ekman, P. Cross-cultural studies of facial expression. In P. Ekman (Ed.), *Darwin and facial expression*. New York: Academic Press, 1973. Pp. 169-222.

Ekman, P., & Friesen, W. V. Nonverbal leakage and clues to deception. *Psychiatry*, 1969, *32*, 88-106.

Ekman, P., Friesen, W. V., & Ellsworth, P. *Emotion in the human face: Guidelines for research and an integration of findings*. New York: Pergamon, 1972.

English, P. W. Behavioral concomitants of dependent and subservient roles. Unpublished paper, Harvard University, July, 1972.

Exline, R. V. *Visual interaction: The glances of power and preference*. In J. K. Cole (Ed.), *Nebraska Symposium on Motivation* (Vol. 19). Lincoln: University of Nebraska Press, 1972.

Fast, J. *Body language*. New York: Pocket Books, 1971.

Friedman, H. Magnitude of experimental effect and a table for its rapid estimation. *Psychological Bulletin*, 1968, *70*, 245-251.

Guilford, J. P. An experiment in learning to read facial expression. *Journal of Abnormal and Social Psychology*, 1929, *24*, 191-202.

Hall, E. T. *The silent language*. New York: Doubleday, 1959.

Hall, E. T. *The hidden dimension*. New York: Doubleday, 1969.

Hall, J. A. Gender effects in decoding nonverbal dues. *Psychological Bulletin*, 1978, *85*, 845-857.

Kleck, R. E., & Nuessle, W. Congruence between the indicative and communicative functions of eye contact in interpersonal relations. *British Jounal of Social and Clinical Psychology*, 1968, *7*, 241-246.

Koivumaki, J. H. Body language taught here. *Journal of Communication*, 1975, *25*, 26-30.

McClelland, D. C., & Dailey, C. *Evaluating new methods of measuring the qualities needed in superior Foreign Service Information Officers*. Unpublished manuscript, McBer and Company, Cambridge, Massachusetts, 1973.

McGhie, A. Psychological studies of schizophrenia. In B. Maher (Ed.), *Contemporary abnormal psychology*. Harmondsworth, England: Penguin, 1973, Pp. 120-133.

Maher, B. A. *Principles of psychopathology: An experimental approach*. New York: McGraw-Hill, 1966.

Mehrabian, A. Nonverbal Communication. In J. K. Cole (Ed.), *Nebraska Symposium on Motivation* (Vol. 19). Lincoln: University of Nebraska Press, 1972.

Meiselman, K. C. Broadening dual modality cue utilization in chronic nonparanoid schizophrenics. *Journal of Consulting and Clinical Psychology*, 1973, *41*, 447-453.

Nierenberg, G. I., & Calero, H. H. *How to read a person like a book*. New York: Pocket Books, 1973.

Rogers, P. L., Scherer, K. R., & Rosenthal, R. Content-filtering human speech. *Behavior Research Methods and Instrumentation*, 1971, *3*, 16-18.

Rosenthal, R. *Experimenter effects in behavioral research*. New York: Appleton-Century-Crofts, 1966. Enlarged, 1976, Irvington.

Rosenthal, R. *On the social psychology of the self-fulfilling prophecy: Further evidence for Pygmalion effects and their mediating mechanisms*. New York: MSS, 1974.

Rosenthal, R. Hall, J. A., DiMatteo, M. R., Rogers, P. L., & Archer, D. *Sensitivity to Nonverbal Communication: The PONS test*. Baltimore: The Johns Hopkins University Press, 1978.

Scheflen, A. E., with Alice Scheflen. *A body language and the social order: Communications as behavioral control*. Englewood Cliffs, New Jersey: Prentice-Hall, 1972.

Scherer, K. R. Randomized-splicing: A note on a simple technique for masking speech content.

Journal of Experimental Research in Personality, 1971, 5, 155-159.
Turner, J. Le B. Schizophrenics as judges of vocal expressions of emotional meaning. In J. R. Davitz (Ed.), *The communication of emotional meaning.* New York: McGraw-Hill, 1964. Pp. 129-142.
Witkin, H. A., Oltman, P. K., Raskin, E., Karp, S. A. *Manual: Embedded figures test, children's embedded test, group embedded figures test.* Palo Alto: Consulting Psychologists Press, Inc., 1971.
Zuckerman, M., Hall, J. A., DeFrank, R. S., & Rosenthal, R. Encoding and decoding of spontaneous and posed facial expressions. *Journal of Personality and Social Psychology*, 1976, 34, 966-977.

TALKING DOWN: SOME CULTURAL SOURCES OF MISCOMMUNICATION IN INTERRACIAL INTERVIEWS*†

Frederick Erickson

Harvard Graduate School of Education

Roo: "Hallo, Piglet! I say, Piglet! What do you think I was doing! Swimming! Christopher Robin, did you see me _____." But Christopher Robin wasn't listening. He was looking at Pooh.

            A. A. Milne, "Expotition to the North Pole"

Christopher Robin, Pooh, and Piglet, as adult members of a speech community (Gumperz, 1968; Hymes, 1972) who were fully socialized into that community's ways of speaking, probably would not have tried to do with words what Roo was trying to do when he did it. He was trying to explain something important. But he was doing so at the wrong time.

Baby Roo was too young to realize the fundamental sociolinguistic fact that one cannot successfully accomplish the speech act /explaining/ without first having the attention of those to whom the explanation is addressed. We can infer that he may have been working from a rough model for speaking that included listener attention as a structural feature. His questions "What do you think I was doing?" and "Did you see me _____." could be interpreted as attempts to get the attention of a hearer as well as to get a turn at speaking (Sacks, 1972). But had Roo been older he might

*This research was supported in part by the Center for Studies of Metropolitan Problems, National Institute of Mental Health (MH 18230, MH 21460) and by the Ford Foundation. The support of both institutions is gratefully acknowledged.

†The author wishes to thank Jeffrey Shultz, Courtney Cazden, and Jan Wilson for advice and assistance. In addition I am grateful for initial conceptual help from Edward T. Hall, and for methodological advice from Hugh Mehan and from John and Jenny Cook-Gumperz. The responsibility for defects in this analysis, however is entirely my own.

have first worked at the more effective strategy of securing fixed attention from his audience before attempting explanation.

How could Roo have determined whether anyone was paying attention or not? By watching and listening to what his addressed audience was doing while he was talking. Listening is not simply the reception and decoding of information, it is social activity that in itself has potential as information. As speakers are doing *speaking,* listeners are doing *listening.* The listening behavior of listeners can be "read" by speakers as indicating attention, understanding, and agreement on the part of the auditors.

This paper is about the effects of auditors' ways of listening on speakers' ways of speaking (and about speakers' ways of giving auditors verbally implicit cues for "what's about to happen next"), as speakers try to accomplish the speech act /explaining/. /Explaining/ is a particular kind of *addressed speaking.* Together with other forms of addressed speaking, such as persuading, inspiring, and deceiving, explaining is essentially rhetorical. A successful explanation cannot be done alone (unless one is talking to oneself). It must be interactionally accomplished. It requires a change in state in the audience being explained to. In terms of a current theory of speech as social action, the *perlocutionary* effect (influence on the hearer) of the speech act /explaining/ is a necessary condition for its *illocutionary force* (nondefectible performance as a social action). For speaking to have any perlocutionary effect, the speaker must have the hearer's attention. Such attention can be signaled by listening behavior.

If there were differences in expectations between listeners and speakers over when and how to realize behaviorally the social function *showing attention while listening,* and how to signal when such attention is appropriate, we could expect attempts at explanation to be troublesome. I have found this to be often the case in a sample of films of naturally occurring interviews between white school counselors and black school students, and between white job interviewers and black job applicants in the U. S. This interactional trouble may result in part from cultural differences in communication style; differences between white and black systems of expecting, performing, and "reading" listening behavior.

In the next sections I will review relevant research and present analytic models for the social and cognitive organization of speaking and listening as interactional partners collaborate in getting from one point to the next in an explanation. Then I will discuss examples of counseling interaction from intraracial and interracial interviews, instances from which the analytic models were derived. I will conclude with a brief statement of implications for educational policy and practice.

Studying how the speech act /explaining/ is accomplished interactionally has special relevance for scholars and practitioners in education because of the ubiquitous presence of /explaining/ in schools of all levels. /Explaining/ is done not only by the counselor in the counselor's office, but by the teacher in the classroom, by the administrator in the administrator's office, and by the secretary in the office outside the administrator's door. School personnel do /explaining/ to students, to fellow staff members, to parents, and to representatives of the public at large. When explanations go wrong repeatedly, systematically, things are likely to be going wrong in the educational process. Before attempting remedies it is useful to have some sense of the kinds of things that may be going wrong.

A DEFINITION OF /EXPLAINING/

An explanation can be defined as a speaking turn (or a part of a turn, or a series of turns) whose function is to clarify something that has already been stated, explicitly or implicitly, the *subject* of the explanation. In the terms used in recent work by Keenan and Schieffelin (1976), the subject of an explanation is a *discourse topic.* Maintenance of the discourse topic is sustained within and across sentences by various grammatical and "prosodic" devices (voice, pitch, intonation contour, stress, and rhythm). An explanation is an attempt to disambiguate the discourse topic.

The simplest type of explanation can occur within a single sentence in the logical and grammatical form of *predication,* a statement made about the subject of a proposition.

(1)   The explanation / is an attempt to disambiguate the discourse topic.

(2)   A box cake / is made from previously measured and packaged ingredients.

Making an explanation point is done by stating in a verb phrase the logical and grammatical predicate of the subject. Predications can be linked together in series, each new predication "tieing" back to the preceding noun that functions as the "subject" or "topic" of the previous phrase. Such linked predications are progressive attempts to disambiguate the subject of the initial proposition in the series, as in the following hypothetical example:

(3a)   The way you get to be a counselor / is to have state teacher certification / which requires that you have a bachelor's degree in education.

As these predications are strung together, the explainer is *persisting at the point.*

Keenan and Schieffelin's (1976) theoretical model for how a speaker maintains a discourse topic includes the *attention of the hearer* as a necessary condition. If such attention is lost, the speaker must attempt some remedy (cf. Goffman, 1967 on "remedial interchanges.") One sort of remedy is hyperexplanation.

Hyperexplanation can be defined as persisting twice or more within the same speaking turn at the same explanation point, as in the following actual example of naturally occurring speech from a film of an interracial interview. The junior college student has just told the junior college counselor that the student wants to be a high school counselor. Then the counselor says:

(3b)   First of all you're gonna need state certification / state teacher certification / in other words you're gonna have to be certified to teach in some area / English / or History / or whatever happens to be your bag / . . . / P. E. // Secondly you're gonna have to have a master's degree /

There seem to be two intersubstitutible forms of hyperexplanation: (1) *talking down* (lowering the level of abstraction from one repetition of the explanation point to the next,) and (2) *giving reasons* (each successive reason justifying the proposition asserted by implication in the discourse topic).

RESEARCH ON REGULATORY FUNCTIONS
OF LISTENING BEHAVIOR

Since there seems to be a relation between speakers' ways of speaking in explaining and listeners' ways of listening so as to show attention while being explained to, it is appropriate here to turn to the research literature on listening. In spite on burgeoning interest in nonverbal communication recently, there has apparently been little investigation of listening as a social activity. The subject indexes of such general discussions and surveys of literature as Mehrabian (1972), Davis (1972), and Argyle (1969) do not contain the category *listening*, although particular listening behaviors, such as eye contact, body motion (kinesic activity), postural configuration, and paralinguistic phenomena (voice pitch, stress, tempo, rhythm) are indexed and discussed. Two of the most well-known experimental studies of person perception in dyadic interaction, Mehrabian (1968) and Ekman & Friesen (1969) focused entirely on the communication behavior of the speaker and did not deal with the listening behavior of the listener.

A few researchers have studied listening as a phenomenon in its own right. Hall has had a long-term interest in listening behavior and in 1969 published the only article I have found so far that was specifically focused on listening (Hall, 1969, reprinted 1974). In a brief discussion he characterized listening behavior as having an extremely important role in the conduct of social interaction; calling listening behavior ". . . the language of 'Yes, I'm listening.' " Obviously, listening behaviors that are interpreted as being a language of "No, I'm not listening" also can have important social consequences in encounters face to face.

Birdwhistell and other scholars following his approach toward studying communicational activity as a total system in which diverse features of the communicative behavior of all parties to an interactional event are considered together (Birdwhistell, 1970), have looked at the listening behavior of listeners as well as the speaking behavior of speakers. Scheflen (1973) identified recurrent patterns in the postural and kinesic activity of listeners in his study of a group psychotherapy transaction. Condon and Ogsten (1967) demonstrated the high degree of synchrony between the kinesic activity of listeners and of speakers. They report that not only is the kinesic activity of listeners synchronized with their speech at microsecond intervals of timing, but that, in addition, the kinesic activity of listeners is synchronized with the speech and kinesic behavior of the speaker. This phenomenon has been observed and reported by other investigators, including myself (Erickson & Shultz, in press; Erickson, Shultz & Leonard-Dolan, 1973).

Kendon (1967, and as reviewed in Argyle, 1969) has presented the most fully developed model for the social and behavioral relationships between the listening behavior of listerners and the speaking behavior of speakers. Since his English subjects, when they were in the role of speaker characteristically looked away from their auditor more than at their auditor, a gaze by the speaker at the auditor at the end of the speakers' utterance could function as a signal that the speaker was finishing; preparing to relinquish the speaking turn. Kendon noted also that auditors' responses to speakers' speech could have regulatory functions; that speakers rely to some extent on such listening behaviors as head nodding and brief paralinguistic ejaculations ("mhm") or lexical items ("yes," "I see") . . . for guidance as to how what he is saying is being received by his listener" (Kendon, 1967). He observed that at the time of writing (1967) little work had been done on identifying features of listening behavior or the varieties of functions such behaviors could perform.

Duncan (1972, 1976) looked at functions of speaker gaze in the regulation of conversational turn taking, and also considered aspects of listening behavior. He characterized the brief noises made by listeners ("mhm," "yes") as "back-channel behaviors," and identified the signal function of such behaviors as potential indicators that the listener was about to claim a turn at speaking. At most turn exchanges between speakers, speakers gave "turn signals" indicating willingness to relinquish the turn (behaviors such as falling intonation at a clause-terminal juncture in speech, the relaxation of a tensed hand position, or stylized verbal fillers, such as "you know," termed "sociocentric sequences" by Bernstein, 1962). At most turn exchange points a turn signal by the speaker was followed or accompanied by "turn claim" signals from the listener. These turn claim signals include back-channels and head nods (Duncan 1976).

What conversationalists are doing, according to Kendon and Duncan, is signaling to each other *moments at which exchange of turn is appropriate*. Role relationships (reciprocal sets of rights and obligations) between speaker and listener at such moments differ from role relationships at other moments in the conversation. Such moments are special times in the continuous flow of interaction. Sacks, Shegloff, and Jefferson (1974) in their work on strictly verbal features of conversational organization term such a moment a "transition relevance place." The turn-relinquishing and turn-claiming signals that mark turn-relevance moments are specific instances of a class of communication signals that Gumperz (1976) calls "contextualization cues." Such cues can have adumbrative functions, foreshadowing changes in social relationship among speakers and listeners.

Exchange of listening and speaking roles at a turn-relevant moment is one way that social relationships can change between conversationalists. Change of social relationships can also occur at special moments within a speaking turn. One such special moment is what can be called a "listening response-relevant moment" (LRRM).[1] At a LRRM, a listener is obliged to show more active listening response

---

[1] By "moment" I mean duration in subjective time, not a duration in technically measured time, i.e., clock time. Thus a moment can be a brief "point" in time, or a longer "space" of time [see Sacks, Shegloff, & Jefferson (1974) for their discussion of "place" as a category of subjective time].

than at other times while the speaker is speaking. Such responses seem to show that the listener is "really listening" and understands what the speaker is saying. The LRRM seems to be signaled by contextualization cues in the speakers' speech. These cues are often similar to the cues by which a speaker signals the approach of a turn-relevant moment. The listening response-behaviors requisite during a speaker-designated LRRM—behaviors such as head nods and back-channel vocalization— are similar in form to those that Kendon and Duncan have shown to function as signals of a listener's intention to claim a turn at speaking. Hence the question arises: "Do the listening responses of listeners at listening-response-relevant moments have a regulatory influence on the speaking performance of speakers?" Since our interest here is in ways of speaking while performing the speech act /explaining/, a more specific question also arises: "Is the way a speaker explains related to the way the listener listens to the explanation?" Finally, since we are also interested in the influence of cultural communication style on the conduct of face-to-face interaction, two more questions are suggested: "Are there cultural differences in the contextualization cues signaling *listening response relevance* and in the listening behaviors that constitute a socially appropriate listening response? If so, what are the consequences of such differences for how explaining gets done, and for how the interactional process of *explaining/being explained to* is handled by conversationalists face to face?"

Recent research by Mayo and LaFrance (1976) speaks to the issue raised in the last question. They conducted an intensive study of two films of interaction between two black and two white conversationalists and generated models for the organization of gaze behavior in conversation in black-black dyads and in white-white dyads. Then they tested their models on a larger sample of encounters, using systematic behavior observations. Their findings corroborated those of Kendon of white-white dyads—whites while speaking tended to look away from the listener relatively continuously and to look at the listener only intermittently, while listeners tended to look continuously at the speaker. In black dyads there was a different allocation of rights and obligations regarding gaze behavior across the two roles *speaker* and *auditor*. Blacks while speaking tended to look at the listener continuously, looking away only intermittently, while listeners tended to look at the speaker only intermittently, except at turn relevant moments, when both speaker and listener would show gaze involvement. The findings of Mayo and LaFrance have great relevance for the study of listening and speaking in encounters between blacks and whites. We could expect that as a white speaker was speaking he would glance briefly at his black listener, who would be likely not to be looking at the speaker (as the speaker would expect an attentive listener to be doing). The black speaker would be looking fairly continuously at the white listener, who would be looking continuously at the black speaker (not looking down as a black listener would be doing). Conversational inferences or attributions of intent that could be drawn by conversationalists under such conditions of mismatch in cultural patterns of socially appropriate gaze involvement could be the following:

Environment 1   *White speaker/black auditor:* The speaker might infer that the auditor was "not paying attention" or "sullen" or "frightened." The auditor might infer that the speaker was "shifty-eyed," "nervous," and/or "trying to whup the game" (trick the auditor).

Environment 2   *Black speaker/white auditor:* The speaker might infer the listener was "insubordinate" or "hostile" because the listener was "staring" at the speaker. The auditor might infer that the speaker was being "overbearing" or "insistent" because the speaker was "staring" at the auditor.

If we consider this set of conditions as structural features in a model of interaction process, we can predict that conversational inferences such as those presented above are likely to occur often in interracial encounters. *Such inferences would be regularly "generated" in and through the interaction itself, given the cultural differences in the organization of interactional behavior that Mayo and LaFrance have identified.*

From the point of view of a white speaker operating from an Anglo-American model of what constitutes "paying attention," the black listener would be doing nonverbal ways of saying "I'm not listening." Returning to our beginning example from the world of Winnie-the-Pooh, we can see that Milne was reporting his intuitive "folk" analysis (as a member of the upper-class British English speech community) of the structural importance of gaze direction in the English cultural system of organizing listening behavior in relation to speech behavior. Milne uses *but* to show that Baby Roo's attempt to do the form of addressed speaking /explaining/ was a futile attempt: *"But* Christopher Robin wasn't listening. He was looking at Pooh." Christopher Robin's listening behavior was a language of "I'm not listening."

A STUDY OF INTERRACIAL INTERVIEW SITUATIONS

I first became interested in the social and cultural organization of /not listening/ when I worked during 1964-1965 as a basic education training consultant to a steel company in a large city in the U. S. I came in contact with white job interviewers at that company and at other companies who told me that when they interviewed black job applicants they had an intuition that something was often wrong in the interviews. Interviewers were vague about what the "something" was. When I pressed them to be more specific some of the interviewers said, "The black applicants don't seem to be listening." In the next few years I met school teachers, school counselors, and teacher education students doing practice teaching who reported the same impressions. In the interview office and in the classroom, black young people appeared to white interviewers and school staff not to be listening or understanding what was being said to them.

Conversely, the black young people I worked with at the steel company and at a YMCA said that when they talked to white job interviewers or school personnel

it often seemed that these adults thought the black young people were stupid because the whites in conversation would keep saying the same thing over and over,
as if they thought the young people did not know what the whites were talking
about. The black young people found such conversations at best tedious and at
worst demeaning.

Reports such as these from interviewers and from those interviewed occurred so
frequently it seemed that something indeed was going consistently awry in interracial interview situations. I decided to try to find out in more detail what took
place in such interviews—and if the interviewers, the interviewed, and I regularly
perceived that things were somehow going "wrong," I wanted to try to determine
how this was happening interactionally.

Accordingly, in 1970 I began a study of interracial and interethnic relations
in school counseling interviews (brief academic advising interviews) and job interviews. In the study my colleagues, Carolyn Leonard-Dolan, Jeffrey Shultz, and
I filmed and analyzed 56 naturally occurring school and job interviews, and 26
"arranged" conversations between pairs of university students in various ethnic and
racial combinations. Procedures for unobtrusive filming and for data analysis have
been reported elsewhere (for detailed description of filming and analytic procedures, see Erickson et al., 1973; for general reports of results and analytic methods
see Erickson, 1975, 1976b). In preparing this paper I have conducted a restudy of
nine films. Eight of them were 10 min in length: one of them is 5 min in length.
Seven films are of school counseling interviews, two are of job interviews. These
last were made by William Condon and Edward T. Hall in a study reported by
Hall (1974). Five of the nine films were of encounters between a white speaker
and a black listener. Two films were dyadic encounters between whites; two were
of dyadic encounters between blacks. I watched and listened to each of the sound
films in detail, making a transcript of the speech involved in each major sequence
of explanation (including rough indications of pause length and intonation contours) and identifying some behavior features of the listening responses of listeners
(head nods, back channel vocalization, lexicalized vocalization). Each listening
response-relevant moment (LRRM) and listening response (LR) was located in the
transcript just above the point in the speech stream of the speaker at which the
LR occurred. There were a total of 133 instances of LRRMs in the explanation-
sequences examined. These LRRM sequences include all instances of hyperexplanation occurring in the nine films. Here is an example of an explanation sequence:

(4a) So what we're gonna have to do first of all is to get you set up . . . for
      an   A C T   test (slight nod) in . . . ah . . . I believe the next one will
      be in July . . . (nod) . . . (nod)

After transcribing a few instances of /explaining/ and watching the listening
behavior of the listener, it became apparent that at some moments during the
explanation more active listening behavior occurred than at other times during
the course of the explanation. These moments seemed to occur regularly at syntactic junctures in the speakers' speech, notably at clause terminal junctures, e.g.,

"is to get you set up" . . . " in example (4a) above. Moreover, it appeared that the *absence* of more active listening behavior at moments it seemed to be required was made an *accountable absence* (Shegloff, 1968; Mehan, 1975: p. 132-134, Garfinkel, 1967: p. 3-24). The speaker makes the absence socially accountable by altering his behavior immediately subsequent to the occurrence of the absence, e.g., in example 4a, the absence of listening response at the first clause terminal juncture followed by a pause ("is to get you set up . . . ") is an accountable absence. Immediately subsequent to the absence the speaker speaks twice as slowly as before the absence and explains in greater detail what will be set up [". . . for an A C T test (slight nod) in"] and then continues on the next speaking point—the next step in the series of procedures for being admitted as a full-time student. By slowing down and recycling the explanation, defining "set up" as *setting up (an appointment) for an ACT test*, the interviewer made interactionally accountable the student's absence of listening response after "set up." In example 4a, at other analogous environments in the speech stream the student provides active listening response and the counselor continues on to the next "point"—the next step in the process of being admitted to the junior college as a full-time student.

It seemed that such moments after clause terminal junctures were LRRMs and that because the LRRM could be thought of as an interactional "slot" with great social consequence for interaction, it should be indicated somehow in the transcription system. Also it seemed as transcription proceeded that the LRRM was often preceded not only by a syntactic juncture, but by intonation contour shifts involving four intonational levels [level 1—low, constricted, 1½—low, nonconstricted, 2—normal, 3—high, 4—very high (see Gleason, 1961)], by intonational contours (falling, rising, sustained), by changes in tempo of speaking, by postural shifts by the speaker (changing seating position, changing hand position, moving toward or away from the listener), or by change in direction of gaze.

Eye contact was not always possible to determine in the films. It was noted when possible. The LRRM was indicated by diagonal slashes across the transcript that connect the line on which the speaker's speech is transcribed and the lines above it on which the listening responses of the listener are noted. Pauses in the speaker's speech are indicated by dots at a rate of approximately 2 dots per second. Thus the last clause terminal juncture in example 1, and the LRRM that follows it can be transcribed in the following manner:

(4b) the next one will be in July / $\overset{nod,\ nod}{\underset{2\frac{1}{2}-1\frac{1}{2}}{.\ .\ .\ .}}$ / and I think that

This transciption system permits more clear illustration of the dynamics of speaking and listening activity than the system used for the first presentation of example (4) in (4a). Next I will present the complete version of example (4) now transcribed more fully than before (the counselor's nonverbal behavior is indicated in parentheses below the line of text, the student's nonverbal behavior is indicated in parentheses or within brackets above the line of text):

                                                            no response

(4c) So . what we're gonna have to do first of all is to get you set up / . . /

                                                  2-2

                       slight nod

for an A C T test / . . / in . . aah . I believe the next one will

1½   *(slows down)*   1½ *(speeds up)*

                     nod, nod

be in July / . . . . / and I think that ah . we can get the informa-

       2½-1½   2   1½ *(speeds up)*

       (student nods slightly and continuously)   *lge nod,sm nod*

tion so that you can get in on that one   / . . / O.K. and then

                              1½ 1   *(rapidly)*

(counselor nods slightly and continuously)

as soon as we get your scores

It is apparent from this way of displaying the speech behavior of the counselor and the listening behavior of the student that there could be some relation between speaking and listening in this performance of the speech act /explaining/. There is an absence of active listening response after the first clause terminal juncture ("set up/") (sustained intonation, followed by a pause). In the next phrase the counselor makes accountable the absence of listening response by the student. The counselor begins to speak more slowly, and elaborates on what he meant by "get you set up" ("for an A C T test"). After the next clause terminal juncture ("A C T test") (sustained intonation, followed by a brief pause) the student nods slightly, and then the counselor proceeds on to the next speaking point (concerning scheduling the student to take the ACT test). As the counselor begins to make the first part of the next point (concerning the next date the test will be given), he lowers intonation level and begins speaking more quickly. At the next clause terminal juncture ("in July") 'falling intonation, followed by a pause), the student gives two nods and the counselor proceeds on to the second part of the speaking point (concerning signing the student up to take the test on the next date it will be given). After a brief slowly spoken phrase ("and I think that ah. . ."), with level 2 intonation sustained throughout, the counselor shifts to a lower intonation level (1½) and begins to speak more quickly, sustaining the lowered intonation level. At the next syntactic juncture ("get you the information"), the counselor and student begin to nod simultaneously. They continue to nod together until the next clause terminal juncture (slight falling intonation, pause) after which the student "echoes" his earlier continuous nodding with a sharply punctuated large nod and then a smaller nod. After this listening response from the student, the counselor changes postural position and proceeds on to the next speaking point ("OK. And then as soon as you get your scores. . .").

Note that after each clause terminal juncture but the first one, the counselor proceeded on to make the next speaking point, or part of a point. There is only one instance in which the counselor persisted at explaining a speaking point. That instance follows the *absence of active listening response* during the pause after the first clause terminal juncture. After that absence the counselor recycled his explanation once ("for an ACT test") and then having received a listening response from the student in the form of a slight nod, the counselor proceeded on to the next speaking point.

From example (4), it seems intuitively apparent that there is something special about those pauses in the speaker's speech that follow the completion of a syntactic unit. Those pauses seem to be LRRMs. Empirical evidence for this conjecture comes from (1) the presence of active listening response *at every instance but one* of a clause terminal juncture followed by a pause, and from (2) the speaker's making accountable the absence of listening response in the one exceptional instance, by recycling the explanation and persisting at the speaking point.

Example (4) is taken from an interview between a white counselor and a white student. A contrasting example, previously presented, comes from an interview between the same white counselor and a black student [example (3)]. In both examples the counselor is explaining steps to be taken by the student across time in the future. In example (4) the discourse topic concerns the steps involved in being admitted as a full-time student in a junior college: (a) finding out when a test is to be given, (b) registering for the test and taking it, (c) reporting the score to the registrar, and (d) registering as a full-time student. In example (3) the counselor's discourse topic concerns the steps involved in the student's eventually becoming a high school counselor: (a) graduate from college and become certified as a school teacher, (b) get a master's degree, (c) get a job as a counselor. In the explanation the counselor persists repeatedly at the first speaking point in the discourse topic (being certified to teach). This recycling of the same point, at lower and lower levels of abstraction, persists until the black student provides active listening response (an "accented" head nod, "mhm," and arm movement) during a pause in the speaker's speech. Then, and only then, the counselor proceeds on to the next speaking point in the explanation, describing the next step in procedure (getting a master's degree):

(3c) *(S. looks intermittently)*
    Essentially . what you need . . . First of all you're gonna need
      2½ 1½   2½   1½   *(C. "counts on finger)*

              no response   *no response*
    state certification /*no pause* / state teacher certification /   .   /
          2 - 2

    (begins very slight, continuous, "unaccented" nods)(nods stop)(nods resume)   no other resp.
    in other words you're gonna have to be certified to teach in some area / . . . /
                                                              2-1½

                                                    (S. brings r. arm to face in synch.
    (slight "unaccented" nods continue (sm. "unaccented" nod) with C's arms)(mhm)
    English or History or whatever happens to be your bag / . P.E. . . /
                                                    (quickly C extends arms in synch.
                                                      with S's arms)

                                                            very slight
    (S. does not move)   *"unaccented" nod*
    ah . Secondly you're gonna have to have a master's degree / .   . /
        2½-2   1½

Such persistence at the same speaking point was characteristic of white speakers doing explaniation to black listeners, in the films I have investigated. In example (3c) the counselor lowers the level of abstraction until active kinesic listening response comes from the listener:

Essentially what you need . . .
   First of all you're gonna need state certification . . .
      state teacher certification . . .
         in other words you're gonna have to be certified to teach in some area . . .
         English or History or whatever happens to be your bag . . .
         P.E.   (listener brings hand to face, nods, "mhm")
   Secondly you're gonna have to have a master's degree (two slight nods)

Only after receiving active listening response does the speaker continue to the next point. Note in the detailed transcription of example (3c) that the student *was actually providing kinesic listening activity* as the counselor spoke. This listening activity took the form of continuous, slight nods that were not "accented," as were all the nods performed by the white student in example (4). This suggests that the black student's slight nods were somehow not enough. Despite these small nods by the listener, the counselor continued to recycle the explanation of "state certification." The counselor, by saying the same thing again and again to the student, was literally "talking down" to him.

The "talking down" continued even after the student showed much more active listening response:

Secondly you're going to have to have a master's degree(accented nod, unaccented nod)
   in counseling (no nod)
     which as you know, is an advanced degree (speaker laughs nervously)

This suggests that regulatory relationships between speaking and listening could not be adequately accounted for by a strictly behaviorist model of organization. The empirical data to support this contention will be presented in the next section of the paper. Here it suffices to say that usually when an absence of listening response occurs at LRRM the absence is made accountable by the speaker through hyperexplanation (talking down, giving reasons). When active listening response occurs at a LRRM the speaker does not usually hyperexplain, but proceeds on to the next speaking point. These are the statistically most frequent relations between speaking and listening behavior in /explaining/—in linguistic terminology, these are the "unmarked forms" of the listening-speaking relationship.

But things are not that simple. There are less frequent ("marked") exceptions when explaining happens. In example (3) the counselor continued to "talk down" after having made the speaking point that a master's degree was needed, "talking down" after the student responded to that point with accented head nods. Some factors other than the form of the listening response itself must account for this. Perhaps a contextual factor—in the LRRMs immediately preceding the student had apparently not provided active listening in a form acceptable to the counselor. At that point the student may have established a "performed social identity." He may have become then for the counselor a *person who does not understand what I am saying.* Having been such a person a few moments ago, the nods given by the student at the next LRRM may not "count." They may not be "enough" to establish a new identity as a *person who I can be certain is understanding what I am saying,* given the counselor's ways of making sense of what is happening.

This discussion suggests that behaviorist models of the relations between explaining and listening are bound to be inadequate. In the following figure I have attempted (1) to specify features of the social and cognitive organization of /explaining/ and of providing listening response while being explained to and (2) to include room in the model for the conversationalists' moment-to-moment ways of making sense of what they are doing.

The diagram is a general model for the joint, collaborative accomplishment by a speaker and a listener of *making a single point in an /explanation/ and going on to the next point.* The most frequently occurring ("unmarked") paths in the model are represented by solid lines, and the less frequently occurring ("marked") paths are represented by broken lines.

From the model one can see that usually a speaker who has just made a speaking point proceeds on to the next speaking point if the first point was followed by some listening response at the LRRM after the first point was made, and no "inculpatory" (blame accruing) contextual conditions applied: $(Path_1 \Rightarrow LRRM \rightarrow + LR \rightarrow RNP-Raise$ Next Point). This can be written in a more differentiated form as $(Path_1 \Rightarrow LRRM \rightarrow + LR \rightarrow -IC \rightarrow (RNP)$. If the listener does not show attention through active listening response, usually the speaker will recycle the explanation and make the point again before proceeding on to the next point. This can be called $Path_2$ $(Path_2 \Rightarrow LRRM \rightarrow -LR \rightarrow PP-Persist$ at Point), which can be rewritten $(Path_2 \Rightarrow LRRM \rightarrow -LR \rightarrow -EC \rightarrow PP)$. In $Path_2$ the speaker recycles the explanation in the absence of any "exculpatory" (extenuating) contextual circumstances (EC). More than one recycle constitutes hyperexplanation, which may appear in the form of *talking down* or of *giving reasons.*

In the model there are two sets of contextual circumstances immediate to the face-to-face interaction situation itself. These sets are *EC* ("exculpatory" circumstances) and *IC* ("inculpatory" circumstances). Members of these sets include:

(1)   previous performance at earlier LRRMs in the conversation,[1] especially those just preceding the current instance. (Negative previous performance can have the effect of establishing the performed social identity of the student as "person who has not been paying attention.");

(2)   other features of social identity, such as grade point average, test scores, race, ethnicity, dress. (Racial and ethnic similarity to the speaker are assumed to

---

[1] The speaker's use of the listener's past performance as a contextual "ground" against which to judge the "figure" of the listener's current listening behavior involves the process of interactional inference that ethnomethodologists term *retrospective-prospective interpretive procedures* (c.f. Mehan & Wood, 1975).

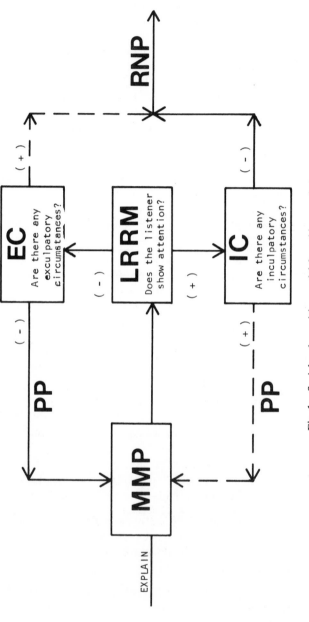

Fig. 1 Social and cognitive model fo making a point.

KEY:

MMP = Moment of Making a Point

EC = "Exculpatory" Circumstances
(Previous performance, social identities, unimportance of point, point made only partially)

LRRM = Listening Response-Relevant Moment

IC = "Inculpatory" Circumstances
(Previous performance, social identities, culturally inappropriate listening responses, listener should have shown understanding as well as attention)

PP = Persist at Point
(Talk down, give reasons, ask point-relevant questions)

——— = Frequent "unmarked" paths

– – – = Infrequent "marked" paths

be positive, or at least potentially positive features. Dissimilarity is assumed to be negative, or potentially negative.)

(3)   unimportance of point (the point is not worth bothering about).

In the context of the *presence* of an appropriate listening response at a LRRM, the overall absence of negative inculpatory circumstances is considered positive. In the context of the *absence* of an appropriate listening response at a LRRM the overall absence of positive, exculpatory circumstances is considered negative. More than one of the circumstances can apply in an additive sense, in each of the sets EC and IC. Some positive features in the set EC may "cancel" other negative features in the set IC, for example, if the listener were black and thus racially different from the speaker (a negative feature of social identity) but had been showing much attention by active listening behavior at prior LRRMs during the interview (a positive feature of past performance), the model allows the speaker to proceed to the next point without recycling the explanation.

The set IC always includes a positive feature that the set [EC] does not; the presence of the feature of performed social identity *person who is now actively showing attention.*

The set IC in the model includes the member *need for the listener to show understanding in addition to attention.* If this condition applies the speaker will recycle the explanation.

The model generates four paths or generative rules, in the Chomskian sense. The first two have already been identified: ($Path_1 \Rightarrow LRRM \rightarrow + LR \rightarrow RNP$) ($Path_2 \Rightarrow LRRM \rightarrow -LR \rightarrow PP$). Out of a total of 133 instances of LRRM sequences examined, $Path_1$ accounts for 42% of the instances (56 cases) and $Path_2$ accounts for 36% of the instances (49 cases) (see Table I). These two paths describe what are the most statistically frequent, "normal" ways by which a speaker and a listener collaborate in the interactional accomplishment of the speech act /explaining/. (In linguistic terminology, $Path_1$ and $Path_2$ are the *unmarked forms.*)

The remaining 22% of the instances are accounted for by $Path_3$ and $Path_4$: ($Path_3 \Rightarrow LRRM \rightarrow +LR \rightarrow PP$) ($Path_4 \Rightarrow LRRM \rightarrow -LR \rightarrow RNP$). These are statistically less frequent, exceptional occurrences (*marked forms* in linguistic terminology) in which special conditions obtain.

In $Path_3$ the speaker, in spite of the presence of active listening response by the listener, does not go on to raise the next point but persists at the previous one: ($Path_3 \Rightarrow LRRM \rightarrow +LR \rightarrow PP$). This occurs in 18 (14%) of the 133 instances coded. In 11 of the 18 instances, the listener provided culturally inappropriate listening behavior. Notice that only one out of the 18 instances came from an intraracial encounter. In that instance the speaker was white and so was the listener. While the listener provided a culturally appropriate verbal and kinesic listening response (back channel and accented nod) another feature of his nonverbal behavior was culturally inappropriate in the white cultural system: he was not looking at the interviewer while providing active listening response. This single case, while ex-

TABLE 1. Path Sequences by Racial Composition of Interview Dyads

	Path$_1$ LRRM (+LR) (RNP)[a]	Path$_2$ LRRM (−LR) (PP)[a]	Path$_3$ LRRM (+LR) (PP)	Path$_4$ LRRM (−LR) (RNP)
Interracial interview dyads (N = 5)	27 (20%)	44 (33%)	17 (13%)	9 (7%)
Intraracial interview dyads (N = 4)	29 (22%)	5 (3%)	1 (1%)	1 (1%)
Total	56 (42%)	49 (36%)	18 (14%)	10 (8%)

[a] RNP = raise next point; PP = persist at point; N of instances = 133.

ceptional, is consistent with the rule that eye contact is a necessary condition within the white cultural system for appropriate listening response at a LRRM.

In 17 of the 18 instances that can be described by Path$_3$, the speaker was white and the listener was black. In 10 of these 17 cases, the black listener provised listening response (LR) in a form appropriate within the black cultural system but inappropriate within the white system. In each of the seven remaining cases, all involve the "inculpatory" contextual circumstances of the past performance of the listener. In these seven cases, the listener had not given any listening response during the previous LRRM and the speaker had persisted at the point and was reiterating it.

Path$_4$ accounts for the remaining exceptional cases (8%). In Path$_4$ the speaker in the absence of active showing of attention by the listener at the LRRM, nonetheless continued on to raise the next point: (Path$_4$ ⇒ LRRM → −LR → RNP). This path accounts for 10 of the 133 instances (8%).

There are two variants of Path$_4$ and they can be designated 4a and 4b. In Path$_{4a}$ the speaker, despite the absence of an active listening response, proceeded on to raise the next point because of some exculpatory circumstance: (Path$_{4a}$ ⇒ LRRM → −LR → +EC → RNP). There is only one instance of this in the 133 cases. It occurred at the beginning of a major sequence of explanation in an interview between a white interviewer who was speaking and a white student who was listening. The point being made had already been discussed in the section immediately prior to the one coded. What the interviewer was doing at this point was tieing back to the prior point just made and then moving on to the next point, which was the important one.

Path$_{4b}$ describes the remaining nine instances. In this variant the speaker proceeded on to raise the next point not because of an exculpatory circumstance but because of an inculpatory one: (Path$_{4b}$ ⇒ LRRM → −LR → +IC → RNP). All nine cases occur in interracial interviews in which the speaker is white and the listener is black. The inculpatory circumstances involved the listener's performance of listening behavior in sequences of hyperexplanation (in which the interviewer had already been "talking down" because the interviewee was not providing active listening response at the points where it was appropriate in the white cultural system). In all nine instances the white speaker had persisted at the same point at least once (and usually more than once) and so finally was "forced" to go on to the next point in order to continue the interview. Path$_{4b}$ represents at once (1) the most extreme form of things going wrong interactionally during explanations, (2) the most structurally extreme exception to the normal discourse rules identified here, and (3) the least statistically frequent occurrences in the empirical data.

These last findings, despite the small numbers involved, have great theoretical salience. It should be noted that *no instances* of Path$_{4b}$ discourse occurred in the films examined in which both speaker and listener were of the same race and shared similar cultural systems for the social organization of discourse and listening behavior in doing /explaining/. While it is theoretically possible for Path$_{4b}$ to occur in the four intraracial, intracultural encounters examined, the empirical data show that this variant only occurred in the five interracial, intercultural encounters. It would seem that this was due to the cultural differences between speaker and listener in the interracial interviews.

CULTURAL DIFFERENCES IN WAYS OF MAKING A POINT AND GIVING A LISTENING RESPONSE

There seem to be culturally conventional ways in which (1) speakers signal listeners that active listening response is about to be appropriate, and (2) listeners signal speakers that they are paying attention. Since the conduct of discourse face to face involves a delicate and simultaneous coordination of communicative performance and interpretation between speaker and listener, cultural differences in their ways of signaling implicitly to each other can result in their misreading or failing to notice all or some of each other's cues as to what the context is—the "state of their union" from moment to moment.

Cultural differences between white people and black people in the U. S., differences in contextualization cue—are illustrated in this section. These are cultural differences that consistently seem to interfere with listener-speaker coordination in getting from one point to the next in an explanation.

First to be considered is the issue of how the behavioral forms a speaker employs in making a point function as *contextualization cues* signaling that a LRRM is what will happen next.

In the white cultural manner of making a point, the point itself (the predication clarifying the discourse topic) is usually made in one syntactic "chunk," the grammatical *predicate* or *verb phrase*, which is then immediately followed by a brief pause during which the LRRM occurs. We can see this by recalling example 3, in which each of the successively linked predications clarifying the subject of the previous point is followed immediately by a LRRM:

(3)   First of all you're gonna need / state teacher certification /LRRM/, that is, you're gonna have to be certified to teach in some area /LRRM/ History or English or whatever else happens to be your bag /LRRM/ P. E. /LRRM/

In the black cultural style of making a point, there is only one general difference from the white style but that difference has profound interactional consequences. In the black style the predication that clarified the previous discourse topic does not always come in a whole "chunk" that is then followed immediately by a LRRM, as in the white style. Within the "chunk" that clarifies the previous point there may be (1) a syntactic break followed by a pause during which listening response is not mandatory (e.g., "when I get here /no LRRM/ they tell me") or there may be (2) an interpolated taglike *filler* that may be preceded by and is always followed by a pause (e.g., "they test /you know / no LRRM/ all my papers"). In both the first and second instances the pause does not constitute a moment at which active listening response is a mandatory obligation of the listener. The pause at a syntactic break before the full predication is complete (instance 1) or the interpolated filler and subsequent silence (instance 2) *postpone the final making of the point,* leaving it, as it were, up in the air. Only then is the final part of the point made and only after that is listening response mandatory.

These ways of inserting a postponing "chunk" between the first part of an explanatory predication and the last part in which the full "point" is finally made are illustrated by the following example from a conversation between a black speaker and a black listener:

<pre>
                                       noLLRRM   +LR
(5a) they tell me they lost you know / . . / all my papers / . . /
                                     no LRRM   +LR
      'n then I had to re- (you know) / . . / reapply / . . /
</pre>

In the black system of contextualization cues for a LRRM, the main point (and the one clause terminal juncture that requires close attention from the listener) is usually marked by a sharp falling intonation, which functions as a LRRM signal. In the white system, the LRRM can be signaled solely by the syntactic juncture, with no downward intonation. The sharply falling intonation shift (from a high pitch level of 4 or 3½ down to a low pitch level of 1) that marks a LRRM definitively for a black listener *is almost never performed by white speakers.* The range of the shift for whites is more usually 3-1 or even 2½-1. In the white system, whichever intonation contour is employed, when the speaker reaches the end of the phrase and falls silent for roughly half a second, that is the moment for listening response by the listener.

The white pattern, in which listening response can be mandatory despite the absence of a steeply falling intonation cue, can be seen in example (4d), which has been previously discussed, and is here presented with subscript numbers indicating intonation contour:

$$-LR$$
(4d)   what we're gonna have to do first of all is to get you set up / . . /
$$2\ \ 2$$

$$+LR$$
for an A C T test / . . / in . . ah . . I believe the next one
$$2\ \ 2\ \ 2\tfrac{1}{2}$$

will be in July.

(speaker slows down)

Here the white speaker makes accountable the absence of listening response during the first LRRM by slowing down his speech and persisting at the point. The first LRRM was signaled by a sustained intonational contour (2-2). The white speaker then signals the next LRRM with a sustained intonational contour plus a slower rate of speech, and the listener provides listening response. After receiving listening response, the speaker goes on to make the next point concerning the date the examination is to be scheduled.

The black pattern, in which listening response is usually mandatory only after a steeply falling intonation contour (which may be followed by an interpolated filler before the point is fully completed) can be seen in example (5b)

no LRRM
(5b) An' then when I get h e e r e / . . / they tell me they
$$2\tfrac{1}{2}\text{-}1\tfrac{1}{2}\ (stress)$$

no LRRM   *(yeah, "unaccented" nod)*
lost you know / . . / all my p a p e r s / .   .   /
$$3\text{-}2\quad\quad 1\tfrac{1}{2}\text{-}1\quad\quad 1\tfrac{1}{2}\text{-}\quad 3\tfrac{1}{2}\ 1\tfrac{1}{2}$$
(stress)

("unaccented" nod)
'n then I had to re- you know re-apply /   .   .   / 'n then they
$$2\quad\quad\quad 2\quad 1\tfrac{1}{2}\quad 1\quad 1\tfrac{1}{2}\text{-}1\tfrac{1}{2}\ 3\tfrac{1}{2}\text{-}1\tfrac{1}{2}$$
(stress)(stress)

told me to resubmit

In example (5b), after the first pause (which is not a LRRM because the point has not yet been fully made), the speaker continues on in the absence of listening response to the second pause, which is preceded by a steeply falling contour (3-1½). In spite of the pitch shift the pause does not count as a LRRM because it was preceded by a tag ("you know") and because the point has still not fully been made syntactically (what was lost was *the papers*). The speaker continues on to complete the point after the second pause, and does so with a steeply falling intonation shift (3½-1½ on "papers"). Here there has been a steeply falling pitch shift *without a subsequent tag,* and the subsequent pause is a LRRM, during which listening response is provided. After that the speaker proceeds on to raise the next point ("then they told me to resubmit"). From this we can infer some things about the interactional knowledge necessary for listeners, in both the black and the white systems. The black listener listening to a black speaker needs to know something like the following two rules: (1) "As the speaker is making a point, if you hear a steep fall at the end of a phrase, or if you hear a steep fall before the phrase is ending and then a tag before the speaker becomes silent, what you should do next is some kind of listening response." (2) "Conversely, if you do not hear a steep fall, or if the speaker is talking in a sustained contour and does not put a tag on the end of that phrase, *you do not need to provide active listening response.*" The white listener listening to a white speaker needs to know something different; something like the following rule: "As the speaker is making a point, if you hear *either* a sustained contour at the end of a phrase *or* a steeply falling contour, *always provide active listening response in the ensuing silence.*"

What seems to have been happening in the interviews in which the speaker was white and the listener was black was that white speakers used the culturally preferred LRRM cue form most often (sustained intonation at clause terminal juncture) and that black listeners "missed" many of those LRRMs that the white speaker was signaling by that cue form. In talking to black listeners the white speakers used sustained intonation 63 times at a clause terminal juncture and only used 29 times a steeply falling intonation at a clause terminal juncture. When the white speaker used the falling intonation as a contextualization cue, the black listener provided listening response in 20 out of 29 instances, but when the white speaker used sustained intonation as a contextualization cue, the black speaker provided listening response in only 20 out of 63 instances; a far different proportion of "hits" to "misses" than that found when the speaker used steeply falling intonation. The misses by the listener were followed by the speaker with hyperexplanation, persisting at the point being made 43 times out of a total of 52 instances (the nine times the speaker went on to the next point despite the absence of listening response are all instances of Path$_4$, in which at least one prior LRRM had not been reacted to by the listener with a listening response). The result of these absences of response to LRRMs that were signaled by sustained intonation was *chainlike sequences of "talking down"* by the white interviewer.

Finally, let us consider differences in the behavioral form of listening responses. In the white system for listening behavior, eye contact is always necessary during active listening response (and before it), while in the black system is appears that eye contact is optional (cf. Hall, 1974). In the black system, if the listener had not previously been looking at the speaker, he could provide active listening response simply by raising the eyes and gazing at the speaker. In the white system gaze involvement by itself is not "enough;" verbal and/or nonverbal response is also required. In the white system vocal back channel responses such as "mhm" are usually accompanied by simultaneous "accented" head nods, while in the black system *either* an unaccented head nod *or* a vocal back channel may be given as a listening response, but both are not usually given simultaneous (see Table 2). In the films investigated here, all nods by white listeners to white speakers were "accented" in form (see Table 3), and were usually performed one at a time, although continuous "accented" nodding also occurred. Conversely, for a black listener with a black speaker, *no "accented" nods occurred* (see Table 3). Instead, the nods were continuous and "unaccented" in kinesic form, with the head moving only very slightly. These continuous slight nods by a listener may begin in the middle of a speaking clause and continue across a number of clauses. Among filmed white listeners lis-

TABLE 2. General Form of Listening Response
by Social Identity of Listener and Speaker

Form of listening response (LR)	Social identity of listener					
	Black			White		
	With black speaker	With white speaker	Total	With black speaker	With white speaker	Total
Verbal LR	12	4	16	–	0	0
Nonverbal LR[a]	5	26	31		4	4
Verbal and Nonverbal LR[b]	2	13	15	–	8	8

[a] N = 34 instances of nodding response; 1 instance of gestural response. [b] For this row all nonverbal LRs are nods. N of black-black films = 2; N of white-white films = 2; N of white-black films = 5.

TABLE 3. Form of Nodding by Social Identity of Listener and Speaker

Behavioral form of nodding	Social identity of listener				
	Black			White	
	With black speaker	With white speaker	Total	With black speaker	With white speaker
Accented	0	14	14	–	4
Unaccented	5	12	17	–	0

N of black-black films = 2; N of white-white films = 2; N of black-white films = 5.

tening to white speakers *slight continuous unaccented nodding never occurs.*

Despite the small numbers of instances involved, Tables 2 and 3 suggest that there are separate white and black cultural rule systems organizing listener's choices of forms of listening response. The tables also show that when black listeners were responding to white speakers, the black listeners adaptively switched cultural listening styles, using the "white" cultural LR form more often with whites than with blacks.

The implication of this style switching is important and deserves brief mention here. The culturally learned knowledge ("communicative competence") necessary to be able to switch listening styles requires that one understand both cultural systems of rules organizing listening behavior, i.e., the person who can do this must be *bicultural*. It has been reported in the sociolinguistic literature that U. S. black speakers of nonstandard Black English" also understand many syntactic and phonological aspects of "standard English" and style-switch freely between both systems (cf. Mitchell-Kernan, 1972; see also Gumperz & Hernandes-Chavez, 1972; Blom & Gumperz 1972 for analogous data on Spanish/English and nonstandard Norwegian/

standard Norwegian linguistic switching.) What Tables 2 and 3 show are analogous examples of style switching in the nonverbal channel of communicative behavior. These nonverbal data support the inferences based on sociolinguistic data that members of cultural "minorities" are not simply monoculturally competent in a "minority" culture, but are likely to be biculturally competent in both the "minority" and the "majority" systems of conventions for interactional etiquette.

In spite of the adaptive ability of the black listeners to style switch and "listen white" part of the time during interaction with a white speaker, there are still negative interactional consequences that derive from differences in cultural interaction style between whites and blacks. After nine of the 12 instances of nods in "unaccented" form by a black listener, the white speaker hyperexplained, persisting at the previous point. In the remaining three instances the speaker responded to the incorrect nod by raising the next point, but these were all cases accounted for by $Path_4$, in which at previous moments of making a point the listener had failed to give a listening response and the speaker had hyperexplained.

Conversely in the 14 instances in which the black listener used the contextually *correct* LR form (accented nod), the white speaker's next move was to proceed to raise the next point 13 times. The one instance in which the speaker persisted at the same point after the listener gave an accented nod is accounted for by $Path_3$, in which the listener fails in preceding LRRMs to provide any listening response and the speaker has already persisted at the point. This one instance was an especially unusual one in which the listener had "missed" giving a LR for four consecutive previous LRRMs. Each time that black and white listeners gave the *most correct* form of listening response (or at least the most emphatic and obvious form), which was to provide a verbal back channel response and a nod simultaneously—provided there were no "inculpatory" contextual circumstances, such as ($\leftarrow$ MMP −LR, PP)− the white speaker always went on to raise the next point. If there were "inculpatory" circumstances, whether the listener was white or black, the speaker invariable persisted at the point even if the listener had provided the culturally correct LR form.

Summary

The main differences between the two systems are that in the white system there is a relatively high threshold for minimal levels of activity necessary to signal attention. Listening attention is signaled in relatively gross ways. Conversely in the black system, listening attention is signaled relatively subtly. It is the LRRM that is signaled in relatively gross ways in the black system, with sharp intonational shifts and considerable kinesic activity. In the black system, LRRMs appear less frequently than in the white system, but they are marked with broad strokes of the pen, so to speak. In the white system LRRMs occur more frequently (at the end of almost every syntactic clause), but are cued much more subtly.

It is apparent from this description that white speakers, viewing black listening behavior from the point of view of the white system, are likely to assume that blacks are providing listening feedback in overly subtle ways that are "not enough." White speakers are also likely to find black listeners "missing" some of the LRRMs entirely (because many LRRMs are not signaled by white speakers with "enough" intonation shifts and body motion, in terms of the black system). From the white speaker's point of view, the black listener would seem to be not providing "any" listening feedback (even though the black listener may be signaling attention with eye contact and with slight, "unaccented" nods, the white speaker would not "read" such listening rsponses as "enough"). White speakers would be likely to react by hyperexplaining.

This is what happens so frequently in the films of interracial counseling sessions that were investigated. Extended sequences of hyperexplanation, talking down or giving reasons, *do not occur* in the black-black encounters or in the white-white encounters. *They occur only in the white-black encounters.* It seems reasonable to conclude that hyperexplanation is caused in part by cultural differences between white and black systems of contextualization cuing; of speakers signaling when listening response is appropriate and of listeners providing listening response at those appropriate times.

IMPLICATIONS FOR POLICY, PRACTICE, AND TRAINING

The work reported here is exploratory, and with such work there is both a danger in taking it too seriously and in not taking it seriously enough. First let me warn against taking too seriously the findings reported here by pointing to some technical limitations in research design.

This is a small sample of cases of intraracial and interracial interaction in only one special kind of social situation. Only one analyst was involved in coding the data off the films, and that was the author. Moreover, the intonation coding system used was very crude. (A more appropriate system for the notation of speech prosody is that currently being developed by John Trim at Oxford and adapted by John Gumperz and associates at the Language-Behavior Research Laboratory, University of California at Berkeley). So the reliability and generalizability of the data reported here should be tested in further research before these findings become a basis for policy decisions.

Even if there were no recurring kinds of errors in the data, there is the problem of competing interpretations of its significance. It could be argued that I have not taken adequate account of the influence of racial prejudice on what happens in the interviews. A white speaker may persist at a speaking point more with black listeners than with white simply because the white speaker thinks the black listeners are likely to be less bright. The prejudice theory could also account for some of the cases described as "marked" exceptions to the general rules for the conduct of explaining: the 22% of the cases in which the speaker either persisted at the speaking point despite the presence of listening response (Path$_3$), or raised the next point despite the absence of listening response (Path$_4$). Almost all these cases occurred in interracial interviews. The differences in listening response form that I think "explain" why the speaker deviated from normal procedure in those cases may be coincidental differences. The real cause may be the racial attitudes of the interviewers. Since I do not have an independent measure of the racial attitudes of the interviewers, the plausibility of this interpretation cannot be ruled out by the evidence I am able to report here. (A more differentiated variation on this explanatory theme is found in the paper by McDermott in this volume. Both he and I are attempting to avoid overly simple causal models in which either *prejudice* by itself, or *communication style difference* by itself is seen as a necessary and sufficient cause of interactional "trouble.")

Still, the coherence and explanatory power of the models I have presented is substantial. There are nine instances of interviewers, not just one or two, and 133 instances of LRRMs. While these are still relatively small sample sizes, the differences in how things went interactionally are very clear when one compares intraracial interviews with interracial ones. These differences are striking enough that one must take seriously the contention that cultural style in communication behavior is at least one of the factors that strongly influence interactional processes and outcomes.

If one takes seriously the idea that cultural differences in communication style can be a source of interactional "trouble" in interracial encounters in settings like schools and work places, what can one do about it?

First, one can become more aware of what the nature of the trouble is. It involves not simply the repetition of explanations long after the listener understands what is being explained, producing a high incidence of "uncomfortable moments" (cf. Erickson, 1975, 1976b); it also involves the inferences people make about one another's intentions when such things go wrong interactionally. I have some evidence about this from interviews with the people I filmed. The evidence suggests that when a listener listens to a hyperexplanation he may say things to himself like "I don't believe that," or "How can I tell that (s)he's not trying to trick me?" When a speaker monitors listening behavior that is inappropriate he may say to himself, "(S)he's not listening—maybe (s)he doesn't understand, or maybe (s)he just doesn't care."

Second, one tries to provide organizational arrangements whereby the *explained to* have some regularly available access, should they desire it, to *explainers* of a culturally similar background. For schools this means the presence of counselors and teachers; for businesses this means the presence of job interviewers and work supervisors. Not the *exclusive* presence of explainers of a culturally similar background. This would mean a kind of resegregation that would be wrong both on the grounds of justice and on the grounds of ignoring the growing body of evidence (including the evidence reported here on adaptive switching of listening style) that attests to the tremendous adaptive capacity of those people called "culturally different" to possess *bicultural competence*—knowledge of both the "minority" and the "majority" patterns for doing things, including the doing of everyday interaction.

But the available evidence also suggests that things are more likely to go wrong interculturally and interracially, that people are usually not consciously aware of what is it interactionally that is going wrong, and that what goes wrong is emotionally painful for both parties involved and may influence them to misunderstand, distrust, and resent one another. So the presence of culturally similar people for at least some of the advising and supervising that happens at school and at work is a reasonable organizational response to the human problems that cultural difference can contribute to. For most "majority" institutions this means substantial increases in minority hiring and attention to the organization of personnel so as to foster face-to-face contact among people of similar racial and cultural background. To reiterate, not *exclusive* contact, but *contact*.

Finally, one tries to improve the quality of interracial interaction face to face. One approach is to train people to communicate better. The evidence that people of cultural minority background are actually bicultural, they already know and practice a good deal of "majority" cultural knowledge, including knowledge of communication style, suggests that the first attempts at training to improve intercultural communication ought to be with people of the cultural "majority." They are likely to know less about the "minority" cultural communication style than the members of the minority group know about the "majority" communication style.

Some cultural differences in communication style can be reflected on consciously and people can be trained to change their behavior to adjust to that of another cultural system. An example from the research reported here concerns the use of a sustained intonation contour to signal listening response-relevance. If my analysis is correct, this is a feature of a listening response cue in the white cultural system but not in the black system. A white interviewer could learn to avoid this intonation contour when making an explanation point with a black listener.

By themselves, however, such behavior changes would probably be ineffective. They would probably be too mechanical; too categorical a response to cultural difference, and they would ignore the micropolitical factors in face-to-face interaction that contribute to interactional "trouble" (see the McDermott chapter in this volume).

Some exploratory work my colleagues and I have begun with teachers in classrooms (and some work being done by Gumperz at the Language-Behavior Research Laboratory at Berkeley) suggests that the first thing to try to change by training is not specific features of the communication behavior involved in doing explaining, but more general features of the processes of ongoing conversational inference by which the *explainer* decides what the *explained to* is up to at the moment—training to change how the *explainer* decides whether the *explained to* is attending, whether (s)he understands, whether (s)he agrees. In other words, I think that making speakers aware of cultural differences by which listeners do listening behavior can help the speaker to avoid "misreading" the meaning of what a listener is doing, and to avoid misjudging the listener's intent. For example, a white speaker could keep in mind that when a black listener is not maintaining eye contact as the speaker completes an explanation point, that does not necessarily mean that the listener is not paying attention. Correct assessment of the meaning of the listener's listening would prevent the speaker from doing such inappropriate things as hyperexplaining when the listener already has shown that (s)he understands what has just been said.

The problem even with this approach, which is likely to be less mechanistic than that involving oversimplified (and stereotypical) exercises in "how to talk to an X" (black, latin, native American), is that even trying to concentrate on one's own processes of conversational inference as one is interacting requires a kind of focused awareness that is alien to the performance of everyday life; a reflectiveness about what one is doing as one is doing it that may well be impossible to achieve, or at least undesireable to maintain, except for brief moments at a time. The kinds of organization of communication behavior and conversational inference I have described in this paper are extremely complex and in everyday social performance are processed cognitively outside conscious awareness, as the grammatical and phonological organization of language is "transparent" to a speaker while actually engaged in conversation. The linguist's insights into the structure of language may not be of much use to the practitioner of ordinary speaking. The same may be the case for the detailed knowledge of the analyst of cultural patterns in nonverbal behavior.

Thus a still less artificial and mechanical approach to training, the last I will speculate on here, might be to develop an interviewer's, teacher's, or supervisor's capacity for retrospective analysis of *what is going on in terms of interactional behavior* when one gets the feeling intuitively that something had just gone wrong. At these uncomfortable moments, or at such moments as *finding one's self hyperexplaining,* it may be possible to check one's normal split-second response of inferring the social intent of the other person ["'(s)he's not interested," "'(s)he's trying to hide something"] and substitute for that knee-jerk reaction of conversational inference an equally brief scanning of the communicational structure of the moment ["Why do I think (s)he's not listening?" "What is (s)he doing?" "What am I doing?"]. Exposure through training to knowledge about the complex ways in which speaking and listening behavior are coordinated in face-to-face interaction, and about cultural differences in the ways such coordination is organized, could provide the trainee with the frames of reference for conducting momentary retrospective analysis of conversation as it occurs, a subjective "instant replay" and analysis during the course of interaction. Through the practice that could come through recurrent participation in intercultural communication situations, combined with self-developed methods of retrospective analysis as a *more observant participant* in interaction, perhaps people can learn to change their patterns of communication behavior and conversational inference in the direction of greater cultural congruence with the people they interact with day by day. Training attempts that move in these directions are, in my current thinking, those most likely to be natural and humane in methods and in outcome; to be responsible in not promising too much for too little effort. We still know very little about all this, and should remain modest in our expectations of applied results.

In sum, three things can be done, each of which alone is a necessary but not sufficient condition for improving the quality of intercultural interaction: (1) increased hiring of ethnic and racial "minorities," (2) planning organizational life to make available intracultural contact, and (3) training for intercultural competence, especially training for those most likely to lack such competence, the members of cultural and racial "majority groups." Each approach adopted in isolation from the others is likely to be inadequate. To adopt any of the approaches requires that one first take very seriously the influence of cultural difference on the conduct of interaction face-to-face.

References

Argyle, Michael. *Social interaction.* Chicago: Aldine, 1969.

Argyle, Michael. *Social encounters: Readings in social interaction.* Chicago: Aldine, 1973.

Bernstein, Basil. Social class, linguistic codes, and grammatical elements. *Language and Speech,* 1962, *5,* 221-240.

Birdwhistell, Ray L. *Kinesics and context: Essays on body motion communication.* Philadelphia: University of Pennsylvania Press, 1970.

Blom, Jan-Petter, and John Gumperz. Social meaning in linguistic structure: Code-switching in Norway. In J. Gumperz and D. Hymes (Eds.), *Directions in sociolinguistics.* New York: Holt, Rinehart, and Winston, 1972.

Condon, W. S., & Ogston, W. D. A segmentation of behavior. *Journal of Psychiatric Research,* 1967, *5,* 221-235.

Davis, Martha. *Understanding body movement: An annotated bibliography.* New York: Arno Press, 1972.

Duncan, Starkey. Some signals and rules for taking speaking turns in conversations. *Journal of Personality and Social Psychology,* 1972, *6,* 341-349.

Duncan, Starkey. Interaction units during speaking turns in dyadic face-to-face conversations. In A. Kendon *et al.* (Eds.), *Organization of behavior in face-to-face interaction.* The Hague/Chicago: Mouton/Aldine, 1976.

Ekman, P., and Friesen, W. V. Nonverbal leakage and clues to deception. *Psychiatry.* 1969, *32,* 88-106.

Erickson, Frederick. Gatekeeping and the melting pot: Interaction in counseling encounters. *Harvard Educational Review,* 1975, *45,* 44-70.

Erickson, Frederick. "Afterthoughts." In A. Kendon *et al.* (Eds.), *Organization of behavior in face-to-face interaction.* The Hague/Chicago: Mouton/Aldine, 1976. (a)

Erickson, Frederick. Gatekeeping interaction: A social selection process. In Peggy R. Sanday (Ed.), *Anthropology and the public interest: Fieldwork and theory.* New York: Academic Press, 1976. (b)

Erickson, Frederick, with J. Shultz, C. Leonard-Dolan, *et al.* Inter-ethnic relations in urban institutional settings. Final Technical Report, Center for Studies of Metropolitan Problems, NIMH (MH 18230, MH 21460), 1973.

Erickson, Frederick and Shultz, Jeffrey J., *Talking to the man: Social and cultural organization of communication in school counseling interviews.* New York: Academic Press, in press.

Gleason, Harold A. *An introduction to descriptive linguistics.* New York: Holt, Rinehart, and Winston, 1961.

Goffman, Erving. *Interaction ritual: Essays on face-to-face behavior.* Garden City, New York: Anchor Books, Doubleday, 1967.

Gumperz, John J. The speech community. In *International encyclopedia of the social sciences.* New York: Crowell, Collier, and Macmillan, 1968.

Gumperz, John J. Language, communication, and public negotiation. In Peggy R. Sanday (Ed.), *Anthropology and public policy.* New York: Academic Press, 1976.

Gumperz, John, & Hernandez-Chavez, Eduardo. Bilingualism, bidialectalism, and classroom interaction. In C. Cazden, V. John, and D. Hymes (Eds.), *Functions of language in the classroom*. New York: Teachers College Press, 1972.

Hall, Edward T. Listening behavior: Some cultural differences. *Phi Delta Kappan* 1969, *50*, 379-380.

Hall, Edward T. *Handbook for proxemic research*. Washington, D. C.: Society for the Anthropology of Visual Communication, 1974.

Hymes, Dell. "Studying the Interaction of Language and Social Life." In *Foundations in sociolinguistics: An ethnographic approach*. Philadelphia: University of Pennsylvania Press, 1974.

Keenan, Elinor, & Schieffelin, Bambi. Topic as a discourse notion. In Charles Li (Ed.), *Subject and topic*. New York: Academic Press, 1976.

Kendon, Adam. Some functions of gaze direction in social interaction. *Acta Psychologica,* 1967, *26:* 22-47. Reprinted in M. Argyle (Ed.), *Social Encounters*. Chicago: Aldine, 1973.

Kendon, Adam, Harris, Richard M., & Ritchie Key, Mary, (Eds.). *Organization of behavior in face-to-face interaction*. The Hague/Chicago: Mouton/Aldine, 1976.

LaFrance, Marianne, & Mayo, Clara. Racial differences in gaze behavior during conversation. *Journal of Personality and Social Psychology,* 1976, *33*, 547-552.

Mehan, Hugh, & Wood, Houston. *The Reality of ethnomethodology*. New York: Wiley-Interscience, 19

Mehan, Hugh, & Wood, Houston. *The reality of ethnomethodology*. New York: Wiley-Interscience, 1975.

Mehrabian, Albert. Inference of attitudes from the posture, orientation, and distance of a communicator. *Journal of Consulting and Clinical Psychology,* 1968, *32*, 296-308.

Mehrabian, Albert. *Nonverbal communication*. Chicago/New York: Aldine/ Atherton, 1972.

Meyer, Leonard B. *Emotion and meaning in music*. Chicago: University of Chicago Press, 1956.

Mitchell-Kernon, Claudia. On the status of black English for native speakers. In C. Cazden, V. John, and D. Hymes (Eds.), *Functions of language in the classroom*. New York: Holt, Rinehart, and Winston, 1972.

Sacks, Harvey. On the analyzability of stories by children. In John J. Gumperz and Dell Hymes (Eds.), *Directions in sociolinguistics*. New York: Holt, Rinehart, and Winston, 1972.

Sacks, Harvey, Shegloff, Emanuel, & Jefferson, Gayle. A simplest systematics for the organization of turn-taking for conversation. *Language,* 1974, *50*, 696-735.

Scheflen, Albert E. *Communicational structure: Analysis of a psychotherapy transaction.* (formerly *Stream and structure in psychotherapy*). Bloomington: University of Indiana Press, 1973.

Shegloff, Emanuel. Sequencing in conversational openings. In John J. Gumperz and Dell Hymes (Eds.), *Directions in sociolinguistics.* New York: Holt, Rinehart, and Winston, 1972.

Shultz, Jeffrey. *The search for potential co-membership: An analysis of conversations among strangers.* Cambridge, Massachusetts: Unpublished Dissertation, Harvard Graduate School of Education, 1975.

THERAPIST TRAINING IN NONVERBAL BEHAVIOR: TOWARDS A CURRICULUM

Peter Waxer

Associate Professor of Psychology
York University

The awareness of the importance of nonverbal behavior in therapy and counseling is long standing. Current articles in this area frequently cite Sigmund Freud's (1959) observation:

> "He that has eyes to see and ears to hear may convince himself that no mortal can keep a secret. If his lips are silent, he chatters with his finger-tips; betrayal oozes out of him at every pore." (p. 94)

Theodor Reik (1948), more than a quarter of a century ago, admonished us to "listen with our third ear." McGowan and Schmidt (1962) suggested that "it may even be that one of the major variables which will help us distinguish the work of the experienced counselor from that of the novice is his ability to pick up and respond to minimal nonverbal cues in an accurate manner." Lewin (1965), focusing on the nonverbal cues (NVCs) of the therapist, alerts us to the fact that it is not only the clients NVCs that are relevant in the therapeutic context. Lewin states, ". . . the doctor should be aware of the importance of nonverbal cues and whether they tend to conceal or to reveal his own personality, so that he may anticipate and deal with the patient's responses. Otherwise certain resistances will develop without the doctor's knowing their source. While he searches fruitlessly for the cause in the patient's past, the answer may lie, neglected, within the confines of the doctor's office." (p. 394)

These are but a few of the numerous observations in past clinical literature underlining the communicative value of nonverbal behavior in the therapy setting. Contemporary analytical and psychotherapy writings show a continuing recognition of the role of nonverbal behavior (e.g., Bateson, 1956; Lowen, 1975; Laing, 1960).

In spite of much cogent comment in the literature about the role of nonverbal behavior from positions of both therapy theory and practice, systematic empirical investigation of nonverbal cues (NVCs) has waited on the development of techniques and apparatus by which NVCs could be properly explored. The advent of relatively low cost videotape recording equipment has now made this type of research possible and has lead to a renaissance of research on NVCs, some of which have direct implications for the area of therapist training. However thought provoking as some current research findings may be, to date there exists no systematic program of therapists training in nonverbal behavior based on a foundation of *empirically* established findings.

The need for such an approach to training is not merely another manifestation of the continuing criticism by behavioral scientists of the clinicians lack of empirical vigor. It is echoed within the directives of the clinician as teacher. Reik (1948), in discussing the role of nonverbal behavior in the therapeutic content, argues: "The greatest danger (and the one favored by our present way of training students) is that these seemingly insignificant signs will be missed, neglected, brushed aside." (p. 145)

This paper explores areas of the therapeutic context in which NVCs come into play, examines some of the existing findings in these areas, and discusses the implications these studies raise for therapy training for subsequent research and practice.

CLIENT-GENERATED NVCs

In order to facilitate discussion of the role of NVCs in the therapeutic context, two major divisions will be made here between NVCs given off by the client and NVCs given off by the therapist.

The areas discussed in each division by no means exhaust even the nonverbal component of the therapeutic context. Rather, they are proposed as basic units in the consideration of any training curriculum attempting to deal with nonverbal parameters of therapy. It is suggested that client-generated NVCs are an important source of therapeutic information in the following ways:

1. *Basic psychodiagnosis.* One fundamental aspect of a counselor's effectiveness is his ability to identify and accurately diagnose the nature of the client's psychological problem. Whether the client may be depressed, anxious, or manifesting some psychotic reaction, the question as to the role of NVCs in this context can be articulated as follows: Does the client's nonverbal behavior tell us anything about the psychological state of the client? Research in this area suggests a definite yes to this question and is in fact, one of the more productive areas of investigation.

2. *Therapeutic progress.* It is essential to optimal therapeutic practice that the counselor develop skills in assessing the rate of therapeutic progress. One has a professional concern not to accelerate the counseling experience beyond the capacity of the client. At the same time, the advance of therapy should not be dictated solely by the client's resistance to therapeutic change. There is a constant balancing act between too much and too little therapist pressure. The role of NVCs in the area

poses the question as to whether NVCs give any information about therapeutic progress. Do client-generated NVCs tell us whether the patient is getting well? Can client-generated NVCs signal a relapse or resistance in spite of client's protestations to the contrary?

3. *Client resistance.* This area focuses on the client's reaction to the counselor and to therapy and asks whether any client-generated NVCs provide information as to how the therapist and therapy is perceived by the client. Obviously the counselor's effectiveness in providing assistance is influenced by the amount of client resistance. It seems a valuable component of counselor training to sensitize the counselor to negative and positive NVC reactions on the part of the client.

THERAPIST-GENERATED NVCs

It is suggested here that therapist-generated NVCs can, if properly employed, exert a positive therapeutic influence. For ease of discussion, therapist-generated NVCs are divided into three sequential steps. In actual therapy practice, the division between these three areas as is often the case would be much less clearly delineated.

1. Establishment of initial rapport. Here the question is asked, are there any pertinent NVCs given off by the counselor that could speed the development of rapport with the client and strengthen the client's initial trust and acceptance? Are there any NVCs a counselor should become aware of and avoid as detrimental to this crucial period?

2. Facilitation of therapy. Are there NVCs generated by the therapist that will facilitate therapy once rapport is established? Do these NVCs differ from those relevant to establishment of rapport?

3. Modeling for growth. One aspect of counseling often overlooked in the effort to provide resolution of psychological crises is that the therapist can directly or unwittingly act as a model for client behavior. Once sensitized to this aspect of the therapeutic context, are there any NVCs that the therapist could employ to the client's benefit? Are there specific nonverbal behaviors characteristic of the therapist that could lead to social reinforcement and psychological growth if adopted by the client? Could such behavior be purposively organized into a therapy program?

RESEARCH ON NONVERBAL BEHAVIOR IN THERAPY

Client-Generated Nonverbal Cues

1. *Basic Psychodiagnosis.* Clinical research has noted in a number of different pathological populations marked deviations in one of the more fundamental nonverbal areas: that of eye contact. Ellsworth and Ludwig (1972) suggest, in fact, that deviation from normal gaze patterns is a hallmark of severe pathology. For example,

Hutt and Ounsted (1966) found that autistics are characterized by extreme gaze aversion, attributing this nonverbal behavior as a NVC signifying fear of rejection. Rutter and Stephenson (1972) found that visual interaction patterns for patients diagnosed schizophrenic and patients diagnosed depressed were significantly shorter in gaze duration than normals.

Waxer (1974) found that raters not informed as to the nature of patients diagnosis, were nevertheless able to identify presence or absence of depression on the basis of NVCs alone. NVCs rated as most salient for depression were poor eye contact, with eyes tending to gaze down and away from the therapist, down-turned mouth, head angled down, and absence of hand movement. Waxer (1976) found that raters naive to the therapeutic context could not only identify depressed from nondepressed patients but could identify how severely depressed patients were on the basis of NVCs alone. In both these studies it was found that raters with therapeutic experience were better able to utilize accurately NVCs in their diagnosis of depression.

In a similar examination of patients diagnosed as anxious, Waxer (1977) found a specific constellation of NVCs for anxiety, distinct in nature from those isolated for depression. Nonverbal cues identified as most salient in conveying anxiety were hands, eyes, mouth, and torso. Anxious patients manifested more stroking, twitching, and tremors in their manual behavior. Eye contact patterns showed the same frequency, but lower duration of eye contact than normals. Normals smiled significantly more than anxious individuals while raters perceived greater torso rigidity for anxious as opposed to normal individuals. In contrasting just the two Waxer studies on depression versus anxiety, the emergence of two distinct nonverbal cue clusters lends support to the historical Darwinian (Darwin, 1872/1955) hypothesis of unique patterns of nonverbal display for each emotion.

If this hypothesis holds up under the light of further empirical examination, NVCs hold the promise of providing a method of trained observation by which the emotional condition of a patient could be assessed in an unobtrusive and nonreactive fashion providing an additional source of convergent validation to existing questionnaires and protocol approaches. Overall, one conclusion to be drawn from studies such as these is that NVCs can provide basic diagnostic information about the client's emotional condition. This knowledge has obvious implications for the direction in which therapy will proceed.

2. *Rate of Therapeutic Progress.*   Hinchliffe, *et al.* (1971) reported an empirical finding supporting a long standing anecdotal observation by many therapists. This is the phenomenon of a client generating more social interaction, being more socially engaging, both verbally and nonverbally with recovery. Hinchliffe examined the amount of eye contact depressed patients engaged in over the course of their therapy. She found that as patients recovered from their depression both the frequency and duration of eye contact increased. Waxer (1974) found a similar difference between depressed and nondepressed patients, in that nondepressed patients generated significantly greater frequency of eye contact. What these studies imply is that NVCs

can provide an economic, nonreactive way to assess a client's therapeutic progress. Simply put, as the client improves, he will be able to look at and engage his therapist significantly more often than at the initial stages of his problems.

The converse would seem to logically hold true also. That is, when a client suffers an emotional relapse or is resistant to attempt new frightening behavioral change, one would expect to see a patient manifest some nonverbal sign of this internal emotional conflict. This issue is perhaps best discussed under NVCs for clients resistance since most clinicians tend to interpret failure to progress on a patient's part as some form, conscious or unconscious, of patient's resistance.

3. *Client Resistance.* Clinical practice reports that patient resistance can take many forms, ranging from withdrawal behavior to angry confrontation. For example, Murray (1964) demonstrated displacement as a resistance reaction. When the verbal content of a patient was analyzed, it was shown that therapist confrontation of the patient's intellectualizing defenses produced an upsurge of physical complaints by the patient. Scheflen (1973) in his content analyses of body movement within therapy employed an approach of observational description. Given this approach, Scheflen notes the occurrence of what he labels a "display of submission behavior" in response to therapist confrontation, consisting of "hunching down, looking down, hiding the hands, cocking the head, smiling, and maybe a conciliatory statement" (p. 135). Many other clinical reports note behavior such as the examples cited above, however the area is one in need of much more empirical investigation into the nonverbal signs of resistance. This research area has not received as much attention as it deserves perhaps due to the ethical problems associated with videotaping clients at a time in therapy when they may feel under attack. As difficult as it is to generate video material in the therapy context in general, the enterprise is even more problematic when the patient is resistant, agitated, or even overtly hostile. Still there is one body of research in the nonverbal area that has bearing on this issue. These are the findings of investigation such as Ekman and Friesen (1972) who report that hand motion, which they label as *self-adaptors,* "increases with psychological discomfort or anxiety" (p. 363). Self-adaptors were defined as gestures such as stroking oneself (ie., hand on hand, hand on face). Similarly, Mahl (1968), Dittman (1962), and Freedman and Hoffman (1967) all note the increase of nervous nonsignalling manual gestures as anxiety increases in a therapy context. These behaviors are argued to be unintentional "emotional leakage" (Ekman & Friesen, 1968) as opposed to purposive communicative gestures. As such they could be argued to function as precursors or concommitants to the patients inner emotional condition during periods of resistance in the therapy process. If patient resistance gives rise to conflict within a patient between the desire to respond to the therapist's directives on one hand and the patient's own fears on the other, it is suggested here that research by Ekman, Friesen, and others is indicative of one external nonverbal manifestation of such internal emotional upheaval. As is often the case, further empirical investigation is in order to lend support to clinical and descriptive observation in this area. When this is done, it is likely that salient

nonverbal communication of resistance will include phenomenon such as inordinate silences, displays of aggression, withdrawal behaviors, and facial reactions of fear, disgust, and confusion, just to mention a few of the more commonly cited nonverbal reactions appearing in clinical literature.

Therapist-Generated NVCs

1. *Establishment of Initial Rapport.* The clinical literature contains numerous *provisos* to novice therapists as to how they present themselves to their client. Berger (1970) provides one example of this in citing the reaction of a therapist-in-training to a videotape of his therapy session. The therapist stated, "I didn't realize how aloof, detached, and intellectual my manner was. I seem to have a superior attitude."

Krumboltz *et al.* (1967) presents empirical findings corroborating Berger's observations. Krumboltz hypothesized that nonverbal activity he labeled "attentiveness" would elicit more information seeking behavior on the part of 36 high school juniors observing videotaped interviews between an "attentive" or an "inattentive" counselor and a client. Krumboltz suggested that nonverbal behavior such as facial expressions of interest, direction, and intensity of gaze, body posture, degree of apparent attention, and number of distracting mannerisms may determine how successfully counseling proceeded. Operationally, the attentive counselor smiled when the student entered, immediately put down her work, turned directly to the student indicating readiness to listen. Throughout the session, the counselor looked directly at the student, nodding and smiling to indicate attention to what the student said. By facial expression and voice tone, the attentive counselor attempted to convey enthusiasm for the student's plans. This counselor refrained from distracting mannerisms (e.g., doodling, fidgeting) and refrained from looking at her watch to indicate the end of the session but rather smiled when the school bell signalled the end of the period.

The inattentive counselor failed to smile when the student entered and continued to work while the student sat down. This counselor responded with a flat tone and seldom looked at the student. This counselor frequently rubbed her eyes, played with her hair, and did some writing while the student talked; she rearranged objects on her desk and folded paper into various shapes during the conversation. The counselor looked at her watch to signal termination and did not smile when the patient left.

Results of this study showed subjects generating two times the number of negative comments about the nonattentive model over the attentive counselor. Subjects were also able to clearly discriminate the differences between the two models.

This study by Krumboltz lends support to earlier work by individuals such as Carkhuff and Truax (1967) with their exploration of dimensions such as empathy, nonpossessive warmth, and genuineness; or Ivey (1971) in his exploration of microcounseling skills. Pulling the efforts of such individuals closer to the nonverbal focus under consideration here, one sees studies such as that of Dong *et al.* (1976)

examining the nonverbal components of microcounseling. Dong reports four NVC areas as relevant to a favorable therapist reception. Therapists were rated more positively when they engaged in high eye contact with patients, maintained a forward, attentive leaning of the torso, showed a concerned facial expression, and maintained a close proxemic distance to the patient (.92 m). Collectively these studies suggest that a rather natural set of nonverbal behaviors conveying friendly, attentive concern acts to communicate a therapist's sincerity to establish a working relation with a client. Such behaviors appear to be an integral part of establishing initial rapport and, as studies in the next section suggest, maintaining such rapport in facilitation of the therapy process.

2. *Faciliation of Therapy.* Strong *et al.* (1971) conducted a study having definite implications for the counselor's conduct in therapy, specifically with regard to his nonverbal behavior. Strong had 86 college coeds rate two counseling models; one where a high frequency of nonverbal movements occurred and one where the counselor restricted his movement. "Still" counselors were seen as more logical, poised, and analytic than active counselors. The active counselor was rated as having greater interpersonal attractiveness; the still counselor was seen as more precise, thoughtful, and reserved. La Crosse, (1975), exploring Strong's discussion of nonverbal movements questioned whether these specific NVCs would have an influence on a therapist's perceived persuasiveness as well as attractiveness. Working with a core of what he labelled "affiliative" nonverbal behaviors, La Crosse found that therapists who smiled often, engaged in head nodding to indicate attentiveness to client's discourse, gesticulated in conjunction with their own speech, maintained high eye contact, and angled their torso and shoulders forward were rated as not only more attractive but also more persuasive than therapists who did not engage in such behaviors.

These studies are valuable in pointing to different nonverbal styles on the part of the therapist that have implications for different stages of therapy and different types of clients. There are times in the therapeutic dialog when the appearance of precise thoughtfulness are in order; there are moments when relaxed, warm accepting responses would be appropriate. Similarly, there are clients who need a warm, supportive atmosphere and then there are those whose adjustment would cause them to be very apprehensive of anything smacking of emotionality. These two studies suggest how the therapist's nonverbal behavior is intimately bound to the creation of therapeutic atmosphere most conducive to the progress of the client.

3. *Modeling for Psychological Growth.* There is a growing interest in the phenomenon of imitative or modeling behavior in the therapy context. For example, in the areas of assertiveness training, there is increasing reference to this type of approach. Serber (1972) discusses a training program focusing on the nonverbal components of assertiveness. In this program, he presented his clients with modeling material in six different areas: voice loudness, speech fluency, eye contact, facial expression, body expression, and body distance. Serber argued for asser-

tiveness gains with such modeling.

Argyle and Trower (1974) discusses a more exhaustive approach to modeling behavior than is usually considered in assertion training within a program they call *social skill training* (SST). Argyle provides a therapy modality attempting to speak to a number of areas of social difficulty, for example, perception of social situations, empathy, nonverbal expression, speech, responsiveness to others, planning and initiating social activity, and presentation of self. As can be perceived, most of these areas possess nonverbal components to be shaped up as part of an individual's total "social-competence." Argyle employs a training paradigm that initially places trainees in a didactic teaching context where procedures and rationale are outlined. Next, trainees receive appropriate role playing exercises slanted to their specific area of social difficulty (e.g., communication of positive and negative feelings to others). Next a trainee is provided with feedback from the trainer in conjunction with video-playback of material relevant to the problem under consideration. The process is repeated to provide further shaping, and finally the trainee is directed to try his new skills in a real-life situation reporting back to the training context for additional assistance. Argyle reports neurotics given this modeling opportunity show in testing and by self-report to resolve their difficulties more rapidly and completely than when provided other therapy modalities.

There appears to be a burgeoning of research and training efforts in the area of directive initiative and modeling approaches to therapy considering both nonverbal and other forms of patient behavior.

At this time, however, there appears to be scant, if any, empirical research focusing on nonverbal cues generated by the therapist as a model in the conventional therapy context that could provide a basis for psychological growth by the client. There is, however, some indirect empirical evidence to the fact that these factors do operate in the counseling context. Rosenthal (1955) found that in spite of the usual precautions taken by therapists to avoid imposing their values on their clients, the clients who were judged as showing the greatest improvement changed their moral values in the areas of sex, aggression, and authority in the direction of the values of their therapist. Similarly, Bandura and McDonald (1963) argue that when the therapist as model adopts a consistent moral orientation, this is likely to be adopted and maintained in turn by the client. The implication of these types of findings for nonverbal research is fairly readily perceived. It is argued here that if therapists took pains not to tell clients of their personal values and attitude and, in spite of their "diplomatic" silence, clients still modeled themselves after their therapists, this information must have somehow been communicated to the client. The most obvious channel is the nonverbal; therapists' nonverbal expressions of approval, disapproval, surprise, disgust, or dismay in reaction to various aspects of the clients behavior, provide the client with an emotional barometer of the therapists' value system and as such can act as a basis for subsequent client modeling. The obvious need in this area of nonverbal communication is to empirically identify and isolate those therapist-generated NVCs that can elicit imitation on the part of the client leading to positive psychological growth.

Implications for Research and Training

In concluding this examination of information currently available for therapist training in the nonverbal area, one factor emerges as most pressing. This is the need for much more in the way of scientific investigation. Heimann and Heimann (1972) suggest "Counselor educators need to be aware of these methodological issues and go beyond simple, gross observation in their attempts to give some meaning to nonverbal research. Training programs need to have a firm research base posited on empirical studies" (p. 453). Both the Heimanns and Gladstein (1974) given an additional *proviso* that such research should be conducted in the therapeutic context. Thus Gladstein argues: "Although it is difficult, expensive and time-consuming to carry out naturalistic studies, they must be done if we are to identify practical applications" (p. 41). Simply stated, more basic empirical information is required on what NVCs are found in the therapy context. It is interesting to speculate that one day an empirically established taxonomy of NVCs for emotional states found in therapy might be established. It appears that basic emotions such as anger, happiness, fear, surprise, disgust, and sadness are universal and the preliterate New Guinea tribesman has no more difficulty in recognizing them in Western faces than does the complaint therapist (Ekman & Friesen 1971). However, the cooccurence and blending of emotions in the therapy context (e.g., aggressive paranoia) may take longer to tease apart. Although recognition of nonverbal displays of emotion may be universal and as hypothesized by Darwin innate to all mammals, research findings (e.g., Waxer, 1974, 1976) suggest it is a capacity that improves with experience. Student-therapists engaging in on-going therapy were better able to recognize NVCs for depression than other students or even clinical faculty not currently in therapy practice. As a learnable capacity, recognition of NVCs would seem amenable to training programs.

Similar dynamics would seem to hold in the training of therapists to recognize nonverbal signs for therapeutic progress and resistance as is the case for psychodiagnosis. Although it is argued here that therapists could be trained to recognize specific NVCs indicative of patient progress and or resistance, additional research is once again in order to more exhaustively fill out the picture of interaction in the therapy context. Accurate assessment of therapeutic progress must not only wait on a fuller picture of nonverbal components in this process, but also the interplay of nonverbal and other behavioral components in therapy (e.g., paralinguistic, verbal, and lexical). For the sake of exposition, this discussion has restricted itself exclusively to the consideration of some basic nonverbal elements in therapy. Effective therapy, of course, involves much more, and sometimes nonverbal content is not the clearest route to understanding.

Also, therapist training, even in the restricted area of nonverbal components would have to provide some consideration of the interaction between such nonverbal components and other channels of information such as paralinguistic and lexical.

Empirical data on therapist-generated NVCs appears to be well on its way.

This, in part, may reflect the fact that it is easier to get an enthusiastic therapist-in-training to sit in front of a videocamera than a troubled patient. However, empirical research in areas where the therapist has a measure of personal vulnerability is just as scarce as material of emotionally troubled clients. Although research forges ahead on areas where therapists purposively present themselves in certain ways and or ask clients to imitate specific models, there is a definite paucity of research dealing with the therapists' unwitting reactions in the therapy context. Such behavior has long been recognized as an important influence on patients. Freud made a point of sitting behind his clients as they reclined on the psychoanalytic couch, expressly so that they could not monitor his expressions and nonverbal reactions to their plight, in an effort to maintain analytic "neutrality." From the lack of empirical investigation in this area, it appears that therapists other than Freud also find it difficult to make themselves subject to this type of scrutiny. Such research is in order to examine fundamental therapeutic processes such as classical transference or relation formation in therapy.

There is no doubt that much work is necessary before a more comprehensive picture of NVCs in therapy can be formulated. This does not mean however, that we must throw up our hands in despair at ever creating a meaningful program of training for nonverbal behavior.

As the empirical data base comes in, it seems valuable to incorporate these findings into a training procedure so that results of such practical applications can feedback and direct basic research to more economical therapeutic practice.

In conclusion, it is apparent that a conscientious training program can only progress at the rate that basic scientific information in this area becomes available. To this investigator, this is not necessarily taken as a discouraging note. Given the relatively recent development of technology permitting scientific exploration of nonverbal behavior, we are perhaps for the first time, in a position where our methodology and perceived applied requirements can be carefully consolidated before we tackle the exploration of nonverbal behavior. Coming late to the point where we are able to systematically explore this area, perhaps we will be able to avoid much of the *post hoc* nature of other earlier considered areas of therapy. The field is wide open, the tools are now available, and all efforts have an equal opportunity for contribution, given the absence of established doctrine.

References

Argyle, M., & Trower, P. Explorations in the treatment of personality disorders and neuroses by social skills training. *British Journal of Medical Psychology*, 1974 (Mar.), *47* (1), 63-72.

Bandura, A., & McDonald, F. J. The influence of social reinforcement and the behavior of models in shaping children's moral judgments. *Journal of Abnormal and Social Psychology*, 1963, *67* (3), 274-281.

Bateson, G., Jackson, D., Haley, J., & Weakland, J. Toward a thoery of schizophrenia. *Behavioral Science*, 1956, *1*, 251-264.

Berger, M. M. *Videotape techniques in psychiatric training and treatment.* New York: Brunner, Mazel, 1970.

Carkhuff, R. R., & Truax, C. B. *Toward effective counseling and psychotherapy.* Chicago: Aldine, 1967.

Darwin, C. *The expression of emotion in man and animals.* New York: Philosophical Library, 1955. (Originally published, 1872.)

Dittman, A. T. The relationship between body movements and moods in interviews. *Journal of Consulting Psychology*, 1962, *76*, 480.

Dong, T. L., Zingle, H. W., Patterson, J. G., Ivey, A. E., & Haase, R. T. Development and validation of a microcounseling skill discrimination scale. *Journal of Counseling Psychology*, 1976 (Sept.) *23* (5), 468-472.

Ekman, P., & Friesen, W. V. Nonverbal behavior in psychotherapy research. In J. Schlien (Ed.) *Research in psychotherapy* (Vol. 3). Washington, D.C.: American Psychological Association, 1968, 179-215.

Ekman, P., & Friesen, W. V. Constants across cultures in the face and emotion. *Journal of Personality and Social Psychology*, 1971, *17*, (2), 124-129.

Ekman, P., & Friesen, W. V. Hand movements. *Journal of Communication*, 1972, *22*, 353-374.

Ellsworth, P. C., & Ludwig, L. M. Visual behavior in social interaction. *Journal of Communication*, 1972, *22* 375-403.

Freedman, N., & Hoffman, S. P. Kinetic behavior in altered clinical states: Approach to objective analysis of motor behavior during clinical interviews. *Perceptual and Motor Skills*, 1967, 24, 527-539.

Freud, S. Fragment of an analysis of a case of hysteria. (1905) In *Collected Papers* (Vol. 3). London: Hogarth Press, 1933, 63-149.

Gladstein, G. A. Nonverbal communication and counseling/psychotherapy: A review. *Counseling Psychologist*, 1974, *4* (3), 34-52.

Heimann, R. A., & Heimann, H. M. Nonverbal communication and counselor education. *Comparative Group Studies*, 1972 (Nov.), *3* (4), 443-460.

Hinchliffe, M. K., Lancashire, M., & Roberts, F. J. Study of eye contact in depressed and recovered patients. *British Journal of Psychiatry*, 1972, *119*, 213-215.

Hutt, C., & Ounsted, C. "The biological significance of gaze aversion with particular reference to the syndrome of infantile autism." *Behavioral Science*, 1966, *11*, 346-356.

Ivey, A. E. *Microcounseling: Innovations in interview training.* Springfield: Charles C. Thomas, 1971.

Krumboltz, J., Varenhorst, B., & Thoresen, C. Nonverbal factors in the effectiveness of models in counseling. *Journal of Counseling Psychology*, 1967, *14*, 412-418.

LaCrosse, M. B. Nonverbal behavior and perceived counselor attractiveness and persuasiveness. *Journal of Counseling Psycology*, 1975 (Nov.), *22* (6), 563-566.

Laing, R. D. *The divided self.* London: Tavistock Publications, 1960.

Lewin, K. K. Nonverbal cues and transferences. *Archives of General Psychiatry*, 1965, *12*, 391-394.

Lowen, A. *Bioenergetics.* New York: Penguin Books, 1975.

Mahl, G. F. Gestures and body movements in interviews. In J. Schlien (Ed.), *Research in psychotherapy* (Vol. 3). Washington, D.C.: American Psychological Association, 1968, 299-346.

McGowan, J. F., & Schmidt, L. D. (Eds.) *Counseling: Readings in theory and practice.* New York: Holt, Rinehart, & Winston, 1962.

Murray, E. J. A case study in a behavioral analysis of psychotherapy. In M. T. Mednick & S. A. Mednick (Eds.), *Research in personality.* New York: Holt, Rinehart, & Winston, 1964, 414-422.

Reik, T. *Listening with the third ear: The inner experience of a psychoanalyst.* New York: Farrar, Strauss, 1948.

Rosenthal, D. Changes in some moral values following psychotherapy. *Journal of Consulting Psychology*, 1955, *19*, 431-436.

Rutter, D. R., & Stephenson, G. M. Visual interaction in a group of schizophrenic and depressed patients. *British Journal of Social and Clinical Psychology*, 1972, *11*, 57-65.

Scheflen, A. E. *How behavior means.* New York: Gordan and Breach, 1973.

Serber, M. Teaching the nonverbal components of assertive training. *Journal of Behavior Therapy and Experimental Psychiatry*, 1972 (Sept.), *3* (3), 179-183.

Strong, S. R., Taylor, R. G., Bratton, J. C., & Loper, R. A. Nonverbal behavior and perceived counselor characteristics. *Journal of Counseling Psychology*, 1971, *18*, 554-561.

Waxer, P. H. Nonverbal cues for depression. *Journal of Abnormal Psychology*, 1974, *83*, 319-322.

Waxer, P. H. Nonverbal cues for depth of depression: Set versus no set. *Journal of Consulting and Clinical Psychology*, 1976, *44*, 493.

Waxer, P. H. Nonverbal sues for anxiety: An examination of emotional leakage. *Journal of Abnormal Psychology*, 1977, *86*, (3), 306-314.

NEW DEVELOPMENTS IN THE ANALYSIS OF SOCIAL SKILLS

Michael Argyle

Department of Experimental Psychology
Oxford University

THE SOCIAL SKILLS MODEL

This approach to social interaction was put forward by Argyle and Kendon (1967) and developed by Argyle (1969). We will not repeat the full details here, but instead show how it can be used as a conceptual model of social interaction.

The model can be represented as in Fig. 1. It is supposed that interactors resemble a person driving a car, or performing other motor skills, in making continual corrective action in response to feedback in order to attain some goal defined as responses on the part of others. This model has been heuristically very useful in drawing attention to the importance of feedback, and hence to gaze; it also suggests a number of different ways in which social performance can fail, and suggests the training procedures that may be effective through analogy with motor skills training.

The Role of Gaze in Social Skill

The social skills model suggests that the monitoring of another's reactions is an essential part of social performance. The other's verbal signals are mainly heard, but his nonverbal signals are mainly seen, the exceptions being the nonverbal aspects of speech, and touch. It was this implication of the social skills model that directed us toward the study of gaze in social interaction. In dyadic interaction each person looks about 50% of the time, mutual gaze occupies 25% of the time, looking while listening is about twice the level of looking while talking, glances are about 5 sec, and mutual glances about 1-2 secs, with wide variations due to distance, sex combinations, and personality (Argyle & Cook, 1976). Kendon (1967) found that long glances are given by speakers at the ends of utterances, and it is likely that one function of these is to collect feedback on reactions to utterances.

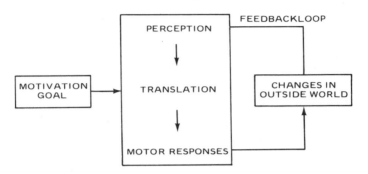

The Role of Reinforcement

This is one of the key processes in social skill sequences. When interactor A does what B wants him to do, B is pleased and sends immediate and spontaneous reinforcements: smile, gaze, approving noises, etc., and modifies A's behavior, probably by operant conditioning, for example, modifying the content of his utterances. At the same time A is modifying B's behavior in exactly the same way. These effects appear to be mainly outside the focus of conscious attention, and take place very rapidly. It follows that anyone who gives strong rewards and punishments in the course of interaction will be able to modify the behavior of others in the desired direction. In addition, the stronger the *rewards* that A issues, the more strongly other people will be attracted to him.

Taking the Role of the Other

It is important to perceive accurately the reactions of others. It is also necessary to perceive the perceptions of others, i.e., to take account of their point of view. This appears to be a cognitive ability that develops with age (Flavell, 1968), but which may fail to develop properly. Those who are able to do this have been found to be more effective at a number of social tasks, and more altruistic. Meldman (1967) found that psychiatric patients are more egocentric, i.e., talk about themselves more than controls, and it has been our experience that socially unskilled patients have great difficulty in taking the role of the other.

Self-Presentation

This is a normal and necessary part of social performance and involves social skills. It is done primarily by nonverbal signals, such as clothes and accent, and can also be done verbally, though in many cultures there are restraints on verbal self-presentation. Jones and Gergen in a number of studies (Gergen, 1971) found that subjects who were motivated to convey a favorable impression of themselves did so with subtlety, drawing attention to assets in unimportant areas, and being modest if they thought the recipient was modest. Marsh at Oxford has analyzed the code for the clothes worn by football hooligans (Marsh, Rosser, & Harré, 1978).

NONVERBAL COMMUNICATION

Human communication consists of an intricate combination of verbal and non-verbal signals. We shall see that the verbal aspects of messages are elaborated and supported in a number of ways by nonverbal communication. To understand human verbal communication, we need to know about these nonverbal components. Non-verbal communication (NVC) can be studied experimentally as a problem in encoding and decoding; it can also be studied as part of a sequence, using the methods of ethology or of linguistics. We shall see that this kind of analysis has theoretical implications for the nature of human communication and has practical implications in a number of fields.

A *sender* is in a certain state, or possesses some information; this is *encoded* into a *message* that is then *decoded* by a *receiver*.

$$\text{Sender} \xrightarrow{\text{(encodes)}} \text{message} \xrightarrow{\text{(decodes)}} \text{receiver}$$

Encoding research is done by putting subjects into some state and studying the NV messages that are emitted. For example, Mehrabian (1968) in a role-played experiment, asked subjects to address a hat stand, imagining it to be a person. Male subjects who liked the hat stand looked at it more, did not have hands on hips, and stood closer.

Decoding research is done by presenting experimentally prepared stimuli to subjects, and finding how they are decoded. Argyle, Lefebvre, and Cook (1974) taught confederates five patterns of gaze, which they used with different subjects who gave their impressions of the confederates in the form of ratings. The main result was that the confederates were liked more if they looked more, unless they looked more than the spontaneous rate, though their perceived activity and dominance increased continuously with their level of gaze.

The meaning of a nonverbal signal can be given in terms of how it is encoded or decoded. These meanings are of two main kinds. Signals may be analogical, as with gestures similar to the object described or some facial expressions, e.g., showing the teeth by animals, which is part of an act of biting. Or signals can have arbitrary meanings as the result of past associations, as with clothes, hair styles, or conventional gestures. Nonverbal signals may have meanings that are not readily expressed in words. There are research methods for finding such meanings, such as multi-dimensional scaling, in which subjects are asked to rate the similarity between photographs of facial expressions; this generates dimensions defined only in terms of the photographs. Some NV signals appear to have no subjective meaning at all, though they do influence behavior, as in the case of small head nods or shifts of gaze. Such signals may be said to have a behavioral meaning. Similar considerations may be applied to some ritual signals, like handshakes, which accomplish a change of relationship but have no obvious subjective meaning.

Nonverbal signals are often "unconscious," i.e., are outside the focus of attention. A few signals are unconsciously sent and received, like dilated pupils, signifying sexual attraction, but there are a number of other possibilities, as shown in Table I. Strictly speaking, pupil dilation is not communication at all, but only a physiological response. "Communication" is usually taken to imply some intention to affect another; one criterion is that it makes a difference whether the other person is present and in a position to receive the signal; another is that the signal is repeated, varied, or amplified if it has no effect. These criteria are independent of *conscious* intention to communicate which is often absent.

The Five Functions of NVC

1. *Interpersonal Attitudes.*   We are concerned here with attitudes toward others who are present. The main attitudes fall along two dimensions:

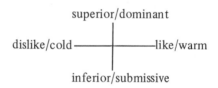

In addition there is love, which is a variant of liking. These attitudes can be conveyed clearly by nonverbal signals, as facial expression, tone of voice, and posture. Liking is conveyed by smiling, a friendly tone of voice, and so on.

The author and his colleagues compared the effects of verbal and nonverbal signals for communicating interpersonal attitudes. Typed messages were prepared indicating that the speaker was superior, equal, or inferior; videotapes of a performer

TABLE 1.   Awareness of Nonverbal Communication[a]

Sender	Receiver	Results
Aware	Aware	Verbal communication, some gestures, e.g., pointing
Mostly unaware	Mostly unaware	Most NVC
Unaware	Unaware, but has an effect	Pupil dilation, gaze shifts, and other small nonverbal signals
Aware	Unaware	Sender is trained in the use of, e.g., spatial behavior
Unaware	Aware	Receiver is trained in the interpretation of, e.g., bodily posture

[a] From Argyle (1975).

counting (1, 2, 3 ... 15) were made, conveying the same attitudes; the verbal and non-verbal signals were rated by subjects as very similar in superiority, etc. The combined signals were presented to further subjects on videotape: superior (verbal), inferior (nonverbal), etc., nine combinations in all, and rated for superiority. It was found that the variance due to nonverbal cues was about 12 times the variance due to verbal cues, in affecting judgments of inferior-superior (Argyle, Salter, Nicholson, Williams, & Burgess, 1970). Similar results were obtained in later experiments using friendly-hostile messages (Argyle, Alkema, & Gilmour, 1972).

The attitudes of others are perceived, then, mainly from their nonverbal behavior. It is found that people can judge with some accuracy when others like them, but are much less accurate in perceiving dislike. (Tagiuri, 1958). The reason for this is probably that expressions of dislike are concealed to a large extent, and only the more subtle ones remain, such as bodily orientation.

2. *Emotional States.* These can be distinguished from interpersonal attitudes in that emotions are not directed toward others present, but are simply states of the individual. The common emotions are anger, depression, anxiety, joy, surprise, fear, and disgust/contempt (Ekman, Friesen, & Ellsworth, 1972). An anxious state, for example, can be shown by (a) *tone of voice,* (b) *facial expression*—tense, perspiring, dilated pupils, (c) *posture*—tense and rigid, (d) *gestures*—tense clasping of objects, or general bodily activity, (e) *smell*—of perspiration, and (f) *gaze*—short glances, aversion of gaze. Interactors may try to conceal their true emotional state, or to convey that they are in some different emotional condition, but it is difficult to control all of these cues, and impossible to control the more autonomic ones. Emotional states can be conveyed by speech: "I am feeling very happy" but such statements will not be believed unless supported by appropriate NVC, and the NVC can convey the message without the speech.

3. *NV Accompaniments of Speech.* These signals are faster moving than those discussed so far, and are closely linked to verbal communication. They take three main forms.

(a) *Completing and Elaborating of Verbal Utterances.* Some utterances are meaningless or ambiguous unless the NV accompaniments are taken into account. A lecturer may point at part of a diagram: a tape recording of this part of the lecture would be meaningless. Some sentences are ambiguous if printed: "They are hunting dogs" but not if spoken—"They are hunting *dogs.*" Gestural illustrations are used to amplify the meaning of utterances, and succeed in doing so, as will be shown below. The way in which an utterance is delivered "frames" it, i.e. the intonation and facial expression indicate whether it is intended to be serious, funny, sarcastic, (implying the opposite), rhetorical, or requiring an answer, and so on; the NV accompaniment is a message about the message, which is needed by the recipient in order to know what to do with it. There are finer comments and elaborations too: particular words can be given emphasis, pronounced in a special accent, or in a way suggesting a particular attitude. The most important NV signals here are the prosodic aspects of vocalization, the timing, pitch, and loudness of speech. The gestural accompaniments of speech are also important, particularly illustrations. Facial expression and glances accompany speech in a similar way.

(b) *Managing synchronizing.*   When two or more people are talking they have to take turns to speak. This is achieved mainly by means of NV signals. For example, if a speaker wants to avoid being interrupted, he will be more successful if he does not look up at the ends of sentences, keeps a hand in midgesture at these points, and if, when interrupted, he immediately increases the loudness of his speech. Another signal that is important here is the head nod: single head nods give permission to hold the floor, double or triple nods show a desire to speak. The actual contents of speech, e.g., asking a question, are also important. Nor only is synchronizing usually successful, but interactors may help each other by finishing their utterances for them. Some interruptions are mistaken anticipations of the other ending, rather than attempts to break in.

(c) *Sending Feedback Signals.*   When someone is speaking, he needs intermittent but regular feedback on how others are responding, so that he can modify his utterances accordingly. He needs to know whether the listeners understand, believe or disbelieve, are surprised or bored, agree or disagree, are pleased, or annoyed. This information could be provided by *sotto voce* verbal muttering, but is in fact obtained by careful study of the other's face: the eyebrows signal surprise, puzzlement, etc., while the mouth indicates pleasure and displeasure. When the other is invisible, as in telephone conversation, these visual signals are unavailable and more verbalized "listening behavior" is used: "I see," "really?," "how interesting," etc.

4. *Rituals.*   By rituals are meant standard sequences of social behavior that bring about temporary changes of relationship (greetings, farewells), more permanent changes (weddings), or changes of state of individuals (puberty rites, graduation, healing rituals). Rituals involve a complex sequence of events, which are able to do the necessary "ritual work," i.e., bring about these changed relationships or states. NVC plays an important role here. The new state may be symbolized, for example, by putting on new clothes, a ring, the mayor's chain. And the acts of the priest or other official are given heightened social impact by the use of bodily contact and mutual gaze.

Van Gennep (1908) postulated that rituals always consist of three phases: separation, transition, and incorporation, which fits puberty rites in primitive societies. Other rituals like greetings appear to move toward and retreat from a point of climax.

5. *Self-Presentation.*   If information about the self is put into words, it must be done very indirectly, or it is likely to lead to derision and disbelief. NV signals are more acceptable, though these too may be misleading. If self-presentation turns out to be bogus, embarrassment ensues, as Goffman (1956) has observed.

Some NV Signals

1. *Gaze.*   This is used by animals as a threat signal and to show direction of attention. In humans it is used more as an affiliative signal and to collect feedback during conversation. The author and colleagues (1968) carried out an experiment that separated some of the different functions of gaze by studying interaction across a one-way screen. It was found that subjects who could see looked 65% of the time on average, presumably in order to collect information. Subjects who could not see looked 23% and their glances and facial expressions were coordinated with speech, evidently to *send* information. When subjects held real conversations, the amount of gaze was greater than when they exchanged monologues, probably because of the use of gaze as a synchronizing signal in conversation.

Gaze operates on three different time scales. The largest is the overall percentage of gaze over a period of time; an interactor looks more at people he likes, and when he is at a greater distance, to compensate for the physical separation. Most research has been concerned with the determinants of the level of gaze and mutual gaze (Argyle & Cook, 1976). However, gaze is intermittent and the detailed timing of glances can also be studied. Glances are typically 1–5 sec long and occur at the ends of utterances, and at grammatical break in speech; there is aversion of gaze at the beginning of utterances, especially after questions; and people look nearly twice as much while listening as while talking. The third time-scale is that of fixations of gaze, lasting about .3 sec; a "glance" of 4 sec consists of about 12 fixations, in a repeated sequence round the other's face, but particularly at his eyes and mouth.

During interaction, gaze is directed to the other person or persons present, at objects of mutual interest like task materials; the rest of the time there is unfocused gaze at irrelevant objects, or out of the window. Argyle and Graham (1976) found that introducing a task-relevant object reduced gaze at the other from 77% to 6.4%. Interactors signal their mutual attentiveness both by periods of mutual gaze, and by jointly attending to the same object; in "deictic" gaze, one interactor follows another's line of regard. During all these processes, gaze functions in two ways at once: it opens a channel of visual information for the gazer and is a signal for others.

2. *Gestures.*   The hands are assumed to have evolved for grasping; however they are also useful for communication. We commonly use the hands while speaking, notably to illustrate utterances. Graham and Argyle (1975) found that decoders could reproduce shapes more accurately when encoders were allowed to use their hands, especially for shapes difficult to describe in words, and especially for Italian subjects. Kendon (1972) and others have shown that there is fairly close synchrony between a speaker's verbal output and his gestures, and that large verbal units are linked with large bodily movements. Other investigations have found that verbal and gestural units start together.

Some gestures have nothing to do with speech, or indeed with communication. Many emotions include "autistic" gestures of self-touching. They occur less in the presence of others, so are not communication, but a kind of NV equivalent of talking to oneself. They can be produced experimentally, and have fairly stable meanings, e.g., covering the eyes (shame), scratching or picking (self-blame), rubbing the face (self-assurance).

In all cultures there are a number of gestures that have acquired conventional meanings. In Britain these include clapping, raising the hand, waving, beckoning, etc., but in some other cultures like Southern Italy there are large numbers of such "emblems." These gestures acquired their meanings at some time in the past, and this history can sometimes be traced. Morris, Collett, Marsh, and O'Shaughnessy (in press) at Oxford, have compiled a "gesture map" of Europe, and have listed the 200 conventional gestures used in Naples.

Why Is Nonverbal Communication Used When We Have Language?

Since we have the power of language, which can carry far more information than NVC, why do we continue to use nonverbal signals at all? There seem to be several different reasons.

(1) NV signals have a greater impact, for expressing interpersonal attitudes and emotions, than verbal messages equivalent in terms of rated meaning on scales like *friendly-hostile*. The reason is probably that NV signals (e.g., bared teeth) immediately put the receiver into a state of physiological readiness to react. NV signals used in rituals appear to have similar powers.

(2) Gestural illustrations, and other accompaniments of speech, are resorted to and communicate effectively, especially for materials of low verbal codability. This applies to shapes and also perhaps to aesthetic experiences, as Langer argued (1942).

(3) When the verbal channel is full, the NV channel is resorted to for feedback and synchronizing signals.

(4) A further reason for the use of nonverbal communication is that it is able to convey messages without directing attention to them and with a degree of ambiguity. While it would be awkward to say "I like you to some extent, about point 3 on a 7-point scale of liking," or "I consider myself slightly more important than you," such messages are constantly being sent via NVC (Argyle, 1975).

INTERACTION SEQUENCES

The problem of understanding sequences, and of explaining them in terms of general principles is the focus of a lot of current research. One contribution from social psychology has been to distinguish four kinds of dyadic interaction (Jones & Gerard, 1967). The social skill model applies best to "asymmetrical contingency," where the interviewer, teacher, etc., is in charge and has plans while the other person does not. However, the model does not fit so well cases of "mutual contingency" where both parties have plans, as in negotiation and discussion.

1. *Ethology.* has been very successful in analyzing sequences of behavior in animals by studying the probabilities that act A will be followed by act X, Y, and Z. Such first-order Markov chains can be elaborated to take account of two or more previous acts.

What is missing from such transition tables are the plans or intentions of the interactors, i.e., what they are trying to achieve. (This can be inferred from longer sequences.) Another problem is that there are a large number of alternative ways of categorizing the same behavior. There are over 100 schemes for recording classroom behavior. Humans, unlike animals, are able to form alternative categories, and can choose the set which are most useful. Another difficulty is that the analysis of overt behavior is not enough when there is a system of ideas behind it. An ethological study of a teacher giving a physics lesson is unlikely to provide us with an adequate account of what is going on.

2. *Linguistic Models of Social Encounters.* A number of investigators have tried to apply ideas from linguistics, using utterances as the units. Clarke (in press) at Oxford has carried out a series of studies of sequences of utterances. In one study subjects were asked to make up artificial dialogues: They were provided with a number of previous utterances and were asked to add one more. It was found that fourth-order dialogues (in which the fourth was added) were regarded by judges as being as acceptable as real dialogue. He also compared the acceptability of nested and cross-nested dialogues like:

Nested	*Cross-Nested*
A. Do you have the time?	A. Do you have the time?
B. Why do you want to know?	B. Is this the way to the station?
A. I have a bus to catch.	B. It's three o'clock.
B. It's three o'clock.	A. No, it's that way.

As expected it was found that nested dialogues were as acceptable as nonnested, but that cross-nested dialogues were acceptable.

Kendon and Ferber (1973) studied greetings and found that they consist of several discrete phases, each of some complexity. For example, the first phase, the "distant salutation," consists of a wave, a mutual glance, a smile, and some vocalization like "Hi." Greetings can be seen as a sequence of complex acts, like a sentence.

Goffman (1974) has used a linguistic model in his account of how social episodes can undergo tranformations of various kinds. Thus a basic pattern of behavior (e.g., a fight, a meal, making love, etc.) can be transformed as in a play, ceremonial, practice, demonstrations, etc. There can also be transformations of a deceptive kind, where some of those present do not realize that the performance is not the real thing, as in hoaxes and various kinds of fraud.

There are several important differences between sequences of words in a sentence and sequences of social acts. Not all social acts take the form of discrete, bounded units. While social acts have a hierarchical structure, this is not clear-cut like the levels of phoneme-morpheme-sentence. A sentence is derived from a plan or idea in the mind of the speaker; an interaction sequence is the product of the plans of two or more interactors, and there may or may not be a shared plan.

Social Episodes

It is necessary to introduce a further concept—the social episode. Ethological studies have found that sequences can be divided up into periods, within which the Markov transition probabilities are quite different, and indeed there can be a Markov chain of these larger units (Dawkins, 1976). Human observers have a high degree of agreement if asked to "chunk" behavior sequences into units (Newtson, in press).

Episodes are signaled by the initiator, either verbally (e.g., "shall we talk about the research you would like to do here?"), or nonverbally (e.g., hostess rises from the table). The main body of the episode may have regular Markovian properties, or a single sequence (as in the case of a greeting). And they have an ending, though this may be the same as the start of the next episode.

Each social episode, of whatever size, is recognized as a bounded unit of inter-action, there are rules governing behavior within it, the internal sequence is highly predictable, and participants cooperate to perform the unit as a joint social act. They will agree to enact a particular episode if this is expected to be sufficiently gratifying for each of them, though there is some scope for negotiating the way the episode goes.

SITUATIONS AND THEIR RULES

The earlier trait model of personality has now been abandoned by most psycho-logists as a result of the findings about the extent to which behavior varies between situations and the extent to which individuals react differently to situations, as shown in a study by Moos of mental hospital patients (Table 2).

A revised approach to personality is now acquiring wider acceptance: the inter-actionist model, which allows for variance due to persons, situations, and P x S interaction, while recognizing that there are stable underlying features of per-sons, though these cannot be defined in terms of behavior (Endler & Magnusson, 1976).

Empirical generalizations can be arrived at, which relate behavior to aspects both of situations and of persons. An example is Exline's study (1963) of gaze as a function of affiliative motivation, sex, and cooperative vs. competitive situations (Fig. 2). This

TABLE 2.   Percentages of Variance in Behavior Categories Accounted
for by Different Sources of Variance[a]

| | Source | | | |
Category	Persons	Settings	P x S	Within
Hand and arm movement	17.2	13.8	29.6	39.3
Foot and leg movement	27.3	13.0	31.2	28.6
Scratch, pick, rub	26.3	18.2	27.6	27.9
General movement and shifting	23.1	4.4	48.2	24.3
Nod yes	4.6	56.5	21.3	18.5
Smile	33.4	8.3	36.1	22.3
Talk	7.4	60.1	19.9	12.5
Smoke	36.5	12.2	10.2	41.1

[a] From Moos (1969).

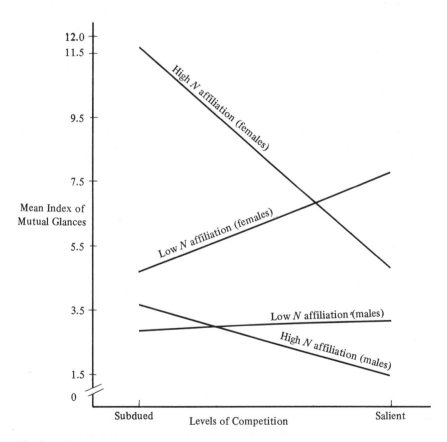

Fig. 2.   Mean percentage of time each sex spends in mutual visual interaction for each of two
levels of n affiliation at two levels of competition. (From Exline, 1963.)

has led to the development of methods of assessing situations. Forgas (1976) at Oxford, carried out a study of the 25 situations most commonly entered by psychology students. He then carried out multidimensional scaling to find the dimensions of these situations as perceived by participants.

However, close inspection of these results disclose a curious feature. Three situations are grouped close together, yet they are a tutorial, a psychology experiment, and a wedding—three situations where the actual behavior is totally different, though evidently they are similar in terms of subjective dimensions like formality.

I suggest that social situations are akin to the chemical elements in being discrete, not continuous elements. Each situation, e.g., a dinner party or an auction sale, is a structured system of closely knit interdependent parts. Certainly there are larger groupings, e.g., team games and meals, which contain a number of related examples, but there appears to be discontinuity both between these groupings and between the specific examples.

How should situations be analyzed then? I suggest that situations have a number of components of different kinds.

Special moves, i.e., elements of behavior. Every situation defines certain moves as relevant. For example, we have carried out several studies that have shown that there is quite a different repertoire of elements in different situations, like going to the doctor, a date, and so on.

Motivational themes. All parties to social encounters are motivated in some way. Sometimes they have different motives (buying and selling, teaching and learning), sometimes the same (affiliative, sexual). There are many combinations of motives not so far used in any social situations, which might be explored.

Traits. Every situation requires different ways of classifying people, e.g., at seminars, morning coffee, etc., and we have found that different traits are used to think about, and to deal with, for example, opposite-sex friends, colleagues, sporting acquaintances, etc.

Pieces. Most situations involve special environmental settings or props. Cricket needs bat, ball, stumps, etc; a seminar requires blackboard, slides, projector, and lecture notes.

Concepts. To play cricket, one must know what "innings" and "over" are. We suggest that more expert and experienced performers use more elaborate concepts, e.g., in Scottish dancing "reels of 3," "rondel," in chess, "fork," "discovered check," etc., or the terms used in different schools of psychotherapy to describe the state of the patient or the therapy—"resistance," "negative transference," etc.

Rules of Situations

All social behavior takes place in specific social situations. In every culture there are rules governing behavior in a larger number of common situations. Unless all those present agree on the definition of the situation and the rules to be followed, chaos usually ensues. Just as two people must agree to play the same game, e.g.,

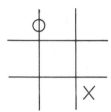

Fig. 3.   Rule breaking in noughts and crosses.

tennis, rather than two different games, e.g., tennis and croquet, so must social interactors. As in the case of games it seems that rules develop in the culture since they provide a satisfactory way of handling certain situations. We can discover which rules are essential by breaking them to see what happens. Garfinkel (1963) used the game of noughts and crosses; and in the middle of a game the experimenter would make a move as in Fig. 3.

In our recent studies of rule breaking, we have found that there is a difference between rules and conventions. There are certain rules that seem to be basic to each situation; for example, at an interview it does not really matter if the candidate wears the wrong clothes, but it does matter if he does not tell the truth or refuses to speak at all (Argyle, 1975).

The study of rules shows that some apparently disorderly situations, like certain schools and British football terraces, are in fact governed by rules that, for example, prevent serious injury occurring (Marsh, *et al.*, 1978).

There are rules governing who may be present, the appropriate setting or equipment, the task and how it should be done, the approved topics and style of conversation, the interpersonal relationships and emotional tone, and the clothes worn.

Situations define the range of possible moves for occupants of different roles and the sequences allowed. An auction sale is a simple example. There are three kinds of social acts open to the auctioneer and one for the customers. All possible sequences of events are covered by Table 3.

TABLE 3.   Following Act

			1	2	3	4	5
	Auctioneer	1. Offers object for sale			√	√	√
		2. States latest bid			√	√	√
Preceding act		3. Closes bidding	√				
	Customer A	4. Bids		√	√		√
	Customer B	5. Bids		√	√	√	

ea of social competence is interacting with members of other
Differences of NVC, rules, ideas, and social structure can give
rise to a var..... nteraction difficulties and to mutual dislike.

NVC

Some areas of KVC have strong innate components and thus do not vary much between cultures. Gestures vary more than facial expressions, which appears to be similar in different cultures, though there are different "display rules" about which emotions may be expressed on different occasions (Ekman *et al.*, 1972), and there is evidence of different "dialects" of facial expression (Seaford, 1975). Shimoda, Argyle, and Ricci Bitti (1978) found that while English, Italian, and Japanese could recognize each other's emotions above chance, the Japanese expressions were very hard to recognize, even by the Japanese themselves, who did better judging English and Italian facial expressions, as shown in Table 4.

Probably the area of NVC that causes the most trouble is bodily contact, since the world is sharply divided into contact and noncontact cultures. There can also be problems about the precise sequence of events involved in greetings, for example.

Rules

As we have seen there are rules for every social situation. However these rules vary greatly between cultures. The way to eat a meal, buy and sell, interact with women, speak to superiors and subordinates, is quite different in different cultures. I have recently carried out small-scale surveys of attitudes to minority groups in Britain, and have found that dislike of these groups is correlated with finding their styles of behavior strange, or incomprehensible, and that each group has a distinctive profile of the kinds of difficulty reported. One example is disliking Pakistanis whose wives walk behind them although they are not aware of the origi-

TABLE 4. Intercultural Recognition of Emotion[a]

| | Performers (12 x 2 = 24 expressions in each) | | |
	English	Italian	Japanese	
English $n = 102$	60.5%	55%	35.5%	50.3%
Italian $n = 32$	52%	61.5%	28.7%	47.4%
Japanese $n = 30$	53.8%	55.6%	43.3%	51%
Average	55.6%	57.3%	36%	

[a] From Shimoda *et al.* (in press).

nal reason—which is brushing away snakes. We plan to study rules of interaction sequences to find some of the points of conflict. There would be trouble, for example, if an outsider in New York became involved in the game of "playing the dozens" in which black youths make obscene remarks about one another's mothers.

Ideas

Social behavior is affected in several ways by ideas, words, and values. There are words to describe what is supposed to happen in psychoanalysis (e.g., "negative transference") and encounter groups (e.g., "roll and rock"), just as there are for cricket and Judo, and cultures may have specific terms for kinds of social behavior (e.g. machismo, chutzpah, honor). There may be cultural ideals about the proper forms of social behavior, e.g., the importance of reciprocity, duty, humility, etc., or there may be cultural ideals, e.g., of the heroes of the hippy movement. There may be beliefs, which affect social behavior; e.g., the evil eye depends on the belief that the perceiver sends a ray to the object or person perceived.

Training

A group at the University of Illinois devised the "Culture Assimilator," which is a programmed text to teach behavior in another culture. The Arab culture assimilator consists of 55 problem episodes based on critical incidents dealing for example with the role of women, the importance of religion in the Middle East, and interaction skills. The trainee assesses the causes of misperception or conflict for each problem, and is then told of the significance of his choice in terms of cultural concepts. Culture assimilators have been constructed for Greece, Thailand, and Honduras. Experiments before and after studies have shown positive but modest effects (Fiedler, Mitchell, & Triandis, 1971).

Collett (1971) trained a number of Englishmen, instructing them to use some of the Arab nonverbal signals: closer proximity, more direct orientation, more looking, more smiling, and more touching. Arab subjects met a trained Englishman and a second, untrained, Englishman. The Arabs like the trained Englishmen more, would like them for friends, and so on. The experiment was repeated with English subjects but they liked the two performers equally well.

Accommodation

There is an automatic process of mutual accommodation, which can go some way to reducing the difficulties of intercultural interaction. Giles and Powesland (1976) have found that when people from different social classes meet, they each shift their speech styles toward that of the other, in order, it is suggested, to be approved of. There is a serious limitation to this process: it is necessary to have the other's style in one's repertoire. Merely hearing him, for example, speak Chinese is not enough, and the same applies to a lesser degree to accents.

Cultural Universals

As we have seen, there are culturally universal facial expressions for emotion. Indeed NVC is used in very similar ways in all cultures, though the details vary. In addition, there are some basic relations (parent-child, friends, etc), and the same basic social situations (eating together, working together, etc.) in all cultures.

The Ways in Which Social Performance May Fail

Social competence is difficult to define. Success at professional social skills like teaching and interviewing can be assessed in terms of results. Success at the miscellaneous encounters of everyday life is hard to measure, though failure is fairly obvious—it leads to isolation, rejection, failure to form and sustain relationships, failure to communicate and cooperate, and so on. The examples given below are drawn from our experiences with socially inadequate neurotic out-patients. Each of the main ideas that have been introduced so far suggests a number of quite specific ways in which social behavior can go wrong, and we have found examples of each of the 20 or so types of failure suggested.

Social skill model.   This model suggests at least six forms of social inadequacy.

1.   Apparent lack of persistent plans in behavior—patients simply respond passively to the immediate behavior of others.
2.   Inadequate planning ahead. As with games, the effective performers think several moves ahead, and think in terms of larger units of behavior.
3.   Peculiar forms of motivation. Berne (1966) describes people whose main aim is to humiliate others.
4.   Inability to produce skilled social acts, for example, friendly or rewarding behavior, or the combination of reward and social influence.
5.   Failure to receive feedback, for example, by not looking at the other, or not listening to him carefully.
6.   Finally the whole performance may be disrupted by anxiety.

Nonverbal communication

7.   People may be extremely inexpressive, with blank facial expression and flat tone of voice, so that no one can tell whether they are happy or sad, or whether they like those present or not.
8.   They may express attitudes and emotions that are predominantly negative: hostile, superior, sarcastic, and so on.
9.   Or there may be failure on the perceptual side—they are very bad at interpreting the emotions and attitudes of others, or interpret them wrongly, for example, thinking that people dislike them, exaggerating the significance of the temporary absence of smiling.

Verbal communication

    10.   Inadequate production of effective utterances, cannot think of what to say.

    11.   Weak NV accompaniments of speech.

    12.   Ineffective synchronizing.

Other interactive processes

    13.   Low reward ingress.

    14.   Failure to take the role of the other.

    15.   Low assertiveness.

    16.   Self-presentation inappropriate—too much, too little, bogus, or simply wrong.

    17.   Self disclosure—too much or too little, or wrong pace.

Interaction sequences and situations

    18.   Not knowing the range of social acts that are appropriate and meaningful in a situation. Candidates at interviews may engage in light-hearted chat, a guest at a party may engage in deep religious-philosophical interrogation.

    19.   Not being aware of the contingency structure of a situation. Socially inadequate patients appear to treat situations as if they are all casual chats, i.e., fail to pursue plans of their own. Candidates at interviews may try to ask the questions, instead of waiting to answer them.

    20.   Patients often report great difficulty with particular situations, or classes of situation. Often this appears to be due to a failure to understand some aspect of the rules, about what is expected, and what can be expected of others. Young people often find parties difficult, since they have not mastered the procedures for starting and stopping encounters with strangers.

    21.   Inability to use signals to negotiate mutually agreeable episodes.

Cultural differences

    22.   The other person is rejected because his behavior is seen as deviating from proper behavior.

    23.   The other's signals are misunderstood. For example, bodily contact (from an Arab, Italian, or African) is seen as a very intimate signal.

    24.   The other's behavior is misunderstood through not being aware of his ideas, ideals, and cognitive world.

    25.   No attempt is made to accommodate, for example by shifting accent toward the other's accent. Attempts are made to impose own rules as being the "correct" ones.

Training in Social Skills

A number of forms of social skills training are now being widely practiced.

Microteaching for teachers is probably the most extensive, and has been found to be very successful (Brown, 1975). It is however mainly confined to forms of verbal interaction in a specific situation.

Assertion therapy is widely used with neurotic patients, and is also successful, though it is directed to one specific form of social inadequacy, and that not the commonest form. (Rich and Schroeder, 1976.)

Culture assimilator.   As described above, this has had some modest success, but is limited to instruction about the conventions and ideas of other cultures.

We have developed a form of social skills training for use with mental patients, though it can be used with any other group. We use a combination of (1) role-playing, with (2) modeling, (3) videotape playback, and (4) verbal coaching and feedback, together with a number of other methods, like training in NVC. This combination has been shown to be the most effective in a number of studies. Our method of social skills training is somewhat different from that practiced elsewhere in that it has been developed in close connection with research on social interaction, that it takes account of the full range of processes now known to be involved in social interaction, and recognizes over 20 forms of social inadequacy, each requiring specific forms of training. For example, failure to emit proper nonverbal signals is treated by practice, using a mirror, and audio- and videotape recorders. Failure in perception is trained by exercises in the recognition of tones of voice, etc. Failure to master the principles of social situations is dealt with by analysis and explanation of specific situations. Patients are assessed, in terms of this range of processes and forms of failure, by means of interview, questionnaires, and observation of social behavior with a male and a female in the laboratory.

Follow-up studies have shown that this procedure is somewhat more effective than psychotherapy, or behavior therapy, meanwhile the application of the findings about social interaction is leading to continuous modification of the procedure (Argyle, Trower, & Bryant, 1974; Argyle, Bryant & Trower, 1974; Trower *et al.*, 1978).

References

Argyle, M. *Social interaction.* London: Methuen, 1969.

Argyle, M. *Bodily communication.* London: Methuen, 1975; New York: International Universities Press.

Argyle, M., & Cook, M. *Gaze and mutual gaze.* Cambridge: Cambridge University Press, 1976.

Argyle, M. & Graham, J. A. The Central Europe experiment—looking at persons and looking at objects. *Environmental Psychology and Nonverbal Behavior,* 1976, *1,* 6-16.

Argyle, M., & Kendon, A. The experimental analysis of social performance. *Advances in Experimental Social Psychology.* 1967, *3,* 59-98.

Argyle, M., Lalljee, M., & Cook, M. The effects of visibility on interaction in a dyad. *Human Relations.* 1968, *21,* 3-17.

Argyle, M., Salter, V., Nicholson, H., Williams, M., & Burgess, P. The communication of inferior and superior attitudes by verbal and nonverbal signals. *British Journal of Social and Clinical Psychology.* 1970, *9,* 222-231.

Argyle, M., Alkema, F., & Gilmour, R. The communication of friendly and hostile attitudes by verbal and nonverbal signals. *European Journal of Social Psychology,* 1972, *1,* 385-402.

Argyle, M., Ingham, R., Alkema, F., & McCallin, M. The different functions of gaze. *Semiotica,* 1973, *7, 19-32.*

Argyle, M., Bryant, B., & Trower, P. Social skills training and psychotherapy: A comparative study. *Psychological Medicine,* 1974, *4,* 435-443.

Argyle, M., Lefebvre, L., & Cook, M. The meaning of five patterns of gaze. *European Journal of Social Psychology* 1974, *4,* 125-136.

Argyle, M., Trower, P., & Bryant, B. Explorations in the treatment of personality disorders and neuroses by social skills training. *British Journal of Medical Psychology,* 1974, *47,* 63-72.

Brown, G. A. Microteaching: Research and developments. In G. Chanan & S. Delamont (Eds.), *Frontiers of classroom research.* Slought NFER, 1975.

Clarke, D. D. The use and recognition of sequential structure in dialogue. *British Journal of Social and Clinical Psychology,* 1975, *14,* 333-339.

Clarke, D. D. *Conversation: Strategy or structure.* Oxford: Blackwell, in press.

Collett, P. On training Englishmen in the nonverbal behavior of Arabs: An experiment on inter-cultural communication. *International Journal of Psychology,* 1971, *6,* 209-215.

Dawkins, R. Hierarchical organization: A candidate principle for ethology. In P. P. G. Bateson & R. A. Hinde (Eds.), *Growing points in ethology.* London: Cambridge University Press, 1976. pp. 7-54.

Ekman, P., Friesen, W. V., & Ellsworth, P. *Emotion in the human face: Guidelines for research and an integration of findings.* Elmsford, New York: Permagon, 1972.

Endler, N. S., & Magnusson, D. (Eds.), *Interactional psychology and personality.* New York: Wiley, 1976.

Exline, R. V. Explorations in the process of person perception: Visual interaction in relation to competition, sex and need for affiliation. *Journal of Personality,* 1963, *31,* 1-20.

Fiedler, F. E., Mitchell, R., & Triandis, H. C. The culture assimilator: An approach to cross-cultural training. *Journal of Applied Psychology,* 1971, *55,* 95-102.

Flanders, N. A. *Analyzing teaching behavior.* Reading, Massachusetts: Addison-Wesley, 1970.

Flavell, J. H. *The development of role-taking and communication skills in children.* New York: Wiley, 1968.

Forgas, J. P. The perception of social episodes: Categorical and dimensional representations in two different social milieus. *Journal of Personal and Social Psychology,* 1976, *33,* 199-209.

Garfinkel, H. A conception of, and experiments with, "trust" as a condition of stable concerted actions. In O. J. Harvey (Ed.), *Motivation and social, interaction: Cognitive determinants.* New York: Ronald Press, 1963.

Gergen, K. J. *The concept of self.* New York: Holt, Rinehart, & Winston, 1971.

Giles, H., & Powesland, P. F. *Speech style and social evaluation.* London: Academic Press, 1975.

Goffman, E. *The presentation of self in everyday life.* New York: Anchor Books, 1959.

Goffman, E. *Frame analysis: An essay on the organization of experience.* Cambridge, Massachusetts: Harvard University Press, 1974.

Graham, J. A., & Argyle, M. A cross-cultural study of the communication of extra-verbal meaning by gestures. *International Journal of Psychology.* 1975, *10,* 57-67.

Jones, E. E. & Gerard, H. B. *Foundations of social psychology.* New York: Wiley, 1967.

Kahn, R. L., Wolfe, D. M., Quinn, R. P., & Snoek, H. D. *Organizational stress: Studies in role conflict and ambiguity.* New York: Wiley, 1964.

Kendon, A. Some functions of gaze direction in social interaction. *Acta Psychologica,* 1967, *26,* 22-63.

Kendon, A. Some relationships between body motion and speech: An analysis of an example. In A. W. Siegman & B. Pope (Eds.), *Studies in dyadic communication.* Elmsford, New York: Pergamon, 1972.

Kendon, A., & Ferber, A. A description of some human greetings. In R. P. Michael & J. H. Crook

(Eds.), *Comparative ecology and behavior of primates.* London: Academic Press, 1973.

Langer, S. K. *Philosophy in a new key: A study in the symbolism of reason, rite, and art.* Cambridge, Massachusetts: Harvard University Press, 1942.

Marsh, R., Rosser, E., & Harré, R. *The rules of disorder.* London: Routledge and Kegan Paul, in press.

Mehrabian, A. The inference of attitudes from the posture, orientation, and distance of a communicator. *Journal of Consulting and Clinical Psychology,* 1968, *32,* 296-308.

Meldman, M. J. Verbal behavior analysis of self-hyperattentionism. *Diseases of the nervous system,* 1967, *28,* 496-473.

Morris, D., Collett, P., Marsh, P., & O'Shaughnessy, M. *Gesture maps.* London: Jonathan Cape, in press.

Moos, R. H. Sources of variance in responses to questionnaires and in behavior. *Journal of Abnormal Psychology,* 1969, *74,* 405-412.

Newtson, D. The process of behavior observation. *Journal of Human Movement Studies,* in press.

Rich, A. R., and Schroeder, A. E. Research issues in assertiveness. *Psychological Bulletin,* 1976, *83,* 1081-1096.

Shimoda, K., Argyle, M., & Ricci Bitti, P. The intercultural recognition of emotional expressions by three national groups—English, Italian, and Japanese. *European Journal of Social Psychology 8,* 169-179.

Seaford, H. W. Facial expression dialect: An example, In A. Kendon, R. M. Harris, & M. R. Key (Eds.), *Organization of behavior in face to face interaction.* Chicago: Aldine, 1975.

Tagiuri, R. Social preference and its perception. In R. Tagiuri & L. Stanford: Stanford University Press, 1958.

Trower, P., Argyle, M., & Bryant, B. *Social skills and mental health.* London: Methuen and Pittsburgh University Press, 1978.

Van Gennep, A. *The rites of passage.* (B. Monika, Vizedom, & G. L. Caffee, trans.). Chicago: Chicago University Press, 1960. (Originally published, 1908.)

PART 3: APPLICATIONS OF NONVERBAL BEHAVIOR IN TEACHING

THE TEACHER AND NONVERBAL BEHAVIOR IN THE MULTICULTURAL CLASSROOM

Aaron Wolfgang

Ontario Institute for Studies in Education
Department of Applied Psychology
University of Toronto

Canada and the U.S. are the leading nations for attracting immigrants of diverse linguistic and cultural backgrounds. It was reported that Canada had a foreign-born population amounting to over 15% of its total population and the U.S. 4% (Davis, 1974). In recent years immigration to Canada has increased from such areas as southern Europe, Asia, South America and the West Indies. The vast majority of immigrants come to the big cities such as Toronto, Montreal, or Vancouver. A large number come from non-English speaking countries or from countries where a dialect based on the English language is spoken. It was estimated that 50% of the school population in Toronto have a mother tongue that is neither English nor French (Carey, 1976). Since many immigrant students and their families cannot communicate in the official spoken languages of Canada, English or French, they may have to rely on nonverbal behavior to make themselves understood and to understand others. Thus, it becomes increasingly important that our teachers understand both the practical and theoretical importance of nonverbal behavior and its importance in cross cultural communication. Anthropologists have sensitized us to the importance of culture in shaping our nonverbal style of communication (Hall, 1959, 1969; Birdwhistell, 1970). Our culture in subtle and sometimes in not so subtle ways tells us under what situations and to what degree we can exhibit certain behaviors. There is also evidence from psychologists and ethologists that there are certain patterns of behavior that are characteristic to the human species that range all the way from simple reflexes to the expression and understanding of certain basic emotions and behaviors (Eibl-Eibesfeldt, 1972; Ekman, 1975; Ekman & Friesen, 1971; Izard, 1977).

The main intent of this paper is to attempt to sensitize teachers or potential teachers to the importance of understanding the role of nonverbal behavior in communication and in particular its role in the multicultural classroom. By focusing

159

on nonverbal behavior I do not mean to minimize the importance of verbal behavior. It is just that our culture emphasizes so much of the verbal aspects of communication that understanding the impact of nonverbal behavior is neglected. My position is that we communicate simultaneously at least on three levels when teaching a student from another culture; on the verbal , non-verbal, and cultural levels, with the third moderating the other two. Neither of the first two levels can be fully understood or expressed in isolation. I hope to show that much of our behavior is on the nonverbal level and that its impact in communication can be powerful and easily misunderstood particularly by students and parents from other cultures who may have learned different cultural rules of *when*, *how*, and *where* and to what *degree* to express certain behaviors.

Another intention of this paper is to discuss ways teachers can learn about their nonverbal communication style and its impact. The ways knowledge of nonverbal behavior can be applied and the ways communication and learning styles of immigrant students might come into conflict with teacher expectations will also be discussed.

INTRODUCTION TO NONVERBAL BEHAVIOR

What is nonverbal? How is it acquired? How is it characterized and related to verbal behavior? Why is it important and neglected? Nonverbal behavior is commonly used to describe behavior that transcends spoken or written words (Harrison, 1974). The study of nonverbal behavior has been divided into at least three areas: *proxemics,* a term coined by Hall (1969) that refers to the study of the ways individuals use space in their enviornment in relationship to one another or to objects. The ways we use space according to Hall (1969) is largely culturally determined. He noted that interpersonal threat or uneasiness results in increasing social distance. Willis (1966) found that when whites spoke to blacks they maintained greater interpersonal distance than when whites spoke to other whites. Several studies have shown that individuals will maintain greater social distance from those identified as having a social stigma or marginal status in society than from normal peers (Wolfgang & Wolfgang, 1971; Wolfgang, 1973a). Another area of nonverbal behavior is the study of *kinesics*, a term coined by Birdwhistell (1970) that refers to the study of the pattern of body movement in human interaction. He maintains that kinesics or "body language" is culturally determined and that he has not found a gesture or body motion that has the same meaning in all cultures. Body language is the popularized term for kinesics (Fast, 1970). It includes such nonverbal behavior as facial expressions, gestures, posture, head nods, etc. The third nonverbal area of study is *paralanguage*, and it refers to the extra verbal elements that are associated with speech, e.g., loudness, tone, pauses, hesitations, etc.

Some of the ways we acquire our nonverbal expressions is through *inheritance, learning, modeling.* Charles Darwin (1965), one of the earliest investigators of nonverbal behavior, came to believe through his research that humans through their common inheritance and genes have a common way of expressing basic emotions, e.g., fear, happiness, sadness, and these emotions can be understood by humans over the world. There has been some recent support for Darwin's findings by several investigators (Ekman & Friesen, 1971; Izard, 1977). Most investigators would agree that the *when, where,* and *to whom* and to what *degree* these basic emotions would be displayed is subject to cultural and situational variations. Another way nonverbal behavior is acquired is through *learning,* which can be quite explicit and subject to cultural rules. Some rules we learn are "Don't stare!" "Don't spit at people!" "Don't gesture too much in public," etc. These "don'ts" are all learned in specific social contexts. The third way is through *imitation.* That is, we incorporate mannerisms, expressions, and even a particular walk by imitating significant people in our life such as our parents, spouses, heroes, etc. Where learning nonverbal behavior is more explicit, imitation is more indirect or implicit. Our learning in school about nonverbal behavior tends to revolve mostly around only a small area of human interaction and about what *not* to do. The teacher or our parents will focus mainly on nonverbal behavior that involves *manners, politeness,* or *social deportment* (Byers & Byers, 1972). Teachers and parents seldom discuss with children what some of the positive nonverbal reinforcers are that would facilitate communication such as head nodding, smiling, keeping eye contact, tone of voice, etc.

Why is nonverbal behavior important, particularly for teachers of immigrant students? Teachers like others have been taught in school that the written and spoken word is supreme and the impact of nonverbal behavior has been largely ignored. Intercultural communication is not only a matter of understanding words but of understanding nonverbal signals as gestures, spatial relations, touch and temporal relationships (Smith, 1966). Because of the focus on verbal behavior, teachers are not normally aware of the nonverbal signals they give off. It has been reported that 82% of the motions used in a classroom by the teacher were nonverbal while only 18% were verbal (Grant & Hennings, 1971). Other research shows that the main impact of communication was from facial expression and least from verbal content (Mehrabian, 1972). In analyzing verbal and nonverbal classroom student teachers' behavior, it was discovered that the teacher's facial expressiveness through the use of smiling exerted stronger effects in obtaining students' attention and responsiveness than speech. The optimal combination was a facially expressive, i.e., smiling or questioning, verbally probing teacher. This was related to student enthusiasm and task relevant behavior. In contrast, frequent use of the blackboard by teachers was related to task-irrelevant and task disruptive behaviors as noisemaking (Keith, Tornatzky, & Pettigrew, 1974). Perhaps teachers who frequently used the blackboard lost eye contact with their students or, as the authors point out, the students had little chance for active participation and thus became inattentive.

Nonverbal behavior can be characterized in the following ways: It normally operates out of the awareness level and unlike verbal behavior it is difficult to manipulate or falsify. It is easier to get out of verbal mistakes than body language mistakes. On the verbal level you can always say "you didn't understand what I was trying to say." On the other hand, try to tell someone that your angry face is not angry. Other characteristics of nonverbal behavior are that it has a greater impact than words, particularly in revealing emotions, and it can be used as an index of assimilation, i.e., students who want to be assimilated may adopt the nonverbal characteristics of Anglo or French-Canadians. Nonverbal behavior can also be used for stereotyping others, e.g., English-Canadians may be described as "cold," "distant," and Italians as "loud" or "emotional" (Wolfgang, 1975).

What are some of the ways nonverbal behavior is related to verbal behavior? It can replace language, add additional information to language, i.e., it can clarify, modify, and confirm language. However, it has a more limited range than language for expressing logical, sophisticated, or creative ideas, whereas nonverbal language is more suitable for expressing feelings and attitudes. Unlike verbal behavior, nonverbal behavior is more ambiguous, more bound by the social context and culture for meaning. That is, there is no common or agreed upon source or reference book to look up the meaning of a particular gesture, emotional expression, or social distance. To reiterate a former point both language and nonverbal language in social interaction are interdependent, used simultaneously and are largely culture bound.

CULTURE AND NONVERBAL BEHAVIOR

In teaching in the multicultural classroom it is important to understand the role of culture and its characteristics and potential impact on individuals engaged in cross-cultural communication. The teacher is one of the primary agents for transmitting Canadian culture to students. Hall (1969) in his book *The Hidden Dimension* makes the point that you cannot shed your culture, you cannot erase it, and that it can penetrate at the very roots of your nervous system. He believes (Hall, 1959) that you can only have a token understanding of another culture and that the real job is understanding your own culture. It makes sense that by knowing your own culture you will know what the immigrant students are seeing or responding to and you can make a comparison. There are data that suggest that problems relating to adjustment of immigrant students were largely attributed to cultural differences (Ashworth, 1975).

What is culture? What are its characteristics and how is it related to nonverbal behavior? Culture is an abstract term that defines a broad range of activities in which individuals express themselves. Culture can be viewed as an organized body of rules, allowing for individual differences, concerning the ways individuals bound together by such things as common boundaries, customs, institutions, values, languages, nonverbal behavior, arts, should behave toward one another and toward objects in their surroundings. Culture is important because it tells us in different degrees what we are expected to think, believe in, say, resent, wear, honor, laugh at, and fight for in typical life situations (Brooks, 1968). Culture like nonverbal behavior tends to be elusive, normally out of our awareness, difficult to control, falsify, manipulate, erase, and has a potent influence in intercultural communication.

SOME WAYS TEACHERS CAN LEARN ABOUT THEIR CULTURE

Teachers in the multicultural classroom have the rare opportunity to examine their own culture and values. Some ways teachers can learn about their own culture is by traveling whenever possible to other cultures, living in another culture, becoming acquainted with people from other cultures abroad or in their own country, becoming involved in multicultural activities in the school or community, visiting the families and neighborhoods of the students. Keep a diary of the things you observe that please you, irritate you, surprise you, on the verbal or nonverbal level. See if you can draw at least one or two conclusions about your culture and about yourself. Then too, teachers could take some risks and challenge some of the accepted ways of behaving in their own culture. For instance, you could go to the front of the line instead of waiting for your turn at the food counter or movies, speak to strangers, sit next to someone in the theatre when there are many empty seats, touch or stand very close to a stranger when asking directions, come 30 min. late for an appointment, and if someone accidentally bumps against you, you could say "thank you" instead of "excuse me." In each of these types of activities notice the facial expressions, if they are hostile, angry, or smiling, and notice what people say.

The multicultural classroom can also be a great resource for learning about your students, and yourself in terms of style of communicating and learning. Notice the students' learning and communication styles and compare them with your own. Discuss the differences with your students. Are there some assumptions you make about the students' intellectual ability, manners on the basis of these observations? Are these assumptions correct? For example if new Canadian West Indian, Chinese, or Italian students fail to participate in classroom discussion can you assume they are not bright, are not listening, or are not motivated? What were the expectations of the teachers in the student's culture? How do they contrast with Canadian classrooms? What was rewarded or punished in the student's former classroom?

NONVERBAL CHARACTERISTICS OF MODEL TEACHERS

In producing and doing background research for the film "Body Language in the Classroom" (Wolfgang, 1974) I had the opportunity to observe teachers of different cultural backgrounds and their use of nonverbal behavior in the classroom. One objective of my research was to select three to four teachers to act as models in the film to show teachers and student teachers how nonverbal behavior can be utilized effectively in the classroom and some techniques that could be used for becoming sensitized to their nonverbal behavior. The good teachers had several characteristics in common; they were all experienced, with at least five or more years of teaching experience, were enthusiastic in teaching their lesson, gestured for emphasis, smiled frequently, showed varied facial expressions, moved toward the class, spent more time in front of the class than behind the desk or at the blackboard, were attentive to students' comments by keeping eye contact and head nodding, showed variation and clarity in their voice, their nonverbal movements were in concert with the verbal and easily decodable, and they used humor in the class. The students were responsive, attentive, and the class atmosphere was relaxed. The Italian-born teacher gestured more, was more animated, spoke louder, moved closer to her students, and touched her students more frequently. The principals of the schools where these teachers taught said that they were well thought of as teachers by their students and by the principals themselves. They also mentioned that the students showed good learning rates in their classes.

The multicultural classroom provides a real challenge for the teacher and student. However, both are normally unprepared for their encounter. The teacher most likely has little direct knowledge about the culture, the language, the educational system of the students, teacher expectations, nonverbal behavior, teaching methods used, values stressed, and learning and communication styles of the students in their own culture. Similarly, the immigrant or new Canadian student knows little about the Canadian educational system and culture.

CROSS-CULTURAL DIFFERENCES OF CLASSROOM ENVIRONMENT AND TEACHER EXPECTATIONS

In Canada the classroom environment and teacher expectations of students' behavior are different from that of many countries (e.g., West Indies, Italy, etc.). The typical Canadian classroom can be characterized as permissive and informal. Students in Canada are expected to speak up in class, raise their hands if they know the answer to a question, and volunteer information. Teachers can be questioned by their students if they do not like an answer the teacher gives. Discipline is often lax and learning by discovery rather than rote is encouraged. Teachers' dress attire can vary from turtle neck, jeans, open shirt, to tie and jacket. Teachers do not automatically assume respect from students and they may be told off by students without reprimand. Students greet teachers informally, e.g., "Hi, Mrs. W." or "Hey, Sir." The classroom environment can be quite competitive, students are rewarded for participation, volunteering information, and for giving the right answers quickly without long pauses.

In contrast, students coming from the West Indies, southern Italy or Hong Kong have come from a relatively more formal and authoritarian school environment. I have seen students in the West Indies and southern Italy stand up when their teacher enters the classroom. Respect is assumed rather than earned. Students wait until spoken to, they learn to listen, they typically do not question the teacher or speak out of turn. Discipline is more strict. I saw teachers using the strap and holding paddle boards in Jamaica. Student's attire may be a school uniform. Schools are generally more oriented toward passing exams, and learning through rote memory. It is not surprising that new Canadian students in the Canadian classroom are generally described by teachers as being passive and nonparticipatory. My own research has shown in using the locus of control scale (Rotter, 1966) that new Canadian-Italian students perceived themselves as being more externally controlled or more powerless in controlling events in their life than native-born Canadian-Italian students (Wolfgang, 1973b). In another study with elementary students, it was shown that high participators in classroom discussion received higher grades than low participators and were more internally controlled (Wolfgang & Potvin, 1973).

What other reasons can be offered besides reported feelings of powerlessness for new Canadian students' lack of participation? In contrasting the two learning environments, one rewards students for participating and the other for being good listeners and speaking when spoken to. Thus, both new Canadian students and their teachers have developed expectancies but in the opposite directions. Other reasons for students not participating may be lack of confidence in verbal skills, or poor self-concept. Students may not have a chance to speak because of the competitive nature of the classroom. Students with poor language skills who are accustomed to a more passive role in learning can hardly be expected to compete with Canadian-born students.

WHAT CAN THE TEACHER DO?

One way teachers can help alleviate the problems of immigrant students in their new environment is to show *patience*, i.e., give the students some time to become accustomed to the new classroom environment before passing judgments. Teachers can explain to the newcomers and their parents what behaviors are rewarded or encouraged and which are discouraged. They can help the students develop cultural and classroom competence. The teacher can show patience, caring, and respect for the students on the nonverbal level by allowing students more time to answer questions, by letting the student know you are listening and attentive, by head nodding, keeping eye contact, leaning forward, or moving toward the student. Approval can be indicated through smiling or head nodding. The teacher can speak slowly, clearly, and in an approving tone to help the student understand in a nonthreatening way. If the teacher does not understand what the student has said, then the teacher can try to paraphrase their statements and ask the students if that is what they said. Teachers can show caring by learning the newcomer's name. They can try to master at least one difficult name to pronounce and use it as often as possible and notice the student's response. If the new students sense that the teacher is making an attempt to communicate, then the chances are better that they will develop a more positive attitude toward their adopted culture and teacher. It has been shown (Lambert, 1975) that students who have a more positive attitude toward another culture will learn the language of that culture more quickly. Perhaps the same would hold true for nonverbal behavior as well.

NONVERBAL EXPRESSIONS OF WEST INDIAN STUDENTS AND ADULTS

What are some of the ways nonverbal cues can be misunderstood in the multicultural classroom? I will try to describe some nonverbal behaviors of students and adults in the West Indies, by the Chinese from Hong Kong and southern Italians in and outside of the classroom that may *confuse*, *annoy*, or *amuse* a teacher.

The students from the West Indies who immigrate to Canada in the largest numbers are from Jamaica, Trinidad, Tobago and Guyana (Immigration, 1975). These students are racially diverse with African, European, East Indian, Indian, Asian, and middle Eastern backgrounds. Until 1962, Jamaica, Trinidad, and Tobago were colonized primarily by the British. Many West Indians speak a dialect of English that differs from the standard British or Canadian-English. It has been argued that if the speech patterns are different from the dominant culture it can be expected that the nonverbal communication patterns would also be different (Johnson,1971).

Immigration from the West Indies to Canada has been steadily increasing since 1967. My descriptions of nonverbal behavior in the West Indies is based primarily on personal observation as well as interviews with teachers, teacher educators, and those in the arts. While spending almost four months mainly in Jamaica, Trinidad, and Tobago, I noticed in the classroom in Trinidad that students when they want to be excused from the class put their two fingers with the inside facing out on their forehead (Fig. 1), while in Jamaica in the primary school the hands are raised high above the head with two fingers up. I observed that students in Jamaica in primary school would flap or snap their fingers if they knew the answer (Wolfgang, 1977). I understand from a Jamaican teacher that this kind of behavior is discouraged. I found myself annoyed when a young Jamaican man snapped his fingers to obtain my attention in asking for the time. When a student is scolded or reprimanded they hang their head and avoid eye contact with the teacher. I was told of a similar incident

teacher complained that in disciplining a West Indian student, the student's head dropped and eye contact was avoided. The teacher was annoyed because the students in Canada are expected to look the teacher in the eye when being spoken to as a sign of respect, whereas in Jamaica the opposite is true. This reluctance to look a person directly in the eye, particularly authority figures was also reported to be found in many West African cultures and practiced by many Black Americans (Johnson, 1971).

Two paralinguistic expressions that were common were *psst, psst*, for gaining someone's attention and "sucking" or "kissing" the teeth for expressing anger, annoyance, or frustration. *Psst* was used among the students for gaining each others' attention but not used to gain the teacher's attention: it would be considered rude. If students "kissed" or "sucked" their teeth to the teacher a Jamaican teacher told me they would be punished. In Trinidad when I had a winning streak in ping-pong, the person I was playing with began "sucking" his teeth when losing a point. In Canada one of my doctoral students, a Trinidadian who immigrated to Canada over 10 yr ago, began "sucking" his teeth when he discovered that some of the analyses of his data for his dissertation were incorrect.

Another common nonverbal expression was *clapping the hands* for attention. In Jamaica when I waved my hands as in Canada for a cab, none came. I asked a Jamaican to show me how he would hail a cab. He told me to clap my hands. I did as he suggested and a taxi stopped in minutes. In Barbados, a waiter in the dining room attempting to get the attention of some Canadian diners to show them to their table by clapping, shrugged his shoulders when they would not respond. In the English-Canadian culture clapping the hands would be considered inappropriate or for that matter almost any expressive or gestural movement for attention would be frowned upon, particularly among those in the middle or upper socioeconomic groups.

These are some nonverbal expressions I saw used in classrooms in the West Indies that are also used in Canada. For instance, putting the index finger to the mouth and saying "shh" for "be quiet" or putting two hands out front with palms facing down with a slight motion to mean "quiet down." Students shrug their shoulders for meaning "I don't know," look at their watch when bored or hungry, and have a blank stare when not listening. Unlike Canadians, girls in the West Indies walk hand in hand and affection is not shown in public between boys and girls. Lastly, in a recent cross-cultural study West Indian students projected similar social distances from teachers, principals, and parents as Canadian students on a figure placement task with the greatest social distances being maintained from the teachers and principals (Wolfgang, 1978).

No discussion would be complete without mentioning West Indian attitudes toward time. They have a reputation of having a more relaxed and flexible attitude than Canadians toward time. With regard to social engagements it is often not uncommon for a West Indian to be between ½ to an hour late. The schools however in the West Indies do stress punctuality.

I noticed that students in the classrooms in Jamaica and Trinidad were quite active; when the teacher asked for a volunteer to answer a question hands went up and students spoke in loud clear voices. In a recent article by a Canadian high school teacher who visited West Indian schools, it was reported that students were eager to learn and participate in the classroom (Wolfgang I., 1976). A former Jamaican educator who has taught in Canada concluded in her research paper on Jamaicans (Glaze, 1975) that when West Indian students are secure and happy they are animated and full of vitality and touch and hug freely. In contrast, in the Canadian classroom she observed they often become withdrawn, shy, and quiet.

My guess is that the more comfortable and accepted these students feel in their new environment the more likely some of the nonverbal behaviors previously described would occur. Many of these gestures and expressions could be misconstrued and lead to misunderstandings and tensions between teachers and students. Teachers must be careful not to practice "nonverbal ethnocentrism" (Eisenberg & Smith, 1971) where it is assumed that their own forms of nonverbal expressions are natural and correct while those of others are unnatural and bizarre. It has been argued that some problems related to racism and prejudice are due to differences in cultural communications systems that are out of the awareness level (Byers & Byers, 1972).

NONVERBAL EXPRESSIONS OF SOUTHERN ITALIAN STUDENTS AND ADULTS

Much has been written about Italian gestural and emotional flamboyance, particularly among the Neopolitans and Sicilians and the more reserved Nordic and Far Eastern peoples, e.g., Chinese (Critchley, 1975). Efron (1941) studied Italian gestures in detail in the U.S. He noticed that assimilated Americanized Italians compared to immigrants showed evidences of "gestural bilingualism" or hybrid gestures, i.e., the traditional patterns of expression were modified to include American stylized movements. In a study by Graham and Argyle (1975) it was shown that performance improved more for the Italians than English subjects when hand gestures were allowed to convey information on a spatial relations task.

Montagu (1971) suggests that there may be national, cultural, and social class differences in expressing tactile behaviors whereby, those who speak Anglo-Saxon-derived languages would be on the noncontact side of the continuum and those speaking Latin-derived languages would be more on the opposite or tactile end of the pole. Thus, people from contact cultures such as those from Latin America, Italy, Portugal, Greece, Spain, and French Canada would tend to touch more frequently, gesture more, embrace or kiss when greeting, and space themselves closer than Anglo-Saxon British, Americans, or Canadians. Montagu (1971) points out that Canadians of Anglo-Saxon origins might even outdo the English in nontactuality. This behavior might lead, he speculates, to Anglo-Saxon Canadians being stereotyped as "unemotional" or "cold" by peoples from contact cultures. He also suggests that the higher the person's social class the less tactile or contact behavior would be shown in interpersonal relations.

A teacher who immigrated from England and has been teaching English to Italian students in the south for about 8 yr said that the first thing an Italian child going to live in an Anglo-Saxon culture would notice is the absence of physical contact between teachers and students. She mentioned that teachers and students, especially young children, touch each other frequently. Children, she said, frequently greet their teacher with a kiss on both cheeks and put their arms around the teacher or the teacher will put her arm around the child. This physical contact, the teacher pointed out continues into adolescence, with boys or girls frequently walking along with their arms around each other or with arms linked.

My observations on the high school level were that classes were quite formal as in the West Indies (Wolfgang, 1973c). Students would stand when the teacher entered and class participation was teacher directed. I saw little contact between teachers and students at the high school level. Thus, contact-oriented behavior may be more pronounced in the classroom in the earlier grades than high school. It is my guess that this would be true also in Canada, but to a different degree than in Italy. I also noted while interviewing in the south of Italy and in Canada that individuals from lower socioeconomic backgrounds frequently were more emotionally expressive, animated, gestural, tactile, and maintained less interpersonal distance than those from the upper and middle class families. This class observation also seemed to show itself in the West Indies. Black West Indians from the middle and upper class, particularly those educated in England seemed more controlled, less contact oriented than those whose roots were in the lower socioeconomic classes. Thus, *age* and *social class* appear to be an important variable to consider before generalization can be made about students coming from contact cultures.

NONVERBAL EXPRESSIONS OF CHINESE STUDENTS

Chinese students who come mainly from Hong Kong are from a noncontact culture. Hong Kong, a British colony, is one of Canada's top 10 primary source countries for immigration. (Immigration Declines, 1976). In a recent value survey (Wolfgang & Josefowits, in press), comparing Chinese immigrant high school students who were primarily from Hong Kong with Canadian-born students, it was found that Chinese students were less accepting of the value that "touching is good to express affection" and would maintain more interpersonal distance from figures representing people showing a great deal of emotion than Canadian-born students. This finding was consistent with Montagu's hypothesis regarding behavior of people from noncontact cultures. However, there was no difference in acceptance of the value that "it is important to be on time."

Chinese students have been described as having a tendency to reticence and reserve on the verbal and nonverbal level in the classroom (Ng, 1975). In the classroom they are usually quiet, show emotional restraint, and are thought of as well disciplined. The Chinese as well as the Japanese are taught that emotional restraint and self-control are signs of maturity. (Sue & Sue, 1972; Kaneshige, 1973). They are taught to respect, obey, and listen to the teacher (Ng, 1975). One teacher who has been teaching mainly girls in a high school composed of 35% Chinese recently told me that the silence in the classroom can be unnerving, i.e., you do not know if you are getting through or if they understand what you are saying. She also remarked that she and other teachers noticed that as the students became Canadianized they often became unruly, overdemanding, hypercritical, speak louder, act more informally, and often times become ashamed of being Chinese. Compared to other Canadians, as they became Canadianized some Chinese students became more nonverbally expressive but on the extreme end of the continuum. However, it was pointed out that these behaviors may be transitory. Thus, another important variable that must be considered before making generalizations about nonverbal behavior is *length of time in the host country* and the desire to lose one's identity and become assimilated.

It is no easy matter to classify students' nonverbal behavior into nice neat cultural packages. In attempting to make predictions or build up expectancies of behavior of students coming from contact or noncontact cultures, the sensitive teacher must consider such factors as social class, age, length of time in the country and desire to become assimilated.

TIPS FOR TEACHERS

Teachers could encourage their students to express themselves as they would in their native culture. In fact, teachers might learn to express some of the new students' nonverbal gestures to show that they are in tune with their students and accept and know them as they are. The probability is high that in a class where the atmosphere is warm and friendly and where attempts are made to make the new students feel secure and accepted, the students would be more expressive, show their emotions more freely, disclose more about themselves, begin to participate more and more in classroom discussions, and thus learn more.

What can the teacher do to help create an atmosphere where students would feel free to express themselves and feel less alienated? Teachers must be culturally flexible and versatile and learn to operate within their students' frame of reference (Thompson, 1973). To do this teachers must make as much effort to become aware of their cultural preferences and values and to respect those of their students. Teachers can help the immigrant student overcome their sense of powerlessness or helplessness by helping the students develop linguistic, nonverbal, and cultural skills that would help them master the environment rather than be controlled by it. In learning these skills students could develop an appreciation of their own culture and an understanding of the Canadian social and cultural milieu and how to participate in it. The teachers' attitudes would also be critical. If the teacher communicates to the immigrant students a positive concern for their problems and respect for their individuality, then this could cut across cultural differences (Rogers,

1964). The culturally versatile teacher in the multicultural classroom can make the classroom environment culturally versatile by hanging up pictures, posters, or having a classroom exhibit that reflects the different cultural backgrounds of the students, including those reflecting the country's culture. This could be an excellent stimulus for discussing cultural similarities and differences among students.

TEACHER TRAINING AND RESEARCH

Teacher training institutions could do more to help train teachers to be more cognizant of the importance of the role and impact of nonverbal behavior in the multicultural classroom. Teacher training still focuses largely on the verbal aspects of communication in spite of the knowledge that indicates that the nonverbal aspects of communication are more potent than verbal, that nonverbal behavior is largely out of awareness, that the majority of classroom motions used by the teachers are nonverbal, that students are more responsive and attentive to teacher's facial expressiveness than speech, that empathy and perceiving and responding with warmth is better conveyed on the nonverbal than verbal level (Gazda, 1973; Grant & Hennings, 1971; Haase & Tepper, 1972; Keith et al., 1974; Mehrabian, 1972). Bancroft (1975) points up the difficulty Ontario teachers experience in understanding the nonverbal behavior of people from other cultures and its implications.

In addition to appraising practice teachers' performance primarily on the verbal level as subject competence, planning, organization, classroom management, rapport, and skill in communication, a special nonverbal category could be developed. This category could include skill in using eye contact for showing and gaining attention, use of space, use of nonverbal reinforcements (e.g., head nodding), use and variety of facial expressions (e.g., frequency of smiling) body movement (e.g., rigid-flexible), use of hand movements, gestures for emphasis, distracting mannerisms, use of touch, etc. A category of student responsiveness could be included as degree of participation, student attentiveness (e.g., degree of eye contact with teacher, posture, nonverbal reinforcements used by students, etc. By including a nonverbal category practice teachers would be motivated to learn about their nonverbal behavior and could receive feedback from the experienced teachers.

There is little systematic research in the area of nonverbal behavior relating such things as teacher-rated skillfulness in using nonverbal behavior in the multicultural classroom and its effects on students' grades, attendance, self-concept, satisfaction in the classroom, student responsiveness, and attentiveness. There is a need to develop an inventory of nonverbal behaviors that accompany the English language or those typically used by individuals from different social classes. Attempts have been made to develop nonverbal inventories of the Spanish, French, and Italian languages (Green, 1971) and such an inventory would be helpful to teachers of English as a second language. Another important area of research would be to assess the effects of matching teachers from contact cultures who have maintained their contact-oriented behavior with the new students from contact cultures vs. students from contact cultures being taught by teachers from a noncontact culture (e.g., English-Canadians).

CONCLUSIONS

Many of the ideas and suggestions put forth in this paper for creating an optimal learning environment in the multicultural classroom would have applications as well for the nonmulticultural classroom. That is, students would benefit and be responsive in almost any classroom environment where the atmosphere was warm and friendly and where teachers were sensitized to their nonverbal style of communication, their culture and values, were flexible, willing to experiment and had genuine concern for their students' problems as well as respect for their individuality.

There are many advantages to being part of a multicultural environment or classroom for both teachers and students. It gives both teachers and new students the rare opportunity and challenge of examining, testing, and becoming better aware of their own cultural values and nonverbal behavior as well as those of others. A great deal of the misunderstanding in intercultural communications that occurs in and outside of the classroom often leads to prejudice and stereotyping. This occurs largely because of our lack of understanding of the powerful effects our nonverbal behavior has on others. This lack of understanding occurs because we have been taught that it is the *written* and *spoken word* that is all powerful and therefore the *nonverbal* part of communication is carried on primarily out of the awareness level and it becomes the *silent* but restless language. When we become aware of how *loud* and *powerful* nonverbal language can be in its silence in communicating our attitudes toward others, our likes and dislikes, our feelings, and make an attempt to understand its social and cultural implications, then we have the seeds for improving and humanizing intercultural communication.

References

Ashworth, M. Results and issues from a national survey of ESL programs. In A. Wolfgang (Ed.), *Education of immigrant students: Issues and answers.* Toronto: Ontario Institute for Studies in Education, 1975. Symposium Series 5, 84-106.

Bancroft, G. W. Teacher education for the multicultural reality. In A. Wolfgang (Ed.),*Education of immigrant students: Issues and answers.* Toronto: Ontario Institute for Studies in Education, 1975. Symposium Series 5, 164-183.

Birdwhistell, R. L. *Kinesics and context.* Philadelphia: University of Pennsylvania Press, 1970.

Brooks, N. Teaching culture in the foreign language classroom. *Foreign Language Annals,* 1968, *1,* 204-217.

Byers, P., & Byers, H. Nonverbal communication and the education of children. In C. Cazden, V. John, & D. Hymes (Eds.), *Functions of language in the classroom.* New York: Columbia University, Teachers College, 1972.

Carey, E. Public fears school ghettos report says. *Toronto Star,* February, 1976, B1.

Critchley, M. *Silent language.* London: Butterworths, 1975.

Darwin, C. *The expression of the emotions in man and animals.* Chicago: University of the Chicago Press, 1965.

Davis, K. The migrations of human populations. *Scientific American,* September 1974, 93-105.

Efron, D. *Gesture and environment.* New York: King's Press, 1941.

Eibl-Eibesfeldt, A. Similarities and differences between cultures in expressive movements. In R. A. Hinde (Ed.), *Nonverbal communication.* London: Cambridge University Press, 1972.

Eisenberg, M., & Smith, R. R. *Nonverbal communication.* New York: The Bobbs Merrill Co., Inc., 1971.

Ekman, P. Face muscles talk every language. *Psychology Today,* September 1975, 35-39.

Ekman, P., & Friesen, W. Constants across cultures in the face and emotion. *Journal of Personality and Social Psychology,* 1971, *17*, 124-129.

Fast, J. *Body language.* New York: M. Evans and Company, 1970.

Gazda, G. M. *Human relations development: A manual for educators.* Boston: Allyn and Bacon, Inc., 1973.

Glaze, A. *The Jamaican child and his background.* Unpublished paper, Department of Applied Psychology, Ontario Institute for Studies in Education, Toronto, 1975.

Graham, J. A., & Argyle, M. A cross-cultural study of the communication of extraverbal meaning of gestures. *Journal of Human Movement Studies,* 1975, *11*, 33-38.

Grant, B. M., & Hennings, D. G. *The teacher moves: An analysis of nonverbal activity.* New York: Teachers College Press, 1971.

Green, J. A focus report: Kinesics in the foreign language classroom. *Foreign Language Annals,* 1971, *5*, 62-68.

Haase, R. F., & Tepper, D. T. Nonverbal components of empathic communication. *Journal of Counselling Psychology,* 1972, *19*, 417-424.

Hall, E. T. *The silent language.* New York: Fawcett Premier Books, 1959.

Hall, E. T. *The hidden dimensions.* Garden City, New York: Anchor Books, 1969.

Harrison, R. P. *Beyond words: An introduction to nonverbal communication.* New Jersey: Prentice-Hall, 1974.

Immigration declines. *Contrast,* February 1976, 12.

Izard, C. E. *Human Emotions.* New York: Plenum Press, 1977.

Johnson, K. R. Black kinesics: Some nonverbal communication patterns in the black culture. *The Florida FL Reporter,* 1971, *9*, 17-20, 57.

Kaneshige, E. Cultural factors in group counseling and interaction. *Personnel and Guidance Journal,* 1973, *51*, 407-412.

Keith, T. L., Tornatzky, L. G., & Pettigrew, L. E. An analysis of verbal and nonverbal classroom teaching behaviors. *Journal of Experimental Education,* 1974, *42*, 30-38.

Lambert, W. E. Culture and language as factors in learning and education. In A. Wolfgang (Ed.), *Education of immigrant students: Issues and answers.* Toronto: Ontario Institute for Studies in Education, 1975, Symposium Series 5.

Mehrabian, A. *Nonverbal behavior.* New York: Aldine-Atherton, 1972.

Montagu, A. *Touching.* New York: Harper and Row Publishers, 1971.

Ng. C. A. The educational background of the adult Chinese student. *TESL Talk,* 1975, *6*, 36-40.

Rogers, C. R. Toward a modern approach to values: The valuing process in the mature person. *Journal of Abnormal and Social Psychology,* 1964, *68*, 160-167.

Rotter, J. B. Generalized expectancies for internal versus external control of reinforcement. *Psychological Monographs,* 1966.

Smith, A. G. *Communication and culture.* Toronto: Holt, Rinehart and Winston, 1966.

Sue, D. W., & Sue, S. Counseling Chinese-Americans. *Personal and Guidance Journal,* 1972, *50*, 637-644.

Thompson, J. J. *Beyond words: Nonverbal communication in the classroom.* New York: Citation Press, 1973.

Willis, F. N. Initial speaking distance as a function of speakers' relationship. *Psychonomic Science,* 1966, *5*, 221-222.

Wolfgang, A. Projected social distances as a measure of approach-avoidance behavior toward radiated figures. *Journal of Community Psychology*, 1973, *1*, 226-228 (a).

Wolfgang, A. Cross-cultural comparison of locus of control, optimism toward the future, and time horizon among Italian, Italo-Canadian, and new Canadian youth. *Proceedings of the 81st Annual Convention of the American Psychological Association*, 1973, 299-300 (b).

Wolfgang, A. (producer). *The Italian in transition.* Toronto: Ontario Institute for Studies in Education, 1973, (Film) Distributed by International Telefilms Enterprises, Toronto (c).

Wolfgang, A. (producer). *Body language in the classroom.* Toronto: Ontario Institute for Studies in Education, 1974. (Film) Distributed by International Telefilms Enterprises, Toronto, and AIMS Instructional Media Services, Inc. Glendale, California.

Wolfgang, A. (Ed.). *Education of immigrant students: Issues and answers.* Toronto: Ontario Institute for Studies in Education Symposium Series 5, 1975.

Wolfgang, A. A locus of control, social distance, and self-concept comparison of Canadian and West Indian students. Mimeographed paper, Department of Applied Psychology, Ontario Institute for Studies in Education, Toronto, 1978.

Wolfgang, A. (producer). *The West-Indian student: A long way from home.* Toronto: Ontario Institute for Studies in Education, 1979. (Audio-visual slide production) Distributed by International Telefilms Enterprises, Toronto.

Wolfgang, A., & Potvin, R. Internality as a determinant of degree of classroom participation and academic performance among elementary students. *Proceedings of the 81st Annual Convention of the American Psychological Association*, 1973, 609-610.

Wolfgang, A., & Josefowitz, N. Chinese immigrant value changes and value differences compared to Canadian students. *Canadian Ethnic Studies*, in press.

Wolfgang, A., & Wolfgang, J. Exploration of attitudes via physical interpersonal distance toward obese, drug users, homosexuals, police, and other marginal figures. *Journal of Clinical Psychology*, 1971, *27*, 510-512.

Wolfgang, I. *Physical education: A personal viewpoint. Orbit*, February 1976, *7*, 16-17.

SOCIAL CONTEXTS FOR ETHNIC BORDERS AND SCHOOL FAILURE

R. P. McDermott and Kenneth Gospodinoff

The Rockefeller University

I. INTRODUCTION

This paper considers the recently popular claim that many minority children fail in school because there is a mismatch between their procedures or codes for making sense with each other and the codes used by their teachers who generally come from a socially more powerful group. In most claims, the emphasis is on the fact that the minority and majority group members have different languages, dialects, gestural systems, or interactional rhythms, etc., that they accordingly produce much miscommunication with each other, and that in the classroom such miscommunication leads to alienation and failure. This paper is different in that, while we do not deny that communicative code differences exist, we emphasize that they are secondary to the political relations between members of the different groups both in the classroom and in the larger community. We claim that constant miscommunication between teachers and their pupils is no accident, that it, in fact, represents an interactional accomplishment on the parts of all those involved given the conditions under which they are asked to come together either to teach or to learn how to read and write.

Primarily, we offer an analysis of only a few moments of some minority children miscommunicating with their teacher and failing in school. But we offer these moments as a systematic part of the contexts in which the teacher and the children are immersed. The most immediate context is that of the children and the teacher trying to understand each other while face-to-face during their reading lessons. At this level, everyone appears to make sense in that they simultaneously act upon and respond to each other's behavior in systematic ways. In terms of the organization of a given piece of face-to-face behavior, what appears to be a miscommunication may be a carefully arranged and sensible way for all the participants to proceed given the interactional and pedagogical problems confronted by members of the classroom.

ISBN 0-12-761350-1

We present an analysis of such a case in Section III.

By itself, the detailed analysis of the good sense of a miscommunication will leave the reader confused. What is needed is an account of how the classroom came to be organized in such a way that the development of codes for miscommunicating came to be a sensible adaptation. The usual account of miscommunication and school failure simply in terms of communicative code differences does not deal with this difficult task. Instead, it usually is assumed that people from different groups are naturally different and that their differences can be in the long run irremedial; with such an assumption in hand, it is not necessary to show how people develop vested interests in being different from one another. Our point is that without such vested interests being created from one moment to the next, people usually develop metacommunicative procedures for altering their communicative codes in order to make sense of each other. When communicative differences become ir-remedial, it is because there are sound political or economic reasons for their being so. No matter how hard the dominant group is trying to equalize access to resour-ces, no matter how downtrodden the minority group, every group is somehow get-ting a maximum payoff given their starting place within a political economy.

In order to give this point some substance, in Section II, we concentrate on the political circumstances in which people alternatively deemphasize, emphasize, and even create communicative code differences. And in Section IV, we attempt to sketch out the higher order contexts in terms of which the sensible, but ultimately damaging, miscommunication analyzed in Section III came to be, in the short run at least, adaptive for all. By way of conclusion, we suggest that in the long run such arrangements are maladaptive in that they have consequences that in no way maxi-mize the potentials for the population under analysis, and we raise questions about the worth and morality of school systems that are geared to sorting young children into successful and unsuccessful categories instead of being geared to socializing everyone for a maximally rich experience of the world.

The setting for our analysis is a first-grade classroom in a comparatively success-ful school in a suburb not far beyond the New York City limits. School failure by minority group children was quite visible in this classroom. Shortly after the start of the school year, most children were ranked into one of three groups on the basis of the teacher's analysis of their reading abilities. The top group consisted of white children, primarily Italian and Jewish. The bottom, or least literate, group consisted of three Puerto Rican, one Black and finally two white children, one of whom was considered the group's best reader and destined to move into a higher group, the other of whom was considered brain damaged. There was one other Puerto Rican boy who was originally assigned to the bottom group, but who had been put out for being too disruptive. Thereafter, the boy had no reading group, and he wandered around the classroom causing trouble. The one other minority child in the class be-longed to the middle reading group.

So five of six minority children are in the bottom group or in no group at all, despite the efforts of a teacher who was considered excellent by her peers, and inci-dently, by us. The teacher of this class gets the most difficult first graders into her room each year and is often successful in teaching them the basics of classroom behavior and reading. However, in the year under analysis, not all the children emerged with such survival skills, and by the end of the second year in school, two Puerto Rican children and one white boy, all from the bottom group, had been reassigned to special schools for various functional handicaps, namely, for being "slow," "emotionally disturbed," and "brain damaged." Essentially, the children were sent to special schools because their teacher found them impossible to work with in the classroom. The other children in the group were not doing too much better in that they were not learning to read up to grade level, a *sine qua non* of institutional success, but at least they had escaped placement (for the moment) in a slowed down program.

The process just described is in no way unusual to schools. Selection for failure is common in many kinds of social institution (Auerswald, 1971; Moore, 1975). There are some who have mistakenly used ethnicity to explain this phenomenon in schools. The claim is that there is something about a child's membership in a certain group that is predictive and causally related to the child's success or failure in school. Two basic versions of this argument stand out. One is that there is something wrong with the children; because they are biologically incapable, cognitively or linguistically deficient, or motivationally misdirected, the children are unable to keep up in school. The other is that the children are merely different and misunderstood. Space does not allow for a discussion of the first set of theories, but there is good reason to reject each of them on the grounds that they are neither logically coherent nor descriptively adequate (Cole, Gay, Glick & Sharp, 1971; D'Andrade, 1973). Fortunately, the work showing the inadequacies of these theories is persuasive enough to allow us to direct our attention to the argument that minority children fail in school because they communicate differently and are accordingly unappreciated and misunderstood.

II. ETHNIC DIFFERENCES DO NOT CAUSE IRREMEDIABLE MISCOMMUNICATION

According to the second set of arguments, which we call the communicative code account, members of minority groups do less well than others in school because the schools generally are staffed by majority group members who do not understand minority group children (more sophisticated versions of this argument point out that even when the schools are staffed by minority group members they are likely to behave in accordance with the majority group communicative code, resulting in the same sort of miscommunication taking place). This argument is most appealing when we consider large differences like those that exist between a teacher who speaks only one language and students who speak only another. The case for the smaller systems of differences, i.e., systems of touching, spacing, gesturing, speaking rights, etc., can be argued along the same lines. People with different communicative codes may want the same things and work equally hard at achieving their goals, but, to the extent that they do not share codes for making sense with members of the dominant groups, they will misinterpret each other's behavior and eventually create unpleasant environments for each other. It is in such unpleasant environments that minority children begin to "act up" and become alienated from the teacher and the learning enterprise.

This stand is attractive. For one thing, it holds out great hope for the children; it assumes they can all do well in school if we could only build more sensitivity for communicative code differences into our teachers. It also has the advantage of not off-handedly condemning the teachers as incompetents or racists. Like all of us, they have had limited experiences with people in different cultures, and once they become sensitive to the codes of the children, they can be the helpful and loving teachers they no doubt would like to be.

As attractive as this stand is, we have been forced to conclude that it is much too simple. Certainly, when the communicative resources of two groups are different, the people will generate much miscommunication. But the question is why this keeps generating problems. Why do the people not repair the miscommunication? This line of thought leads to an even more difficult question, namely, why are there communicative codes at all? Increasingly, there is reason to take the position that different communicative codes represent political adaptations; in the course of talking or moving in one way rather than another, children and teachers are doing politics. If this is so, we all not only suffer from communicative conflicts, we help to make them. Our communicative codes, as persuasive and entrapping as they are, do not turn us into communicative robots incapable of coming to grips with other people simply because they communicate differently. The social world is subject to negotiation. If codes exist, it is because we all help create them in the very process of communicating. If codes are keeping us apart, it is because it is adaptive for us to do so given the constraints imposed on our behavior in the social order constituted by the codes. Ways of speaking and moving harbor political systems that we all help to recreate with our every movement and utterance (Beck, 1975; Hymes, 1961, 1973; Labov, 1972a, b; Scheflen, 1973, 1974).

There are a number of reasons for understanding the communication problems between members of different groups as the accomplishments of people trying to get the most out of the political and economic contexts for their being brought together. We will briefly mention some examples from the growing literature on interethnic communication and then present a detailed analysis of a case of a child supposedly miscommunicating with his teacher. From the literature, three kinds of examples stand out: (1) there are cases in which members of different groups make an effort to move beyond a major communicative code difference, for example, a difference between two mutually unintellegible languages; (2) there are cases in which one would think it would be easy for members of different groups to put aside their communicative differences, the difference between dialects, for example, but they maintain them anyway in the face of differential institutional payoffs; and (3) there are cases in which members of different communities work hard at establishing communicative code differences in order to mark themselves off as coherent and often antagonist groups.

Before proceeding with the examples, we want to take care to point out that our position rests on some assumptions about the nature of ethnic groups and that these assumptions have proved helpful in explaining interethnic relations around the world. The case we are making for classrooms is manifested in many diverse situations in which groups of people find themselves at odds. In most cases, it has become clear that the differences between people are only incidentally a problem; the differences between people are as much a resource for mutual exploration and celebration as they are a resource for conflict (J. McDermott, 1976; R. McDermott, 1975). Our problem is not ethnicity, but ethnic borders. Our problem is not that people are different, but that the differences are made to make more of a difference than they must, that the differences are politicized into borders that define different kinds of people as antagonists in various realms of everyday life (Frake, unpublished manuscript).

Barth (1969a,b) has articulated this view and shown how we must understand the ethnic identities of many people in terms of how these identities are related to the maximization of physical and economic security and/or identity enhancement in contrast to other available alternatives. Moerman (1965, 1968) has made the same point for groups in Northern Thailand. His point of departure was to try to answer the question, "Who are the Lue?," with a description of the behavior and attitudes of the Lue people. His job proved so difficult that he had to rephrase his questions to when, where, why, and how are the Lue. The complexities of having a Lue identity could not be understood without a specification of the circumstances under which it made sense for the Lue to emphasize their Lue identity over the various alternative identities available to them. As we shall see, this phenomenon of identity switching in certain situations is not any less prevalent even in societies in which ethnic groups are divided by a clear physical marker such as skin color; for example, many whites and Blacks in urban American cities have developed competencies for communicating and identifying with each other in certain situations in which racial differences are temporarilly brushed aside.

(1)   The position that communicative codes do not form a simple exact calculus determinative of behavior is perhaps most available to us in the records of millions of immigrants who move to other lands and pick up new and diverse languages and customs in only a few years. Here the political circumstances for learning the ways of the people who control the resources of the new land is obvious. Sometimes, it is even necessary for immigrants to learn two languages, one of the poorer working-class people who surround them upon their entrance to the country, the other the language of the politically more dominant group. For example, the Italians who immigrated to the bilingual city of Montreal work with, live near, and intermarry with the French. But the majority of Italian parents send their children to schools to learn English, which the parents feel is the language of the successful, a feeling they apparently share with both French and English speakers of Montreal (Boissevain, 1970; Frender & Lambert, 1973; Lambert, 1967). In New York City, Puerto Ricans are exposed mostly to Black neighbors and co-workers,

and the children first become competent in Black language (Wolfram, 1973). Although Black English is useful in the most immediate politics of everyday life, in the long run the children are forced to learn a more standardized English in order to get by in the larger urban scene. The result in both these cases are populations with three different codes for their participation in the three different communities. People who do not become trilingual can suffer exclusion from certain institutions.

Along with their adoption of languages, immigrants and their children also make drastic shifts in their kinesic behavior. In a stunning effort, Efron (1941) long ago showed that the Jews and Italians of New York City altered their gestural patterns in accordance with the demands of the immediate situation. The same Jewish student who would barely gesticulate when he talked with his professors at Columbia University would be far more active the next day back in the Jewish community where he could wave his forearms and button-hole his friends without being considered conversationally aggressive.

Even without the extreme example of immigration, the social science literature is filled with accounts of people overcoming structurally complex communicative code differences in order to make sense of each other on certain occasions. The fascinating records of whole groups together generating pidgin and creole languages come from all parts of the world. Usually the processes are more complex than the "Me Tarzan, you Jane" model of pidginization, but this example serves the purpose of showing that when the circumstances are such that people must understand each other, they will find a way. Most often, such pidgins develop among different groups of people who have much interaction with each other in the market place of a third and more powerful group and, under such conditions, it is good to have a way of communicating with each other without becoming part of the dominating market society (DeCamp, 1971). Similar processes have been demonstrated on the kinesic level by Erickson (1975, 1976 and this volume), who has shown that members of different ethnic groups alter their communicative styles to fit "panethnic" groupings made up of various ethnic groups aligned according to the dictates of local politics; for example, Blacks and Puerto Ricans in Chicago would fall together against Irish, Poles, and Italians on one hand, and WASPS on the other.

(2)   The case of people refusing to repair minor communicative code boundaries also makes the point that the divergence of communicative patterns into mutually exclusive codes must be understood in terms of their function in interaction and not simply in terms of structural differences. The differences between the vernacular English of many American Blacks or the creole English of many West Indians are minute compared to the differences between mutually intelligible languages. Yet these smaller barriers to mutual intelligibility appear to be much more difficult to overcome in schools and other institutional settings (Cazden, John & Hymes, 1972; Craig, 1971). What makes a difference is the politization of language and dialect differences in the schools in which the children are asked to learn.

In fact, some research efforts are beginning to show that dialect use by Black children in American schools actually increases as children proceed through school (Hall & Freedle, 1975; Labov, 1972a; Piestrup, 1973). Given the correlation between dialect use and success in school in numerous minority-dominant group settings, this is an important finding that can give us a rough sense for the social processes underlining the emergence of communicative code boundaries together with failing school records. Labov and Robins (1969) have shown, for example, that the use of dialect increases as peer-group participation increases and school performances decline. This result is further illustrated by Piestrup (1973) who found that in the first grades she analyzed, the Black children's use of dialect either stayed the same or soared in direct proportion to how much the children were hassled for their use of dialect. The more their speech was corrected, the more they used dialect, and in such classrooms, reading scores were low. In classrooms in which the children were allowed to express themselves and read orally in dialect, the use of dialect did not increase and their reading scores were higher, with many children above the norms.

The presence or absence of dialect in the children's speech is not the crucial determinant of successful communication in school. Rather, dialect appears to function as a focus for the relational work of the children and the teacher. If the teacher and the children are alienated from each other, their dialects will take center stage and the teacher and the children will battle each other about the proper way to speak. In this sense, the emergence of a dialect in each new generation of different minorities represents more than a passing on of a set of speaking skills. It also represents an active adaptation to conditions in classrooms across the country. And the conscious claiming of a dialect, or any other aspect of a communicative code, from a clenched fist to a particular kind of walk, represents a political activity, a statement of one's identity as a member of a particular community.

(3)   The point that communicative codes are not determinants of people's relations with each other, that they are in fact adaptations to the various relations between the people who use the codes, is most clearly made by cases in which a group invents a communicative code in order to build cohesion into the home community and to block out the surrounding communities (Halliday, 1976; Gmelch, Langan & Gmelch, 1976). The Pennsylvania Dutch (Amish) are a good example of people who work at keeping themselves different, and they specify these differences not only at the level of general values against modern life, but at the level of the minutiae of everyday communication, at the level of language and dress, right down to the kinds of hooks used to fasten their clothing together. Such communicative strategies can have an effect on classrooms. The code differences do not in and of themselves enhance or detract from the children's learning. But the work that the Amish do to make themselves different apparently does interfere with the children's performance in public schools, where they do not do well academically. But this same work apparently creates a communal learning environment in their own schools in which Amish children do well, even by the standards of state tests (Hostetler & Huntington, 1971). These differential school results can only be un-

derstood in terms of the mutually distrustful relations between the Amish and the surrounding communities, on the one hand, and the positive relational environments generated by Amish teachers and children, on the other (McDermott, 1977).

The same may be true for Black Muslim schools, which have apparently been more successful than public schools in the education of Black children in America (Shalaby & Chilcott, 1972). Certainly the Black Muslims work hard at defining their school as a special place carved out of an ugly racist and criminal environment, and this work can be seen in their efforts to create a unique communicative system for members of their community to use in their dealings with each other and outsiders. The use of Islamic symbolism and food taboos does much to accomplish this goal and the Black Muslims until recently have given the impression of being dominated by the secrets of the esoteric wisdom of the East, by what new adolescent initiates in the mid-1960s called "heavy knowledge" (Labov, Cohen, Robins & Lewis, 1968). Members also developed a special code for addressing each other in Arabic and fictive kinship terms, and they dress in ways that mark them off from the Black and white communities in which they are immersed. Upon entering school every day, each child is searched for candy and other prohibited items, a fascinating communicative device that informs every child that the door to the school or mosque is no ordinary door and that behind it lies a whole new world of meaning. This is further reinforced by the children, particularly the boys, being taught to adopt a special military, square-cornered walk for their time in school. By building such elaborate communicative code differences with the surrounding communities, the children are made to feel like part of a coherent community that is cut off from the evils of the outside world.

The three kinds of examples we have just cited should demonstrate that an account of minority group problems in school in terms of communicative code differences is too simple. Certainly communicative differences exist across groups. And certainly, we notice these differences more among the children who are failing in school. But to suggest that these differences cause misbehavior and failure in school is to make a cause out of what is more likely only an effective medium for expressing the political and economic relations between the different groups. In order to disentangle this hypothesis, we will have to locate some situations in which some minority children are failing and specify the role of communicative code differences in their behavior with the teacher. Our notion is that when ethnically specific patterns are used and appear to cause trouble, the cause of that trouble will not be with the communicative code disparity but with the function of the disparity in the relations between the students and the teacher in the classroom. The relations between the teacher and the children will be the key to the member's interpretations and evaluations of the importance of ethnic borders and school learning in their lives with each other (McDermott, 1977). With this in mind, we will present an account of a teacher and a child having trouble with each other in ways that could be understood in terms of a communicative code conflict, but which upon analysis appears to be a function of much mutual understanding of their circumstances by the child and the teacher.

III. A CONTEXT ANALYSIS OF THE FUNCTION
OF A MISCOMMUNICATION

In the classroom we introduced above, there was a Puerto Rican boy who was assigned to the bottom group for most of the year. There Juan (as we shall call him), made life miserable for all, and much of his time was spent being put out of the group or chastised while in the group. Although we never tracked this boy's activities alone, there were times when he would show up in our notes more than ten times an hour as the focus of a disruptive incident in classroom routines. Later in the year, the teacher became concerned enough to have the school officials discuss his case as a candidate for a special school for disturbed children. And this is where he is today. By the time the films were taken, this child was no longer a part of the bottom reading group. He was in no group at all, and he either busied himself with little projects the teacher gave him or he wandered around the classroom interacting with the other children, interactions that often led to disagreements. When the bottom group was at the reading table, he appeared to monitor their actions carefully, and any disturbance usually was followed by his showing up at the table anxious to participate.

We should mention how we came by our observations; one of us was in the classroom throughout the year observing behavior and recording it in a notebook, on Super-8 film mounted in one corner of the room and on videotape often centered on the reading groups. We did not attempt to code the data that we abstracted out of the records for purposes of statistical manipulation as it was our conviction that the patterned nature of the behavior in the classroom must emerge on the participants' own terms from an intensive analysis rather than by being imposed a priori. With that in mind we carefully analyzed tapes of the top and bottom reading groups at work and identified how the participants struggled to understand and organize their own behavior. The result was a complex structural analysis, only a diluted example of which will be presented in this section. By virtue of the extended observation in the classroom and a more detailed interactional analysis, as in McDermott (1976), we feel our statements about Juan and ethnic borders are warranted.

On one occasion, Juan came to the teacher complaining that another child was bothering him and that her intervention was necessary. It came at a time that the teacher was working with the bottom group in a reading lesson. She was standing in front of the group writing a word on the board. All were quite involved. At this point, the young boy started across the classroom shouting the teacher's name, "Hey, S_____, you better tell him to stop!" The teacher ignored the boy until he reached her and made contact by touching her on the buttocks. Thus, the boy violated two apparent rules of mainstream culture. He skipped the teacher's title and used only her last name in trying to get her attention. Further, he got her attention by contacting a prohibited area. The teacher immediately responded to the boy's touch and gave witness to the violation status of his attention-getting techniques. She turned quickly and left the bottom group without instruction as to what they should do next. She took the boy by the arm to a corner near her desk where she had a brief conversation with him before they broke contact.

The discovery of this behavior was easy. The boy violated not only the teacher's rules for contact, but our rules also, and we attended to his violation almost immediately. With a little more looking at the video tape, it became probable that the teacher was not pleased with the boy, for throughout the year, when the teacher was annoyed, the same arm raising procedure was used. The procedure consisted of the teacher raising the child's arm to a height that made the child dependent on her guidance for a means of transport.

So we have some behavior that can be used as an anecdote relating ethnicity to miscommunication. The child wanted the teacher's attention, went about it in the wrong way, and got nothing but trouble for his efforts. The teacher in turn has the trouble of being hassled and having to hassle the child. No one is getting what they want. Or at least no one is getting what the institution has defined as desirable. At first, we thought that the problem was simple. People from different cultures have different systems for doing touch. The teacher is a rather classic Northern and Eastern (non-Jewish) European in this regard, and she has little tactile involvement with other people in public. This should be difficult on the Mediterranean and Caribbean children who come from more tactile cultures and who could suffer relational mishaps with the teacher because of their different ways of making sense (Efron, 1941; Hall, 1966; Scheflen, 1974). This little anecdote supports this notion. Numerous other examples can be found in the literature on cross-cultural communication in educational settings (Byers & Byers, 1972; Collier, 1973; Dumont, 1972; Erickson, 1975, 1976; Mehan, 1973; Philips, 1972).

With this supporting literature, it is easy to jump from the anecdote to conclusions. One is that the boy is working with a different communicative code than the teacher and unwittingly causes some trouble for himself by not learning her code. The second response is that the teacher should be aware that the child has a different way of proceeding and should be more adaptable in order to give the boy the most satisfying relational environment in which to learn and adapt to mainstream culture. In this way, it might be possible to minimize miscommunication and restrict the possibility that the boy might eventually work at achieving school failure, rather than school success.

But two other questions have forced themselves on us. One, given the adaptability children display in many of their activities, why is it that this boy is not using the mainstream code to get the teacher's attention? Why is it that after nine months in school, he still has not figured out the teacher's rules for addressing and touching? Is it possible that there are other contexts for this behavior than is obvious in the adecdote? Two, might there be more reasons for the teacher being annoyed than is obvious in the anecdote? The teacher generally displays tremendous patience with the children. Is there something else going on than simply a touch deemed inappropriate in the teacher's native culture? Is it possible the boy is breaking more rules than those of the culture at large? Is it possible the boy is breaking rules that govern the relational work between the children of the class-room and the teacher? And is it possible the teacher's annoyance is only a part of more inclusive contexts for the sequencing of their behavior? The anecdotal des-cription we offered cannot be used to address these questions. Instead, we need a description of the people's contexts for their behavior as they are defining those contexts and using them in the organization of concerted behavior. Fortunately, both the theory and the method of context analysis has been well worked out (Bateson, 1955; Birdwhistell, 1970; McQuown, Bateson, Birdwhistell, Brosin, & Hockett, 1971; Scheflen, 1966, 1973).

Perhaps the most immediate context or environment for people's behavior is the answer they might collectively give to the question "What is it that is going on here?" or "What's happening?" (Frake, 1964, 1976; Goffman, 1974). Many have shown that it is possible to locate people's answers to this question, because people must constantly inform each other of what is going on in order to continue pro-ducing concerted behavior with each other. So much of the behavior of members when face to face is related to this task that it would seem to be the *sine qua non* of any interaction (Birdwhistell, 1970). Verbally, they keep each other informed by formulating or keying what it is that they are doing for everyone to hear, most clearly by naming, although usually members are less explicit (Hymes, 1974; Sacks, 1974; Wieder, 1974). Kinesically, they do this by moving and positioning their bodies in relation to each other in particular ways at particular times. Thus, what it is that people are doing together can be seen in the positions or postural config-urations they work out with each other   (Kendon, 1973; McDermott, Gospodinoff, & Aron, 1976; Scheflen, 1964, 1973).

In the bottom group, the children and the teacher move in and out of three different major activity types, only three of which will be considered in this paper. These are the most immediate contexts for their answers to the question that they constantly put to each other and to themselves, namely, "What's going on?" As these were located primarily by an analysis of postural shifts performed by the members, we will call them positionings (Fig. 1-3).

For our present purpose, it is only important to know that each of these posi-tionings is marked by a different kind of work at the outer boundaries of the group. That is, depending upon which of the three positionings the children and the teacher assume, outsiders to the group appear to have different degrees of license to enter the group. This is not an unusual phenomenon, and an outsider's rights to enter a group have been clearly documented as subject to the postural work of the people already in the group (Kendon & Ferber, 1973; Scheflen, 1971, 1976; Shultz, 1976). For example, in the bottom group, when the teacher is out of the group and the children are waiting for her return (positioning III), outsiders are invited in to visit. When the children are struggling to get a turn to read from the teacher (posi-tioning II), the children carefully monitor the teacher's activities; accordingly, no

Fig. 1. Positioning I: Looking at the book.

Fig. 2. Positioning II: Getting-a-turn to read.

Fig. 3. Positioning III: Waiting for the teacher.

one is invited in, but if outsiders have business with the teacher, they will usually make an entrance. However, when the children are actively engaged in reading with the teacher (positioning I), no outsider enters the group. Interestingly, the top reading group assumes this organization throughout its reading lesson and is never disturbed by outsiders.

Now we must reconsider the boy's attention-getting behaviors in terms of the immediate contexts in which they occur. The behaviors occur at a special time and must be understood as they function at that time. With such a reconsideration, for example, the teacher does not have to be such a cultural imperialist to respond in the way that she does. No one except this boy enters the reading table while the group is reading (positioning I). The top group is never disturbed, and when a member of the bottom group even went near the top group while the members were reading (positioning I), the teacher, three top group members and one member of the bottom group at the other end of the room conspired to prevent a possible disturbance by chasing the boy back to his part of the room. On the other hand, children from the top group often disturb the children of the bottom group while they are at the reading table, but never enter the table while the bottom group is reading (positioning I). This avoidance is no accident, for there are examples of a top group child entering the periphery of reading activity (positioning I), waiting until it is complete, and finally moving in to address the teacher at the start of the children calling for a turn (positioning II). The only case of a child violating a reading positioning comes when Juan enters and contacts the teacher's buttocks. Suddenly, this episode does not look like a simple case of culture conflict. The conflict at hand is not between the patterning of behavior of Caribbean Spanish versus that of Northern and Eastern European. It is far more localized than that. Given the particular ways of doing the order of the classroom, as that order is negotiated, formulated and done by the teacher and the students for their mo-ment-to-moment life in school, the important question asks how it is that this particular boy becomes involved in conflicts of scheduling as well as conflicts of naming and touching. Whatever the reasons, the teacher's reactions appear to be quite sensible.

More context must be considered for the boy's behavior. Recall that the boy was formerly a member of the bottom group and has since been put out. However, the boy still monitors the group's activities quite carefully. For example, every time there is a disturbance while the teacher is away from the reading table and the children struggle, squirm and fight, this boy shows up on the scene. During one such episode, a child takes a pencil belonging to another child and throws it to the floor at the other end of the reading table. The pencil has barely hit the ground as the boy in question runs across the room and picks the pencil up. Later, when two children square off in an argument, the prodigal child again appears on camera examining the scene. The boy monitors the group carefully and gives evidence of knowing the difference between the three positionings. More examples are possible, and each of them would contrast the boy's entering behavior in the buttocks scene to the boy's usual behavior during a reading positioning, in which he moves past the table the same as everyone else, without any disturbance whatsoever. So there is some reason to think that the boy moves to the table misaddressing and mistouching the teacher at a time that he understands as inappropriate.

Can we still talk about the teacher and the child miscommunicating? The child appears to have mastered the basic rules of the classroom and simply uses them for a different purpose. What could be the function of his behavior? Remember that the teacher takes the child to a corner and chastises him (unfortunately out of the range of the microphone). What happens next is interesting. The teacher then goes off camera to the back of the room where she is picked up by another camera. There she chastises the boy that Juan was complaining about. On her way, she is followed by Juan, in no way crushed, clapping his hands and delighting in the fact that his adversary is also getting into trouble. The plot thickens. In short, he received from the interaction what he might have wanted all along, namely, to get the other child in trouble, no mean feat in a classroom in which the teacher discourages snitching, particularly while she is busy working with a group. So the small anecdote locating a miscommunication, if properly contextualized, shows the miscommunication not only to be sensible, but quite functional as well.

It is not as easy to locate the teacher's behavior as functional. By placing her behavior in its larger context, we have located that her annoyance was based on more than a misunderstanding of cross-cultural norms for touching. Rather, her behavior appears to be based as well on a "knowledge" of the interactional norms governing her particular classroom. The boy breaks the rules and the teacher chastises him for it. Up to this point, her behavior makes sense, but then she crowns his efforts by attending to the matter he brought before her in the way he might have hoped. She breaks the first rule of classroom management by rewarding a person for breaking the rules and norms she otherwise enforces. Meanwhile, the bottom reading group is wasting its time on the other side of the room; a fight has started and reading has stopped. A good portion of the class is also disrupted by this episode. There is little reason for him not to proceed in the same way at another time. How then can we say that the teacher's behavior makes sense? The answer to this question is in no way complete, but consider the following pattern.

Often, as the bottom group gets into a positioning II in which they are struggling for a turn to read or a positioning I in which they are engaged in reading or some other lesson activity with the teacher, they are disrupted by the teacher yelling at the rest of the class or actually leaving the group to attend to outsiders. The teacher's attending to the boy's behavior in both a negative and positive way at a particular time may have to be understood in terms of this larger pattern of the teacher exiting from the bottom group at key points, when the group is highly focused around a particular task. By way of inference, it can be claimed that the teacher is uncomfortable with the bottom group once it is settled and ready for instruction. In terms of the readiness of some of the children to engage in reading activities, the teacher's response to the bottom group is quite understandable. It is easier to teach children how to read when they already know how to read. The top group does not present the problems the bottom group does. If this is the case, then the teacher's positive response to the boy's requests appears to be a self-serving activity in that it is a way of getting out of the group for a little while. In the long run, everyone pays heavily for this escape, but in the short run it is to everyone's advantage; the boy gets someone in trouble and the teacher and the children in the bottom group get a brief rest from their intense organizational negotiations.

By placing the behaviors described in the anecdote within the contexts in terms of which the people engaged could possibly understand and act upon them, a quite different interpretation of this anecdote is possible. A miscommunication cannot be understood without asking about the constraints on each person in terms of which their miscommunication may be adaptive. After this question is answered in terms of the contexts negotiated by the participants, a miscommunication may look quite sensible. The little boy and the teacher appear to understand each other quite well, and they prey on each other's circumstances in order to enhance their respective standings within those circumstances. How then can we talk of communicative code differences causing misbehavior and failure in school? Juan demonstrates an understanding of the world in which he operates. It is hard to imagine how Puerto Rican culture inhibits his participation in the classroom. He and the teacher get a maximum amount of use of each other given the pressures of the classroom on each of them at that moment. The consequences of the adjustments they make to their circumstances are the mutually regressive understandings we see at evidence in this account. Juan and the teacher seem to have agreed unknowingly on how to miscommunicate with each other. Their choices are adaptive given their circumstances. We will now have to give some attention to what these circumstances might be and, in terms of these circumstances, we will have to consider the long-term consequences of their behavior.

IV. THE CIRCUMSTANCES AND CONSEQUENCES OF MISCOMMUNICATION IN SCHOOL

Just what are the circumstances that make this miscommunication functional? In other words, how is it that things are set up so that many children, particularly minority children have the kinds of problems just detailed? Our argument is that schooling situations offer less of a payoff for many minority and poor children. Most often, it is not the case that the schools are staffed with teachers consciously trying to keep minority children from succeeding in school. Nor is it generally the case that there is something wrong with the children as they enter school. Although these two explanations are the most popular accounts of minority school failure, we suspect that cases to which they actually apply are rare, and we will not deal with them as such. Our problem is neither racist teachers nor dumb kids. Our problem is that our school systems are set up to have conscientious teachers function as racists and bright little children function as dopes even when they are all trying to do otherwise.

More specifically, our claim is that poor and minority children start school knowing less about how to read and write than do the children of the enfranchised groups that survive in the modern nations via literacy skills. This is in no way a deprivation argument. We are not suggesting that the children of the minorities do not have the skills for immediately learning how to read; we have only suggested that many have not learned how to read before they come to school. From every-thing we know about the proper age for starting to learn how to read around the world, being more or less prepared at age six should have no effect on the eventual acquisition of literacy by the children (Wanat, 1976). Yet, given the nature of the classrooms in which the children are asked to catch up, learning to read at school becomes an organizational impossibility.

In the early grades, schools are best set up for reinforcing and practicing what children have already learned at home. When minority children show up in school not knowing how to read, they are placed in special groups like the one described in this paper. The teacher's job is not only to teach them how to read, but to make sure that they achieve a certain competence and demonstrate it on a standardized test by a certain date. In other words, the teacher is trained, paid, and held account-able for producing certain kinds of reading children by a certain date. Children in the bottom group create difficult organizational and pedagogical problems for the teacher. Many of the communication problems that exist between teachers and minority children can be understood as mutual adaptations to these organizational problems. For example, in the classroom we analyzed, the teacher handled the top and bottom groups quite differently. With the top group, the teacher likes to have the children take turns reading, one after the other, from left to right, around the table. This is not possible with the bottom group, because there are children who cannot be expected to read any page that comes along. So the teacher spares them some embarassment and picks a special reader for each page. This means that she cannot divert here attention from this group for more than a moment with-out their needing her direction in picking a new reader. Concentrated attention with the bottom reading group is hardly possible while the teacher has two other groups and some stragglers busy (and not so busy) in other parts of the room. Accordingly, the members of the bottom group are often left without direction about how to proceed in their reading lesson, and they spend more than half their time waiting for the teacher or trying to get the teacher's attention to their pleas for a turn to read.

Recall the three positions that the members of the bottom group achieve with each other; two of them, getting-a-turn and waiting for the teacher (positionings II and III respectively) pit the children and the teacher in a struggle for each other's attention. The top group shares only the first positioning with the bottom group, the one in which all the members focus on reading. Now recall that these three positionings are different in that they allow different visiting rights for outsiders. The fact that the top group stays in the reading positioning (even when they are not actually reading) means that no outsiders enter the group during its lesson. However, by adapting to the teacher's procedures for calling on special children for special pages, the children in the bottom group arrange themselves into positionings II and III, and suffer constant interruptions from the children in the top group entering to ask the teacher questions during the bottom group's time at the reading table. Each of these interruptions further necessitates the elaborate procedures the children in the bottom group develop to get the teacher's attention in order to get a turn to read. Juan became so good at getting the teacher's attention in unorthodox, but situationally adaptive ways that he was put out of the bottom group. As we have seen, he still exercises his communicative skills by entering the group in the way that he does. Other children in the bottom group are developing similar skills.

The case we have made for circumstances that nurture miscommunication in the classroom is as follows: Various children, most of them poor or minority children who are not submerged in literacy skills at home, come into school behind their peers in reading and present difficult organizational and pedagogical problems for their teachers who are pressured to produce children with certain kinds of reading skills by a certain date; the teacher and the children make adjustments to each other's organizational quandaries; and the consequences of these adjustments are institutionally regressive, but sensible and functional forms of communication that appear to us as cases of miscommunication and misbehavior.

There are two important consequences of such apparent agreements to miscommunicate in the classroom. By way of their participation in such classrooms, the children from the bottom group fail in school and achieve the same places their parents hold in the social structure of the community. And in the case of the minority children in the bottom group, they acquire an ethnic identity that is not defined simply in terms of the values and behavioral styles of the group, but in terms of their group's antagonistic relations with the more dominant groups. Both these statements deserve some warrant.

We have suggested that the children in the bottom group come into the first grade not knowing how to read. They start off behind. Then they are put into the bottom group where they suffer the organizational problems we have described. The significant fact is that although they spend the same amount of time at the reading table as the children in the other groups, due to all the interruptions, two-thirds of them initiated by the other groups, they get only one-third the amount of time as the children in the top group get in a reading positioning. The rest of their time is spent in attentional struggles with the teacher. The net effect of this is that the children in the bottom group fall further behind the children in the top group for every day they spend in the classroom. The alternative to this is that they learn how to read at home. If they do not do this before school, they apparently do not do it after they enter school, and they get caught in the communicational systems that accentuate this discrepancy. Placement in the bottom group of this classroom (and classrooms without such tracking into ability groups appear to get much the same job done in different ways) works like a self-fulfilling prophecy in that the children in this group consistently get less concentrated, quality instruction than the children in the other groups. And this is the case for an excellent teacher who cares deeply about the children. We all know that teaching a first grade is a difficult job, and this particular teacher is excellent under the circumstances. We are only suggesting that learning to read in a first grade classroom may be an even more difficult job for the organizational reasons we have highlighted.

Without learning how to read, there are few other paths for upward mobility for minority children in modern nations. Thus the children achieve the same adaptational skills of their parents, and a new generation of the so-called disadvantaged takes its place in the world. If we wanted a mechanism for sorting each new generation of citizens into the advantaged and the disadvantaged, into the achieving and the under achieving, we could have done no better than to have invented the school system we have. Not only is it efficient in assigning many generations of the same people to the top and bottom slots, but, and this is one of the ironies of contemporary life, it does so in ways that make sense to the hard working, caring, and talented people who are trying to help break the cycle of the disadvantaged becoming more disadvantaged and the advantaged becoming more advantaged.

Lastly, we want to note that the ethnic border conflicts that mark all the nation states and plague most modern cities are reinforced in the classroom. People need a way to explain the persistent failure of minority children in schools. Rather than taking a look at how this is done, as we have tried to do here in only a limited way, most of us have ethnic labels available for talking about and explaining the failure of the different kinds of children. Ethnic group membership does not cause school failure or success, but after different kinds of children differentially succeed and fail, ethnicity becomes salient in negative ways. In the classroom we have just analyzed, at the beginning of the year, the white, Black, and Puerto Rician children divided their time with each other without regard to ethnicity. By the end of the year, the two Black children, the four Puerto Rican children and the eighteen white children began to form isolates. By late May, the terms "nigger" and "spic" began to show up, and border fights between members of the different groups became a daily occurrence. How this happened is worth another paper. We are pointing to this phenomenon now because we believe that it flows rather directly from the experiences we have described for the children in this classroom. For it is the minority children who engage in the bulk of the miscommunication with the teacher. Under these conditions, ethnic solidarity becomes a refuge from the negative relationships offered to the children in the classrooms. In this way, the experience of belonging to a group was transformed into an experience of having enemies. The problem in this classroom was not ethnicity, but a set of contexts in terms of which ethnic differences were turned into ethnic borders.

Hopefully, ethnic differences will survive the many homogenizing influences of the modern world. We will need these differences to keep us alive to the variety of ways we potentially have available for celebrating and humanizing each other. However, when ethnic differences become a source for ethnic borders, we must attempt to overcome the conflicts; we must attempt to locate for ourselves how we are helping to create the conditions for transforming differences into borders.

Unfortunately, even if we achieve some semblance of intellectual clarity on the subject, there is considerable question as to whether we will be able to stop our own participation in the creation of borders without considerable change in the institutional demands with which we must deal in our everyday life. Many of our institutions certainly get in the way of maximizing the social and psychological potential of our children, and most of us do not have the foggiest notion of how to proceed in rectifying the situation. Efforts at achieving institutional reform consistent with our growing knowledge of the constraints and possibilities of human behavior, efforts such as those formulated in a stimulating paper by Church (1976), will have to form a far greater focus for our activities.

Acknowledgements

Most of the research reported in this paper was supported by predoctoral research grants to McDermott by the National Institute of General Medical Studies, the National Institute of Mental Health, and the National Science Foundation. McDermott's writing time was supported by Carnegie Corporation funds to Michael Cole and the Laboratory of Comparative Human Cognition at the Rockefeller University. We both are indebted to Albert Scheflen who gave us some difficult problems to work on and the inspiration (and a place) to work on them. Bernard Strassberg did an expert job on our drawings. In addition Gospodinoff wishes to acknowledge numerous discussions over the past six years on many of the issues of this paper with Dr. E. H. Auerswald of the University of Hawaii Department of Psychiatry and the Maui Community Mental Health Center, who also provided financial support and critical comments. About one-third of this material has been adapted from the doctoral dissertation submitted by McDermott to the Department of Anthropology, Stanford University, 1976.

References

Auerswald, E. H. The noncare of the underprivileged: Some ecological observations. *International Psychiatry Clinics,* 1971, *8,* 43-60.
Barth, F. Introduction. In F. Barth (Ed.), *Ethnic groups and boundaries.* Boston: Little, Brown, and Company, 1969. (a)
Barth, F. Pathan identity and its maintenance. In F. Barth (Ed.), *Ethnic groups and boundaries.* Boston: Little, Brown, and Company 1969. (b)
Bateson, G. The message "This is play." In B. Schaffner (Ed.), *Group processes.* New York: Josiah Macy, Jr. Foundation, 1955.
Beck, H. Ethological considerations on the problem of political order. *Political Anthropology,* 1975, *1,* 110-132.
Birdwhistell, R. *Kinesics and context.* Philadelphia: University of Pennsylvania Press, 1970.
Boissevain, J. *The Italians of Montreal.* Ottawa: Crown Copyrights, 1970.
Byers, P., & Byers, H. Nonverbal communication and the education of children. In C. Cazden,

V. John, & D. Hymes (Eds.), *Functions of language in the classroom*. New York: Teachers College Press, 1972.

Cazden, C., John, V., & Hymes, D. (Eds.). *Functions of language in the classroom*. New York: Teachers College Press, 1972.

Church, J. Psychology and the social order. *Annals of the New York Academy of Sciences, 1976, 270,* 141-151.

Cole, M., Gay, J., Glick, J., & Sharp, D. *The cultural context of learning and thinking*. New York: Basic Books, 1971.

Collier, J. *Alaskan Eskimo education*. New York: Holt, Rinehart, & Winston, 1973.

Craig, D. Education and Creole English in the West Indies. In D. Hymes (Ed.), *Pidginization and creolization of languages*. London: Cambridge, University Press, 1971.

DeCamp, D. Introduction, In D. Hymes (Ed.), *Pidginization and creolization of languages*. London: Cambridge University Press, 1971.

D'Andrade, R. Cultural constructions of reality. In L. Nadar and T. Maretzki (Eds.), *Cultural illness and health*. Washington, D. C.: American Anthropological Association, 1973.

Dumont, R. Learning English and how to be silent. In C. Cazden, V. John, & D. Hymes (Eds.), *Functions of speech in the classroom*. New York. Teachers College Press, 1972.

Efron, D. *Gesture and environment*. New York: King's Crown Press, 1941.

Erickson, F. Gatekeeping and the melting pot. *Harvard Educational Review, 1975, 45,* 44-70.

Erickson, F. Gatekeeping encounters. In P. Sanday (Ed.), *Anthropology and the public interest*. New York: Academic Press, 1976.

Frake, C. A structural description of Subanun "religious" behavior. In W. Goodenough (Ed.), *Explorations in cultural anthropology*. New York: McGraw-Hill, 1964.

Frake, C. Interpretations of illness. Paper presented to the New York Academy of Sciences, March 8, 1976.

Frake, C. The emics and etics of ethnicity: Cultural boundaries in the Sulu Sea. Unpublished manuscript, n.d.

Frender, R., & Lambert, W. Speech style and scholastic success. In R. Shuy (Ed.), *Sociolinguistics*. Washington, D. C.: Georgetown University Press, 1973.

Gmelch, S., Langan, P., & Gmelch, G. *Tinkers and travellers*. Montreal: McGill-Queen's University Press, 1976.

Goffman, E. *Frame analysis*. New York: Harper, 1974.

Hall, E. *The hidden dimension*. New York: Anchor, 1966.

Halliday, M. Antilanguages. *American Anthropologist, 1976, 78,* 570-584.

Hostetler, J., & Huntington, G. *Children in Amish society*. New York: Holt, Rinehart, & Winston, 1971.

Hymes, D. Functions of speech. In F. Gruber (Ed.), *Anthropology and education*. Philadelphia: University of Pennsylvania Press, 1961.

Hymes, D. Speech and language: On the origins and foundations of inequality in speaking. *Daedalus, 1973, 102,* 59-86.

Hymes, D. *Foundations in sociolinguistics*. Philadelphia: University of Pennsylvania Press, 1974.

Kendon, A. The role of visible behavior in the organization of social interaction. In M. von Cranach & I. Vine (Eds.), *Social communication and movement*. New York: Academic Press, 1973.

Kendon, A., & Ferber, A. A description of some human greetings. In R. Michael & L. Pearson (Eds.), *Comparative ecology and behavior of primates*. New York: Academic Press, 1973.

Labov, W. *Language in the inner city*. Philadelphia: University of Pennsylvania Press, 1972. (a)

Labov, W. *Sociolinguistic patterns*. Philadelphia: University of Pennsylvania Press, 1972. (b)

Labov, W., & Robins, C. A note on the relation of reading failure to peer-group status in urban ghettos. *Florida FL Reporter, 1969, 7,* 54-57, 167.

Labov, W., Cohen, P., Robins, C., & Lewis, J. *A study of the nonstandard English of Negro and Puerto Rican speakers in New York City.* Cooperative Research Project No. 3288, Office of Education, 1968.

Lambert, W. A social psychology of bilingualism. *The Journal of Social Issues,* 1967, *73,* 91-109.

McDermott, J. *The culture of experience.* New York: New York University Press, 1976.

McDermott, R. Toward an embodied map of urban neighborhoods: how it may be that New York City taxicab drivers make sense and generate social structure. Paper presented to the Anthropological Sociey of Washington, May 14, 1975.

McDermott, R. Kids make sense: An ethnographic account of the interactional management of success and failure in one first grade classroom. Unpublished doctoral dissertation, Department of Anthropology, Stanford University, 1976.

McDermott, R. Social relations as contexts for learning in school. *Harvard Educational Review,* 1977, *47,* 298-313.

McDermott, R., Gospodinoff, K., & Aron, J. Criteria for an ethnographically adequate description of concerted activities and their contexts. *Semiotica,* 1978, *24,* in press.

McQuown, N., Bateson, G., Birdwhistell, R., Brosin, H., & Hockett, C. *The natural history of an interview.* University of Chicago Library Microfilm Collection of Manuscripts in Cultural Anthropology, series 15 (nos. 95-98), 1971.

Mehan, H. Assessing children's school performance. *Recent Sociology,* 1973, *5,* 240-264.

Moerman, M. Ethnic identification in a complex civilization; who are the Lue? *American Anthropologist,* 1965, *67,* 1215-1226.

Moerman, M. Being Lue: Uses and abuses of ethnic edentification. In J. Helm (Ed.), *Essays on the problem of tribe.* Seattle: University of Washington Press, 1968.

Moore, S. Selection for failure in a small social field. In S. Moore & B. Meyerhoff (Eds.), *Symbol and politics in communal ideology,* Ithica: Cornell University Press, 1975.

Philips, S. Participant structures and communicative competencies. In C. Cazden, V. John, & D. Hymes (Eds.), *Functions of language in the classroom.* New York: Teachers College Press, 1972.

Piestrup, A. *Black dialect interference and accommodation of reading instruction in first grade.* Berkeley: Monographs of the Language-Behavior Research Laboratory, 1973.

Sacks, H. An analysis of the course of a joke's telling. In R. Bauman & J. Sherzer (Eds.) *Explorations in the ethnography of speaking.* London: Cambridge University Press, 1974.

Scheflen, A. The significance of posture in communication systems. *Psychiatry,* 1964, *27,* 316-331.

Scheflen, A. Natural history method in psychotherapy. In L. Gottschalk & A. Auerback (Eds.), *Methods of research in psychotherapy.* New York: Appleton-Century-Crofts, 1966.

Scheflen, A. Living space in an urban ghetto. *Family Process,* 1971, *10,* 429-450.

Scheflen, A. *Communicational structure.* Bloomington: Indiana University Press, 1973.

Scheflen, A. *How behavior means.* New York: Anchor Press, 1974.

Scheflen, A. *Human territories.* Englewood Cliffs: Prentice-Hall, 1976.

Shalaby, I., & Chilcott, J. *The education of a Black Muslim,* Tuscon: Impresora Sahuero, 1972.

Shultz, J. A microethnographic analysis of game playing in a kindergarten/first grade classroom. Unpublished manuscript, Harvard University, 1976.

Wanat, S. Reading and readiness. *Visible Language,* 1976, *10,* 101-127.

Wieder, D. *Language and social reality.* The Hague: Mouton, 1974.

Wolfram, W. Objective and subjective parameters of language assimilation among second generation Puerto Ricans in East Harlem. In R. Shuy & R. Fasold (Eds.), *Language attitudes.* Washington, D. C.: Georgetown University Press, 1973.

TEACHING AND NONVERBAL BEHAVIOR

Charles M. Galloway

The Ohio State University

Over 15 yr ago when I began to study teacher-student nonverbal communication patterns, I never imagined the prominence the field would attain. An awareness of the value of nonverbal communication appears everywhere: businessmen and salesmen, administrators and managers, actors and dancers, as well as teachers and parents have voiced an interest. Why the popularity of the subject? Why the interest in the unspoken, the unsaid, and the silent expression?

The answer is simple: Human beings do not understand themselves or other persons as well as they would like. We do not understand the complexities of what it means to communicate well, to understand or to be understood. We are not in touch with our deepest feelings and thoughts; we hide from ourselves and we fail to share what we think and feel.

Nonverbal sources of information represent an expressive network that reveals and informs. Some of us however, remain out of touch with this source of information. We refuse to honor the wisdom of body signals and signs, and we blind ourselves to nonverbal effects. In a need to fool ourselves we believe that self-control is a verbal achievement; that only verbal consequences matter.

Someone says, "You don't like me, do you? You don't believe I can do it?" Our response verbalizes, "Did I ever say that? What makes you believe I feel that way?" The assumption is clear: Only words count. I am in no way responsible for the countless expressions, gestures, faces, or actions you see. I control my world with verbal logic, the silent languages of attitude, value, and preference must be ignored because I take no responsibility for their expression.

When an individual takes the study of nonverbal communication seriously these questions serve to guide inquiry (Galloway, 1976):

Am I aware of my nonverbal messages?
Am I willing to take a responsibility for my nonverbal influences and effects?
Am I aware of the nonverbal messages of others?
Am I willing to be influenced by nonverbal messages?

Early in my own work I was convinced that nonverbal influences and effects were connected to classroom life. Nonverbal exchanges between teacher and student abounded throughout the contexts of teaching and learning. Not until recently have I realized the full significance nonverbal communication has for educators and students. The forces of power, control, influence, motivation, self-esteem, and interpersonal understanding are all related to the interplays of nonverbal exchange in the classroom.

If talking and listening were the only aspects of teaching, the problems of being understood would be difficult enough. But the difficulty is even more complex. When a teacher talks, students are watched to see how they are receiving and responding to what is said. When students listen, they hear the words (hopefully) and they observe the behaviors and expressions of the teacher to obtain further information. These behavioral cues and expressive displays fill in the blanks of missing information. Does the teacher mean what is said? Is the teacher sincere? What is the teacher's attitude toward me? There are countless questions that form in the mind.

Since the student is not talking, the advantage of observation without performance exists. The teacher must think ahead to what to say next, (this keeps one occupied), but students are watched for expressive signs. The teacher's mindedness is future oriented as thoughts and emotions race forward. The student thinks retrospectively. What did the teacher say? What do I think about what the teacher said? What is the teacher expressing nonverbally that was not said? The student deals with multiple channels of information and has to "put it all together."

Much emphasis has been given in the literature (Fast, 1970) to reading signs and signals, simple gestures and facial expressions that might signify how someone feels. If a person clenches his teeth or his fists, he is angry; if a person looks down or avoids eye contact, he is embarrassed or fearful; if he opens his arms, he is receptive or can be trusted. Such references to gestures and expressions, as indicators of emotionality, have been overplayed. (Publications that deal exclusively with body language or "how to read a person like a book" are predominant examples.) Because few nonverbal gestures, perhaps none, represent precise internal states and because it is dangerous and presumptuous to assume that reading specific signs and expressions can reveal what a person is thinking or feeling, we need to emphasize a different purpose for understanding nonverbal communication. We need to look at nonverbal realities in a broader context of human existence and experience. Why should we be concerned with nonverbal communication at all? The simplest answer is unpromising and vague: to better understand ourselves and others. The key to uncovering the value of the nonverbal is to recognize its relationship to what we are and to what we communicate. There is no truth like the whole truth. And nonverbal expressions provide a fuller measure of what we mean to communicate.

As a professional educator, I have been more interested in research that sheds light on the practical problems of teaching and learning. As a researcher I have focused on the necessary descriptions and data outcomes of teacher-learner behavior that have implications for improved practice. In a fundamental sense I have been most interested in teacher performance, learner productivity, and exchanges of meaning that facilitate distinctive human results. While these are tough-minded targets, I remain humanistic in style and purpose.

The study of nonverbal communication converts you toward the humanistic tradition whether you like it or not. When you come close to the variables that influence nonverbal understanding, you see the frailty of the human condition and the powerlessness of human beings to be understood well, if at all. The cries and calls of nonverbal messages scream out to an unperceptive and insensitive world that you are here, you exist, you need to be recognized, and you want to be given a chance to live your life with meaning.

Studies of nonverbal communication teach you that humanistic leanings create communicative contexts of the courage to be, the responsibility to act, and the consequences of choice. Humanistic tendencies toward students never guarantee humanism, nor do they insure good behaviors or positive results from students, but the approach makes it difficult (not impossible) for the client or student to act badly. Nonverbal concerns focus on the qualities of person-to-person relationship, and make evident the evasive difficulties of interpersonal understanding.

THE DIMENSIONS OF TEACHING

In my studies of the nonverbal behaviors of teachers in classrooms, three large dimensions of teacher activity have been witnessed. These dimensions have been recognized as the institutional, task, and personal behaviors of teachers. In some of the earlier research, institutional forms of teacher behavior were frequently observed during classroom observations. In Jackson's (1968) *Life in classrooms* and later in Smith and Geoffrey's (1968) *Complexities of an urban classroom*, similar data were provided to substantiate this claim: The press of institutional expectance in schools is so strong, teachers and students can be observed to behave in ways that are unique to the school environment. Indeed, these same behaviors rarely occur outside the school context.

While teachers and students are rarely instructed to behave in institutional ways, they soon learn. For instance, teachers often snap their fingers to achieve silence, fold their arms to signify impatience, point at students to give directions, stare directly at students to correct misbehaviors, and signal students to get ready to work. Students learn to look like they are studying, listening, or thinking. They learn to raise their hands to seek teacher attention; to cradle their arms in their hands to persuade the teacher of an earnest desire to be chosen. Eventually students learn to raise their hands so they will not be called on by the teacher. Standing in line, waiting your turn, eating, singing, and exercising on schedule are well-known institutional forms of school life. These manners and mores of school activity may be sympathetically enforced or they may be harshly administered.

In the last few years I have noticed a decline in the force of these institutional expectations. School life seems to be changing gradually, but institutional behaviors still persist to some degree. What appears to be a more dominant form of school life today is task behavior. Teachers are spending more of their time in the explaining, clarifying, question asking, praising, task-setting mode. More time is spent arranging learning activities for students and specifiying objectives for skill achievement. Even city schools are using less time for institutionalizing the student in school. Either the student complies with certain requirements or he is withdrawn from the classroom. Sometimes the student drops out himself. At other times he is simply ignored or avoided.

Recent developments have conspired to diminish the power of institutional and task demands. Students no longer seem disposed to go along with school requirements just because you are supposed to. Students have begun asking questions about school expectations. Why? So what? What difference does it make? Who cares?

> *Item*: A student recently asked why he should do school work the teacher assigned. The teacher wanted to know if he wanted to achieve a good grade and pass the course. The student replied that he wanted to do well, but did not understand what the teacher's demand had to do with learning anything important. The teacher's report was quick and to the point, "Don't you want to graduate from high school, go to college, or get a job?" The student responded that he understood those goals, but he thought the teacher had misunderstood him. His further clarification went something like this: "I don't mean to be disrespectful, but I am asking you what this assigned work means to you. It doesn't mean anything to me. If I could understand what its significance meant to you beyond its representing something for me to do, then I might get turned on. I might not either. But at least I would have the benefit of your thinking and feeling toward the work. Otherwise, I am left to my own limited devices and to your insistance without knowing its value." The teacher hesitated momentarily then answered, "I really do not grasp how this discussion is related to your reluctance to do the assigned work. If you fail to see its value, then I am afraid I cannot tell you." The student said no more. The conversation was terminated. The student turned to the task at hand and began to work.

The personal dimensions of teaching were more difficult to observe in the past. Intimate contact between teacher and students such as a pat on the back, an arm around the shoulder, or a gentle touch were rarely seen. Primary teachers, coaches, vocational teachers, and other nonacademic areas were the exception to this general observation. Teachers usually agree that a psychological distance between teacher and student is desirable. Getting too close causes the student to lose respect for teacher status and position, or to take advantage of the familiarity.

question ???

THE PERSONAL DIMENSION

While teachers acknowledge the recognition of nonverbal behaviors, they pretend that their influence on educational and social life are irrelevant. In the school situation, nonverbal expressions are considered an unwanted intrusion, an unnecessary diversion. The argument goes something like this: Teachers must not show their feelings. Expressed values can be wrong and misconceived. Not liking a child is immoral and unethical. Hair style, dress, and personal manner must conform to social taste. Personal life outside the school is private business. Do not bring your private experiences into the school building; leave them behind you at the front door. You job is to teach, to instruct, to do your duty. Your personal life may be interesting, but it has nothing to do with your professional task of teaching the young. You are a role-taker, a technician, and a taskmaster. Your job is to find ways to motivate without using yourself. Your job is to instruct the curriculum. Your job is to measure learning by every standard external to your own life.

Here is the problem: Few of us can hardly strip ourselves of our personal experiences and perceptions when we come to school so we end up merely fooling ourselves. Leakages of nonverbal expressions appear to others but we are frequently the last to know their effects. Our pretense of not revealing ourselves is just that— a masquerade for the benefit of the role. This action rarely works on its own, much less in a culture that abhors phoniness and facades.

Nonverbal expression of the teacher's outlook have always been available to students. Values and attitudes reveal that the teacher does not like his subject matter, or prefers certain kids, or smokes during break. In such instances no direct verbal information is necessary. The students know.

Throughout this culture we have teachers who go to schools with one thought in mind: I have a job to do today, I teach, I must leave my personhood outside the school door when I enter the building. I dislike mathematics, I resent those two troublemakers, I distrust the principal, but no one need ever know as long as I do my job. I am safe. Unfortunately, we have insisted on viewing the student from a psychologically safe distance. But students are neither invisible nor are they objects to be taught.

SCHOOLING AND NONVERBAL CUES

When teachers and administrators are confronted with the idea that nonverbal cues are a significant part of school life, they appear interested. While they believe that nonverbal contacts occur between teacher and student, they have difficulty in identifying specific behaviors. Since a reliance on verbal messages is common to educators, this lack of recognition is to be expected.

What sources of information are most helpful? References to research or theory? Not quite. I have found that a short demonstration of common gestures and expressions works. Recognition of these signs and signals comes easily since they are observed with such regularity in schools: a crooked finger beckoning a student to come here; the straight finger that points directly to student eyes; the elliptical finger movement that directs the student to move from one place to another; the wagging finger of accusation.

Although these expressive gestures are made everyday, the crucial conclusion is that we rarely point at others whose status is greater than ours. Principals do not point at superintendents while talking, and it would be a rarity to observe a student finger-pointing in the eyes of a teacher during a conversation. In this respect, we can identify a cheap rule: Rarely do we point or gesture aggressively at a person whose status is greater than ours. It is easy to point at students because teachers assume a dominant-submissive, superior-subordinate attitude.

If gestures reveal the basis of relationships, what can the eyes express? Staring is the visual counterpart to pointing. Ogling a student operates to remind a student of his place. A stare across space expresses a visual reminder: "I see you," and I want you to notice that I see you, the accompanying expectation is simple: your behavior is unacceptable (cut it out!).

Do teachers and administrators use their eyes to control student behavior? A downcast expression of condescension, an eye-roll of disapproval, a glance of acceptance, a wink of encouragement, a twinkle of affection, and a blink of disbelief are a few examples. The eyes also overlook, see around, look over, and indicate nonrecognition. A fear of closeness to students creates visual cues of avoidance. Eye contact not only presumes acknowledgment and recognition but implies a responsibility for further interaction. The well-known admonition: "Don't smile until Christmas," is apt here. To become too close to students is to take the risk of intimacy. Since such risks cannot be taken with objectivity and impartiality, distance is necessary.

> *Item*: After locking the doors of the car with careful certainty, the English teacher walked quickly and efficiently to the front of the school building. A few students converse near the entrance but the teacher fails to see them. The teacher hurries through the door. The students notice the quick movement and think nothing of the absence of acknowledgment.
>
> Moving through the inside corridor of the building the teacher is greeted with "good morning," but fails to look in the direction of the voice. The person who spoke thinks nothing of it. Walking at a fast rate, the teacher arrives at the classroom. Unburdening his arms with materials, the teacher is ready to begin the day.

What meaning can we infer from this simple description? These events mean little, except when you realize that they form a pattern that is repeated every morning. This is a teacher who rarely speaks to teachers, who never speaks to students unless they are in difficulty, and who prefers to be left alone. Or, so it seems.

This is a teacher who sits behind a desk and who rarely moves around the classroom during a teaching day. When the teacher speaks, an avoidance of eye contact prevails. The basic line of communication between teacher and student can be found on graded papers and critiqued exams that are returned to students with side comments. If an observer were asked what he saw, he might infer that this teacher makes an extra effort to keep a safe psychological distance from students.

How could an observer make such a comment? His inferences are based on what this teacher does and does not do. Observing everyday classroom events, the observer infers from the consequences of actions and behaviors. Would it be possible for the observer to have faulty perceptions? To see what was not intended? To fail to understand actions and events from the teacher's point of view? This is possible but the data are clear: behaviors and attitudes from the basis of impression and evaluation. Without different data to observe, it is difficult to infer something else.

A facial expression, gesture, posture, glance, vocal pause, or a dozen other actions can express a message: for instance, that the teacher dislikes papers turned in late, dirty blue jeans, or long hair. A teacher can convey to a student that he is smart, dumb, pretty, ugly, dirty, or unimportant, without reference to a single word—and the student gets the message! Indeed, nonverbal messages can be too easy to deliver. Teachers can express information without words that they would never have the courage to state verbally, and would retract if they only knew what the students had decoded.

NONVERBAL OBSERVATION AND FEEDBACK

During the past several years and in recent years many category systems have been developed for observing and analyzing classroom interaction (e.g., Galloway, 1971; Grant, 1977, Grant & Hennings, 1971). These observational approaches are useful. When patterns of teacher-student interaction are described and analyzed, feedback can be realized. By analyzing patterns of teacher behavior, decent inferences can be made regarding the style of the teacher, teacher expectations, or learner response. These analytic efforts must of necessity rely on statistical frequencies, pattern counts, cyclical episodes, or category combinations. They are deductive in nature, providing observational data from which specific conclusions and implications can be drawn. This is their elegant parsimony.

For instance, a category system provides a trained observer with reliable assurance that his observations are objective. The value of such a system goes beyond its scientific merit, for it can be learned by the actor as well as the observer. This advantage insures that the use of feedback data for the actor as well as the observer can be interpreted accurately with a minimum of distortion.

Observational approaches for nonverbal phenomena fail precisely on this count. If observations are made of simple acts and events, then high measures of reliability can be achieved. Noting the number of smiles, pats on the back, head nods, travel patterns, or nonverbal demonstrations that are given can obviously represent data of a certain kind. The very purpose for observing nonverbal phenomena precludes

any easy or convenient measure that falls short of capturing the essence and meaning of behavioral acts or events. It is evident that reliable observations of nonverbal
influence are most difficult to make when the requirement is to observe what is
significant rather than what is apparent.

The advantage of using category systems for observation is obvious. Their use
implies economy of effort and their utility affords an abbreviated version of note
taking. But the data provided by category schemes can be limited in value and the
shorthand advantage can preclude observations of behavior that are not included in
the definitions of categories. A promising approach for observing behaviors, which
has received limited use, is the recording of nonverbal acts in narrative descriptions.
Taking the role of participant observer, narrative accounts of what is seen and understood about classroom activity is written. Such an approach has heuristic advantages and is not limited to the deductive limitations of predefined categories. Indeed, categories can emanate from the data that the observer records.

Two benefits of observational systems have been achieved (Galloway, 1971).
First, we have needed descriptive data relative to what teachers do. Research data
on teacher behavior has provided these descriptions. Then we have needed to de-
vise means for sharing these observations with teachers. Feedback has been given
to teachers through matrices, audiotape soundings, videotape recordings, and criti-
ques with the teacher. In effect, we have succeeded in describing what teachers do
and we have devised a means to give the teacher feedback of pedagogical performance. In this spirit several approaches and observational methods have value.
There is no such thing as *the* observational approach or *the* method for the teacher.

If the teacher wants to understand nonverbal influences, a monumental problem
exists. How to change classroom practice is no easy task. In our preliminary work
with teachers we have detected a defensiveness about observations with which
teachers disagree. Intense defensiveness occurs when the teacher is confronted with
disagreeable data or evidence. While value differences have always been evident
regarding what should occur in classrooms, observations or evaluations of nonverbal
phenomena seem to dramatize value differences.

If the teacher and helper trust each other, then open-sharing takes care of itself.
Otherwise, you have to work on value differences in a mood of understanding and
acceptance. We have learned that the teacher is a more critical factor than the helper. If the teacher is willing to take an attitude of attending to the observational data in
an open fashion, then this represents the best basis for resolving potential conflicts.
A mood of mutuality must prevail and the teacher is the prime agent for insuring
profitable exchanges. If the teacher denies observations or discounts data as invalid,
then an impasse of distrust is created. Once a barrier of mistrust is erected, data
become irrelevant and disfunctional.

The elegant beauty of using an observational system, which both helper and
teacher agree is valid, is that it removes the difficulty of value conflict. Especially
is this true when both parties have been trained in the purpose of usefulness of the
system. This is the supreme value of observational systems.

A model for understanding the appearance of nonverbal phenomena in classrooms can be found below. These ten dimensions of nonverbal activity have served us well for identifying nonverbal influences that are significant in classroom life. Category systems that describe narrow behavioral referents for observation have their purpose. We prefer broad outlines of behavioral activity, which these dimensions represent, rather than a specific glossary of observational definitions (Galloway, 1976).

Indeed, an entire dictionary of signs does not exist for observers to memorize or to learn. The theme of the situation provides a backdrop for making interpretations of behavior. Reading the meaning of behavior and knowing its definition depends on the context. For instance, sitting on the forward edge of a chair and leaning forward may suggest the beginning of an exchange, the acceptance of an idea, or the initiation of confrontation. It all depends on the situation and what other simultaneous signals are perceived.

To become more knowledgeable and sensitive to the influences of nonverbal communication is difficult. The best way to start is to develop an awareness of the multiplicity of messages. Human beings send and receive information multisensorily. If we observe more sensitively, then a richer more available source of data exists. Awareness does not come all at once. Accuracy improves as perception increases. When we perceive to greater depths, we are more attuned to those around us and we begin to employ nonverbal cues for positive purposes. We begin to recognize that expressive cues transmit emotions and feelings more quickly than speech. An appearance of these cues especially reveal attitudes and evaluations. Understanding what we say without words is important to the establishment of good rapport and understanding. Through this awareness we come a little closer to being understood and to communicating more effectively, as well as understanding the silent messages of others.

ENCOURAGING-RESTRICTING MODELS OF NONVERBAL COMMUNICATION (Galloway, 1976).

1.   Congruous-incongruous. This dimension refers to the congruity or incongruity that exists between the voice tone, gesture, and actions of the teacher and verbal messages. Congruity occurs when the teacher's verbal message is supported and reinforced by nonverbal behaviors. A mixed message or incongruity exists when there is a descrepancy or contradiction between the verbal message and the teacher's action or gesture. For example, demanding that assignments be turned in on time but forgetting the assignment was given. Saying that a student has done good work, but looking unsure and lacking certainty.

2.   Responsiveness-unresponsiveness. A responsive act is a modification in the teacher's behavior as a result of feedback. Verbal feedback occurs when the teacher hears himself talking, but nonverbal feedback is based on the reactions and responses of pupils to the teacher. A responsive act occurs when the teacher alters the pace or direction of a lesson when misunderstanding or pupils' distress is detected.

Unresponsive acts ignore the behavioral responses and reactions of pupils.

3.   Positive-negative affectivity. Positive nonverbal expressions convey warm feeling, high regard, cheerful enthusiasm, display of liking and acceptance. Negative nonverbal experssions convey aloofness, coldness, low regard, indifference, or displays of rejection.

4.   Attentive-inattentive. Nonverbal expressions that imply a willingness to listen with patience and interest to pupil talk. By paying attention, the teacher shows an interest in the pupil. By being inattentive or disinterested, the teacher inhibits the flow of communication, and neither sustains nor encourages sharing information or expressing ideas.

5.   Facilitating-unreceptive. The teacher is facilitating when she performs a function that helps a pupil, usually in response to a detection of pupil needs, urgencies, or problems. An unreceptive act openly ignores a pupil when a response would ordinarily be expected. The teacher may ignore a question or request.

6.   Supportive-disapproving. Expressions that clearly show the teacher is pleased and approves of student behavior. Disapproving expressions convey dissatisfaction, discouragement, disparagement, or punishment. The facial expression may be one of frowning, scowling, or threatening glances.

7.   Intimate-distant. Teachers indicate how close and intimate are their contacts with students. Intimacy is revealed by physical proximity and psychological closeness while distance is created by an absence of contact and treatment of of aloofness and withdrawal.

8.   Inclusive-exclusive. Nonverbal cues of action and glance reveal who is included or excluded. Inclusion is marked by exchanges of mutual glance and acknowledgment while cues of exclusion suggest a denial that the other person is there or deserves recognition. Evidences of human existence or invisibility can be noted.

9.   Free-restricted time. Definitions of our uses of time with others create realities beyond words. How much time we spend with others and how our time is used makes a difference. Uses of time and the values we hold have a positive correlation.

10.   Open-close space. Classroom spaces outline travel routes of movement and desks take on the property of territorial rights. Accessibility to the spaces and territories of the school becomes available or restricted.

Recognizing the meaning of nonverbal realities has begun to make a difference in classrooms, and teachers have sharpened their sensitivities. Desks are no longer stationed at the front of the room like solitary sentinels of status. Students have more freedom to walk around the classroom without the imposition of artificial restrictions. Space has been expanded and enlarged with greater flexibility of movement. Uses of time have become less restrictive.

Teachers can be seen to give positive glances and head nods that reinforce positive student behaviors. It is now recognized that visual contact reveals attitudes and feelings.

Teachers are learning to read the nonverbal feedback of students and to respond appropriately. If a student misunderstands or fails to comprehend an idea, teachers are picking up the cues and putting the student at ease without putting him down.

Many teachers can be observed to be talking less. They know that silence can be preferable to words; that a nonverbal response can reveal a more eloquent understanding than an oververbalization. Indeed, to sustain a class discussion through nonverbal cues is a real skill, especially when it is important to get student ideas.

Whether we are considering changes in the uses of space and time, patterns of travel and body movement, expressions of face and gesture, or the nuances and subtleties of the pause and eye glance, it is clear that the realities of nonverbal contact are important to human understanding. But the most significant implication for the teacher has to do with having more valid data that relate to teaching and learning.

References

Galloway, C. *The silent language of the classroom.* Phi Delta Kappa Fastback Series, Bloomington, Indiana, October 1976.

Grant, B. M. Analyzing teacher nonverbal activity. *Theory into Practice,* 1977, *16,* 200-206.

Grant, B. M., & Hennings, D. G. *The teacher moves: An analysis of nonverbal activity.* New York: Teachers College Press, 1971.

Jackson, P. *Life in classrooms.* New York: Holt, Rinehart, and Winston, 1968.

Smith, L., & Geoffrey, W. *The complexities of an urban classroom.* New York: Holt, Rinehart, and Winston, 1968.

COMMON MISCONCEPTIONS ABOUT NONVERBAL
COMMUNICATION: IMPLICATIONS FOR TRAINING

Robert M. Soucie

Seneca College
Toronto, Ontario

There are few human activities we value more, understand less, and perform worse, than person-to-person communication. Despite its critical role in the success of countless other activities, we have until fairly recent times neglected to study it with the intensity and thoroughness it deserves, and we have certainly not attempted to teach this process widely and with conviction to the members of our society.

Nonverbal processes, as a whole, operate at lower levels of consciousness than verbal ones, and no doubt this fact partly explains why we have traditionally paid far more attention to the linguistic, than to the nonlinguistic aspects of human interaction. But this picture is changing rapidly. It is instructive to note that since Darwin's publication of *The expression of the emotions in man and animals* in 1872, the increase of scientific interest in nonverbal communication has roughly paralleled the increase in the distribution of visual, lifelike images of the human body through the media of the photograph, the film, and television. These technologies have enormously facilitated the study of nonverbal communication by providing scientists with invaluable tools, but more importantly, I think, by directing their attention to the power and the subtlety of these phenomena that, from man's earliest days, have functioned in the background of human affairs. The result has been a kind of "surfacing" of nonverbal variables within the scientific community, comparable to the "surfacing" of the psyche following the pioneering work of Sigmund Freud and the psychoanalytic school. Indeed, McLuhan (MacRae *et al.,* 1975) sees a connection between Freud and Darwin and other explorers of "the depths":

> The rapidly extending concern with nonverbal communication needs to be put in the entire ecology context of environmental studies. Our time has discovered that there is a language of Forms and Gestures—a language which has its own grammar and syntax. *The expression of the emotions in man*

and animals by Charles Darwin was part of his own biological study in heredity and environment. . . the characteristic mark of twentieth century studies and awareness has been the increasing tendency of all subliminal *ground* to surface. Freud's *Interpretation of dreams* was published in 1900, which provides a very convenient time mark by which to measure the steady rise of the subliminal to the surface of consciousness. Psychology and art and advertising alike provide wide testimonies to this pattern of change of awareness. It was Harold Innis who initiated communication studies into the observation of the hidden consequences of technical innovation in changing the environment. (*Foreword*)

During the past ten years we have witnessed a great explosion of interest not only in nonverbal communication, but in the entire process of interaction. As this process moves from the background to the foreground, or surface, of our awareness, it is becoming more and more difficult to take good, effective communication for granted. We are now at the stage where we are examining in detail what happens when people meet face-to-face, and out of this examination has come a concern for the development of interactional skills, a concern that is central to the objectives of this book.

Yet, while no informed person doubts the crucial importance of nonverbal communication skills, there is considerable room for debate about the issue of nonverbal training. Is formal training desirable in the first place, and why? Desirable for whom? Under what circumstances? Who ought to conduct the training? What ought to be taught, and when, and how?

I do not intend to answer any of these questions, but I do intend to deal with issues that have a direct bearing on them. In this paper I will examine three common misconceptions about nonverbal communication, and show how these misconceptions confuse and complicate the discussion of training issues. Though I have taken no formal survey, I have listened carefully during the past four years to thousands of students and educators, and people in businesses, professions, and the home. This experience has convinced me that clarifying fundamental concepts in the field would be a worthwhile contribution to the public's understanding of the training question.

I will take a look at three popular notions. The first is that nonverbal communication is a very minor part of interpersonal communication. Because there is not a great deal to learn about it, the idea of nonverbal training makes no sense at all. Such training would be merely an expensive educational frill, which we cannot afford. The second notion is that, while there is undoubtedly a great deal to learn about nonverbal communication, and while it surely plays very important roles in our daily encounters, sheer life experience implicitly, automatically, teaches us all we need to know about it. Because of this "natural" process of education, explicit, formal education would be redundant and a waste of time. The third misconception is that the average person does not know much at all about nonverbal communication, and what he does know he has little awareness of. Furthermore, this is a most desirable state of affairs, because "too much" knowledge of nonverbal communication will create a direct threat to the privacy we claim for ourselves even during face-to-face interaction. "Too much" knowledge will also have the effect of reducing interactions to the level of strategic games, with the participants attempting to outguess and out-maneuver each other, and lying and withholding information from each other. Therefore, some people say, formal training in nonverbal communication would be a dangerous mistake.

FASHIONABLE NONSENSE

Some people find it difficult to take nonverbal communication at all seriously. To them, anything remotely connected with "body language" smells strongly of fad and frill, and the sooner all those phony "experts" exhaust their welcome on the TV talk shows and take their deserved tumbles from the bestseller lists, the better. Needless to say, this view is a superficial one. The field has been done a great disservice by those who have glamourized and simplified research findings to satisfy the popular tests for instant solutions to complicated communication problems. It is hardly any wonder then, that the field appears to be populated by quacks and Madison Avenue hucksters, and that many intelligent people have only been strengthened in their conviction that language is the prime and the only major communication medium working during interaction. This conviction seems to be rooted in a profound appreciation of the tremendous civilizing power of language, particularly written language, a power that is immediately apparent everywhere in man's history, yet nowhere to be found in the histories of all other species. People who take this point of view often tend to adopt a somewhat bemused attitude to nonverbal communication, and tend to derive a great deal of satisfaction from juxtaposing in their minds the images of the articulate human and the dumb animal. And yet this understandable preference for the word as against the deed is also rooted many times in a profound ignorance of what really transpires during face-to-face encounters.

There is first of all the matter of *how much* we communicate nonverbally. In an average day we may meet a great many persons, may speak to very few of them, and yet, unavoidably, we will communicate with every one of them. Language as a medium of exchange is an on-off system which is most of the time in the off mode. As Birdwhistell puts it, "Man is a multisensorial being. Occasionally he verbalizes." As long as we are in another's presence, we cannot fail to communicate nonverbally, for even the very attempt to suppress communication is, in itself, communication (Watzlawick, Beavin, & Jackson, 1967). Furthermore, in those few interactions that do involve words, a large proportion of messages are still nonverbal ones, a fact that has been stressed by practically every researcher in the field (e.g., Birdwhistell, 1970; Argyle, 1975; Scheflen & Scheflen, 1972). Almost invariably, therefore, it is our nonverbal system, and not our language system, that receives the greater interpersonal action during the typical day.

But there is a far more compelling reason than sheer *quantity* of information for arguing the importance of nonverbal communication, and that is the critical functions that this information performs. Both Goffman (1959, 1963, 1967, 1971) and the Scheflens (Scheflen & Scheflen, 1972; Scheflen & Ashcraft, 1976) have spelled out in great detail how dependent, as a process, interaction is on nonverbal information. While the data, or contents, of interaction tend to be carried mainly (though not exclusively) in the verbal channel, the nature of the relationship between the participants is usually determined largely by nonverbal information (Watzlawick, *et al.,* 1967). In other words, *what* people communicate *about* is normally the function of language, whereas *how* people *relate* to each other is normally the function of the nonverbal media. In fact, a major part of the nonverbal stream contains information about the participants themselves—their attitudes, their emotions, their personalities, their cultures, their societal positions, and so on. Nonverbal information reveals people in depth, and it is this sort of information that plays a huge role in determining how others relate to them, because it allows others to make crucial decisions from the very beginning of the interaction through to the end. It is often on the basis of nonverbal information that we decide whether or not to interact at all; that we decide on how to dispose our own faces and bodies as we make our approach; that we decide on a suitable topic for discussion, and when to change topics; that we decide on our tone of voice, our pitch, and our volume; that we decide when to speak and when to listen; when and how to withdraw from the interaction; and a whole host of other extremely important decisions. This is not to say that language information plays no part in these decisions; it most certainly does. It is only that very often language is not well suited to reflect quickly and efficiently the highly detailed and constantly shifting facts about a person to which another must have access on a continuous basis if he is to initiate and sustain contact with him.

Another way to look at the importance of nonverbal communication is to conceive of the high volume of nonverbal messages as context, or environment, within which words occur. All words are ambiguous, out of context, and what nonverbal information provides is a massive system of cues that serves to shed light not only on the literal meanings of words, but on what they mean to the person speaking them—right here, right now. A manuscript of a conversation is a very poor substitute and description of what really occurred. And while one may make guesses from such a manuscript about the nature of the relationship involved, these guesses may be completely at odds with the impressions one obtains from *being there.* The richness and subtlety and clarity that nonverbal behaviors impart to language, and therefore to the relationship itself, is a measure of its extreme importance to the process of talking. Those who view interaction as merely or mostly an exchange of words fail to appreciate what interaction is. Small wonder they feel nonverbal training would be a frivolous and expensive undertaking that we cannot afford.

A WASTE OF TIME

A second common notion is that most of us already know how to communicate perfectly well nonverbally. We may not have much *awareness* of all that we actually know, but awareness is not important, and may even be a drawback. Training would therefore be redundant and a waste of time.

Certainly ordinary life experience *does* equip the average person with an immense competence in nonverbal communication, and in a manner similar to that in which he learns an oral language. We *do* learn an enormous amount about faces and bodies and postures and appearances just by growing up. Yet, on the way, we also pick up bad habits of perception and interpretation. Some of us have patterns of experience that leave large and serious gaps in our repertoires of skills. And worst of all, a good many of us simply peak out after a while. We stop learning, stop developing, and coast along, frozen at whatever level of proficiency we have reached. It happens to our oral skills, and it happens to our nonverbal skills too.

One of the most fatal assumptions we make is that, because we have spent days and years communicating, we must by this time be pretty good at it. Yet this is not necessarily true for verbal, nonverbal, or any number of other skills. In fact, over the years we may even get worse. It is not just experience that we need; we need the right kind of experience—experience in trying out new skills in new situations, and analyzing and reshaping old ones. Faulty habits must be detected and broken, often a very difficult process; rusty skills must be brought back into shape. Unfortunately, our experiences vary greatly, and it seems plain that many of us have had less than ideal ones on which to hone our communication abilities. Often it is sheer motivation that is lacking. We simply stop trying to improve ourselves.

Study after study has established the fact that large individual differences exist in people's ability to accurately encode and decode facial, bodily, and other nonverbal stimuli (cf. Knapp, 1972; Hinde, 1972; Argyle, 1975). Rosenthal's PONS Test reveals that there are even significant group differences in decoding skills, such as between males and females, and between members of various occupations (Rosenthal *et al.*, 1974).

We suffer from several kinds of deficiencies as nonverbal communicators. We may, for example, be processing information generated by others quite satisfactorily, but be considerably out of touch with the impressions we are creating in others. We may be sensitive to obvious or reoccurring behaviors, particularly when several channels yield information that is more or less congruent, but we may fail to perceive behaviors accurately when they are small in scale, or rapid, or subtle, or not found in other channels. When we are distracted by emotion or prejudice or some vivid event, we may be far less capable of controlling our own behavior, or of processing information from others, than we normally are. Perhaps our problem is that we pay little attention to the body, or to the voice qualities, and focus mainly on facial expressions (or vice-versa), and thus miss important information entirely. Our ability to form accurate first impressions quickly may be extremely limited. A further difficulty is that when we encounter people from different cultures we may become confused, or anxious, or irritated because of our unfamiliarity with the strange nonverbal patterns.

These are merely a few of the difficulties people experience in their relationships. The shame of it is that, unless we receive sufficient feedback from others or from careful self-analysis of our nonverbal skills, we may go through our lives suffering from distorted, unrealistic conceptions of our talents and weaknesses. Among the most tragic misconceptions is the belief that we have little or nothing to learn about nonverbal communication, that nonverbal communication training would be redundant and a waste of time.

DANGEROUS MEDDLING

Some people, particularly those who have had some acquaintance with the research in the field, feel that the average person does not know much at all about nonverbal communication, that what he does know he has little conscious awareness of, and that everyone would be better off if things remained that way. There seem to be two closely related reasons for this position, and both of them are emotionally tinged. The first is a belief that privacy and the very process of interaction will be threatened if people learn "too much" about nonverbal communication. The second is a fear that such knowledge will inevitably produce a society of liars.

Both concerns can be related to what Goffman (1971) has called "information preserves." A person's information preserve is the

> . . . set of facts about himself to which an individual expects to control access while in the presence of others. There are several varieties of information preserve. There is the content of the claimant's mind, control over which is threatened when queries are made that he sees as intrusive, nosy, untactful. There are the contents of pockets, purses, containers, letters, and the like, which the claimant can feel others have no right to ascertain. There are biographical facts about the individual over the divulgence of which he expects to maintain control. And most important for our purposes, there is what can be directly perceived about an individual, his body's sheath and his current behavior, the issue here being his right not to be stared at or examined. Of course, since the individual is also a vehicular unit and since pilots of other units have a need and a right to track him, he will come to be able to make an exquisite perceptual distinction between being looked at and being stared at, and, God help us, learn to suspect, if not detect, that the latter is being masked by the former; and he will learn to conduct himself so that others come to respond to him in the same way. (pp. 38-40)

While Goffman discusses information preserves primarily with respect to behavior between strangers in public places, the concept applies in principle to any interaction, though in some situations—for example when lovers or very close friends meet—obviously less is claimed as an information preserve.

The concern for the security of this kind of preserve is encountered frequently by those who study or teach nonverbal communication, most often in the form of a question like: "Oh! (nervous giggle). You're in nonverbal communication. What is my body revealing to you?" The assumption here is that the person trained in nonverbal communication is busy reading all kinds of deep, dark secrets, or at the very least, that he is super-capable of doing this. Thus the nervous giggle. People often become visibly uncomfortable in the face of what they perceive to be a direct threat to their information preserves. Or, to put it another way, they seem to feel like the Emperor in his new clothes, right after the kid on the sidelines, unsocialized brat that he is, started pointing his finger at him. The kid cannot be trusted. He is a social menace because if everyone gets to know what he knows, sooner or later none of us will have the guts to step out in public.

It is an interesting scenario. The belief is that widespread nonverbal training will have the disastrous effect of engendering a painful self-consciousness about our appearance and behavior that, at best, would interfere with the spontaneity and flow of interaction, and at worst reduce interactions to strategic games, where success turns on a person's ability to out-maneuver the other guy (cf. Goffman, 1969). A trump card in these games is the ability to lie successfully nonverbally, both to withhold information and to send false and misleading information (cf. Ekman & Friesen, 1969). Best we not know too much about our faces and bodies, and what we do know already on a subliminal level, we best not fuss over. We must maintain the illusion of privacy, through respect for the information preserve, that we so carefully foster to smooth the course of interaction—an illusion that, in the last analysis, is a cornerstone of civilized communication.

This is a very compelling argument because it contains a number of valid premises. We *do* conspire together to preserve each other's "face" during interaction. It *is not* polite to stare and to examine another closely. A good many aspects of our appearance and behavior are unofficial, in the sense that, though they are visible, we do not consider or wish them to be part of the content of interaction. Calling attention to them verbally or nonverbally *will* violate the information preserves to which we have assigned them. This is particularly true in cases where the information exposes some irregularity, such as an amputated limb (Kleck *et al.*, 1968), or a facial tic. But it is also true in quite normal circumstances. Commenting on another's posture or eye movements, or staring intensely into someone's eyes, for example, will often disrupt the flow of interaction and cause feelings of irritation.

It is also accurate to say that these and other face-saving tactics are necessary if our daily interactions are not to degenerate into strategic games, or worse, into violent confrontations. Exposing oneself to interaction always entails some degree of risk-taking, and the process is stressful enough without a person having to worry that his clothes, his voice, and his slightest moves are fair game for minute and open scrutiny by anyone who wishes to do so. It is a relatively simple matter to control, and thus assume responsibility for, our words. It is quite a different thing to control, and assume responsibility for, the entire set of information generated by our bodies. Without the help of face-saving techniques, the information preserve is one, we would find it difficult to commit our bodies to interaction unless we were prepared to defend to the last detail the images they projected. And that is the road to anxiety-ridden communication.

This position, however, overlooks a central fact: The average person *already* knows a very great deal about nonverbal communication; he *already* knows enough to violate information preserves right, left, and center, and to see accurately whether or not Emperors have their clothes on. He can size up people, sometimes in seconds. He can read facial expressions and postures, and he knows the language of the eyes and hands. Nonverbal training would not be training that pretends to turn rank amateurs into seasoned professionals. Rather, the goal is to build upon and to refine an extraordinarily complex repertoire *already* in place by virtue of countless hours of implicit learning and practical experience. As was mentioned earlier, most people still have a lot to learn about nonverbal communication, but this training is not going to turn dummies into professionals. Yet this is the impression some people have. What *is* extremely fascinating is discovering from the research just how much we already know without being conscious of it, in much the same way that we might be fascinated to learn about the complexities of the language we have been speaking since childhood.

So, the conclusion to be drawn is that if man was capable *without* nonverbal training, of seriously jeopardizing the privacy afforded by devices such as the information preserve, *yet has not*, then *with* nonverbal training, he hardly seems more likely to do so. The fear that he will seems to arise out of an overestimation of nonverbal training, and an underestimation of the value we place on face-saving techniques.

It could be argued that training will raise the level of consciousness we have about nonverbal behavior, and that *this* is the dangerous part, not the mere possession of knowledge. That is, we have not violated the preserves before *only* because we were not sufficiently aware of the knowedge we possessed. This seems most unlikely. There are many occasions when we *are* fully conscious of another's behaviors, verbal and nonverbal, and yet refrain from drawing attention to them. What keeps us *then* from violating social norms? Our commitment, obviously, to the norm itself, which is stronger, at least on those occasions, than our desire to violate it for some other end. Goffman (1967) has written eloquently on this subject, stressing the great lengths to which people will go in cooperating with each other in the task of preserving public order through the mutual preservation of face.

On the other hand, in individual cases people have always flaunted conventions, and most certainly will continue to do so. There is every reason to believe that training in nonverbal communication will provide some fuel for these kinds of fires just as language training has done for verbal communication. People use the same language to compliment others as they do to insult them.

Also, a certain amount of awkwardness and self-consciousness is almost bound to occur from time to time, and particularly during the training period. But after four years of teaching intensive courses in nonverbal communication, I have yet to run across a former student for whom this became a problem, and who exhibits any symptoms of induced self-consciousness.

It is likely, too, that in concert with the influence of film and television, which provide plentiful images of the human body in action, nonverbal training will raise the general level of anxiety about our behavior, in much the same way the Freudian concepts, as they filtered down into society, have probably raised the general level of anxiety about our psyches.

Finally, it is possible that widespread nonverbal training, say through our school system, will effect major changes in the ritual of interaction itself after some time. After all, such changes have been a fact of life, a fact of history. We do not interact with each other today exactly the way we did in the last century. For that matter, it would seem that young people have rung several changes in our styles over the past 20 years or so. But again, I see no reason for fearing that any changes that occur will be in the direction of anarchy, that they will be changes that work against the common good. We are far too interdependent to allow that to happen.

Would nonverbal training produce crops of skilled liars? This is a most sensitive issue, and one that continually arises. If, and it is a very large if, people will learn, as a side effect of nonverbal training, to lie any more successfully than they *already can,* then, by the same token, other people should be able to *detect* liars more successfully than *they* already can. There would be a cancelling effect. In fact, if we assume that there are fewer liars than nonliars in our society, the rate of successful lying ought to go down, not up. Furthermore, to lie or not to lie is a moral choice each individual makes for himself; even if there were no cancelling effect (which is possible), to deny nonliars the positive benefits of nonverbal training by refusing to train anyone would be like refusing to teach rhetoric on the grounds that future Adolf Hitlers may be sitting in the classroom. We do not ban knives from the table simply because individuals have been known to sink them into their neighbors' backs.

Perhaps the most important point to make is that, to date, no one is claiming he can train people to lie really effectively; it is simply not that easy to lie nonverbally, but if and when that day arrives, unless we have become completely perverse in the meantime, we surely will not rush out to install lying courses in our curricula. Certain individuals would no doubt be very interested in registering in whatever underground courses they could find—and I am sure there would be many—but such a prospect is not only remote and hypothetical, it in no way bears upon the issue of legitimate, responsible training.

CONCLUSION

Is formal training in nonverbal communication desirable? For whom, and under what circumstances? Who should teach and what ought to be taught? When should the training occur? What methods should be used?

These questions remain. They are difficult to answer, and deserve a very great deal of thought and debate. What I have tried to do in this paper is point out that large numbers of people have already decided that formal training would be fashionable nonsense, or a waste of time, or dangerous meddling; that they have reached these conclusions because of their misconceived notions about the nature of nonverbal communication itself. I feel that we have not succeeded, if indeed we have tried at all, in educating the general public about fundamental concepts in the field. If the discussion of nonverbal training is to take place in public, and I think it ought to, then it seems likely that, until we clarify what we are about, we are going to encounter a fairly widespread resistance that will be based on ignorance, and that will confuse and complicate the issues involved.

I have not taken the position that formal training *is* desirable. There may very well be good reasons why it is not. But what I am saying is that arguments against formal training that spring from the popular notions I have described in this paper are not arguments at all. If we can agree that there is a great deal to learn about nonverbal communication, that many of us have not learned an adequate set of skills, and that learning these skills would not threaten the process of interaction, then perhaps we can get on with the task of answering the many and difficult training questions that, to this point, have received little attention.

References

Argyle, M. *Bodily communication.* London: Methuen, 1975.

Birdwhistell, R. *Kinesics and context.* Philadelphia: University of Pennsylvania Press, 1970.

Darwin, C. *The expression of the emotions in man and animals.* Chicago: University of Chicago Press, 1965.

Ekman, R., & Friesen, W. Nonverbal leakage and clues to deception. *Psychiatry*, 1969, *32*, 88-106.

Goffman, E. *The presentation of self in everyday life.* Garden City, New York: Anchor Books, 1959.

Goffman, E. *Behavior in public places.* New York: The Free Press, 1963.

Goffman, E. *Interaction ritual.* Garden City, New York: Anchor Books, 1967.

Goffman, E. *Strategic interaction.* Philadelphia: University of Philadelphia Press, 1969.

Goffman, E. *Relations in public.* New York: Basic Books, 1971.

Hinde, R. (Ed.) *Nonverbal communication.* Cambridge, England: Cambridge University Press, 1972.

Kleck, R. Physical stigma and nonverbal cues emitted in face-to-face interaction. *Human Relations*, 1968, *21*, 19-28.

Knapp, M. *Nonverbal communication in human interaction.* New York: Holt, Rinehart, & Winston, 1972.

MacRae, D., Campbell, R., Gunckel, V., Hartlieb, C., & Soucie, R. *You and others: An introduction to interpersonal communication.* Toronto: McGraw-Hill Ryerson, 1975.

Rosenthal, R., Archer, D., DiMatteo, R., Hall-Koivumaki, J., & Rogers, P. Body talk and tone of voice: The language without words. *Psychology Today*, 1974, *4*, 64-71.

Scheflen, A., & Scheflen, A. *Body language and social order.* Englewood Cliffs, New Jersey: Prentice Hall, 1972.

Scheflen, A., & Ashcraft. *Human territories: How we behave in space-time.* Englewood Cliffs, New Jersey: Prentice Hall, 1976.

Watzlawick, P., Beavin, J., & Jackson, D. *Pragmatics of human communication.* New York: W. W. Norton, 1967.

PART 4: CONCLUSION

What can be concluded from this book about the field of nonverbal behavior? What is the state of the field of nonverbal behavior? Have the issues that have evolved been resolved? How does the future look?

From the papers, one can see that there has been in the past two decades, and right up to the present, a great deal of interest in this field of study, as shown by the increasing number of books, courses, journal publications, and new journals. The multidisciplinary nature of this field should help guard against provincialism and narrowness in thinking. There seems to be a willingness among investigators from the different disciplines to share, discuss, and debate their ideas, read each other's works, and even quote each other, thus helping breakdown some of the artificial barriers or lines set up by their different disciplines. Being in a multidisciplinary field puts some pressure on the investigator to take a broader and more holistic view in attempting to explain and understand such things as the role of human expressive behavior and motivation in interpersonal communication. There seems to be a growing awareness and concern among investigators in this field of the necessity for developing means or strategies for integrating information of how the different levels of nonverbal behavior are interrelated and how they are related to such variables as personality, social situations, cultures, etc.

There was concern voiced in this book about the ethical issues of how knowledge gained in this field could be misused. That is, if nonverbal behavior normally operates outside of awareness, are we potentially equipping experts, politicians, governments, advertisers, salesmen, etc., to manipulate and control people by teaching them how to understand and use these channels of communication? The issue is partially resolved by the argument that people are intelligent enough to see through such manipulations and can look for contradictions or verification from other sources. One can also argue that language can be used to control and manipulate people that the same arguments could be used about teaching people to read and write. There was one basic issue among others not dealt with in this book and that was: When is nonverbal behavior nonverbal communication? That is, do all human expressive behaviors have meaning?

In conclusion, in looking to the future of the field of nonverbal behavior, notes of optimism and caution were expressed by the contributors. On the bright side, there is a great deal of multidisciplinary activity, interest, research, and publishing in the field. The importance of nonverbal behavior in human communication has been demonstrated, as well as its possible applications. Through the study of nonverbal behavior there has been progress in understanding and improving intercultural communication, as well as in understanding and analyzing the underlying structure in social interactions. Notes of caution, however, were voiced by some contributors about not expecting too much too soon, because this is an exploratory and relatively complex field where we are being exposed to large amounts of information, so much so that it is hard to keep up with the literature even in one's own area of specialty. There is concern that the field in its diversity may become fragmented and piecemeal in its approach. Thus, it becomes important in the future to develop ways to integrate this information with other variables. There were notes of caution expressed in attempting to interpret accurately what a person feels or is experiencing on the basis of what a person is willing to show through his nonverbal behavior.

Although the contributors to this book come from diverse backgrounds, each bringing with him his own unique perspective to the field, it seems that some common areas of agreement have emerged. For instance, most of the investigators would agree that at this point the diversity in approaches and perspectives in this relatively new science of nonverbal behavior is welcome and that nonverbal behavior should not be studied in isolation but in relation to such areas as language, culture, social context, and biological influences. Also, there would seem to be agreement that nonverbal behavior can be studied by using natural observations in the field as well as in the controlled laboratory environment. Lastly, most of the contributors would concur that the results of research in nonverbal behavior has a good potential use for humanistic purposes in helping improve communication between human beings from the same or from different nations.

INDEX

A

Academic achievement, sensitivity to nonverbal communications and, 88–89
Accommodation, social interaction and, 153
Adaptiveness, of emotions, 46
Adults, expression motivated behavior in, 41
Age, sensitivity to nonverbal communication and, 84–86
Aggressive displays, 26–27
Alcoholics, sensitivity to nonverbal communication, 77, 79, 88
Altruism, cognitively induced, motivation and, 36, 37
Anger, facial expressions and, 32
Anxiety, diagnosis of, 130
Apotropaic displays, 27
Arousal, physiological, facial expression and, 44–45
Assertiveness training, modeling in, 133–134
Attachment, mother–infant, emotion communication and, 39–40
Attention, *see also* Listening behavior
explanation and, 99–100
Attentiveness, 206
rapport and, 132
Attitudes
communication of, 142–143
toward emotion, cross-cultural differences in, 41–43

B

Behavior, universals in, 18–19
Biological unity, cultural diversity versus, 17–18

Body movements, *see also* Gestures

Body movements, *see also* Gestures
applications of research in, 61–63
current research developments in, 57–61
facilitation of therapy and, 133
historical perspective on, 51–57
notation systems for, 55–56

C

Change, metabehavior and, 13–14
Children
emotion perception in, 44
expression motivated behavior in, 40–41
sensitivity to nonverbal communication in, 84–86
Classroom, *see also* Teachers
cross-cultural differences in, environment and teacher expectations in, 164–165
Cognitive ability, sensitivity to nonverbal communications and, 87–90
Cognitive complexity, sensitivity to nonverbal communications and, 90
Cognitive transformations
in delay of gratification, 35–36
distress, altruism, self-gratification, and conscience development and, 36–37
Communication
concept of, 2–3
structural view of
evolution of, 9–10
paradigm and operations, 10–12
Communicative fields, neural organization and, 14–15
Congruity, between verbal and nonverbal communication, 205

Contextualization cues, listening behavior and, 115
Coyness, cross-cultural comparisons of, 23–24
Cross-cultural comparison
  of attitudes toward emotion, 41–43
  of body movement, 54
  of classroom environment and teacher expectations, 164–165
  of facial expression, 32
  of motor patterns
    analogies in principle, 25–27
    homologous, 20–24
    inborn, 24–25
  of nonverbal communication
    of Chinese students, 169–170
    of Southern Italians, 168–169
    of West Indians, 166–168
  of perception, 43, 70–76
  of ritualization, 29
  of verbal clichés and strategies of social interaction, 28–29
Cues, schooling and, 201–203
Cultural differences, *see also* Cross-cultural comparisons
  biological unity versus, 17–18
  in communicative behavior, 13
Culture
  how teachers can learn about, 163
  nonverbal behavior and, 162–163

D

Decoding, 141
Delay of gratification, cognitive transformations versus affect induction in, 35–36
Depression, diagnosis of, 130
Dialects, political factors and, 180–181
Disapproval, 206
Distance, 206
Distress, cognitively induced, motivation and, 36, 37

E

Electromyographic (EMG) studies, of facial expression and emotion, 33–34
Emotion(s), *see also* Psychodiagnosis
  attitudes toward, cross-cultural differences in, 41–43
  communication of, 143
  control of, psychotherapy and, 45–46

expression of, *see* Body movement; Facial expression
as motivation for individual action, 34–35
  cognitively induced distress, altruism, self-gratification, and conscience development and, 36–37
  delay of gratification and, 35–36
perception and expressions of, in psychological assessment, 43–44
Emotion Attitude Questionnaire (EAQ), 41–42
Encoding, 141
Epistemology, 3–4
  real truth and, 6–9
  reductionism and, 4–5
  reification and, 5–6
Ethology, interaction sequences and, 147
Event, communicational, description of, 10–11
Exclusiveness, 206
Expectations, mediation of, 67
Explanation, 100–101
  cultural differences in, 115–118
  definition of, 101–102
Expression, inborn motor patterns of, 19–20
Eyebrow flash, cross-cultural comparisons of, 22
Eye contact
  in psychodiagnosis, 129–130
  schooling and, 202–203
  therapeutic progress and, 130

F

Facial expressions
  in deaf and blind, 19–20
  emotion and, 31
    psychophysiological studies of, 33–34
    universality of facial expression and, 32
  historical perspective on, 53
  as motivation in social interaction, 37
    face as social stimulus, 37–38
    mother–infant attachment and, 39–40
    in older children and adults, 40–41
    smiling and laughing and, 38–39
  physiological arousal and, 44–45
  in psychological assessment, 43–44
Facilitation, 206
Failure, selection for, 177
Feedback, 144
Field independence, sensitivity to nonverbal communication and, 84
Funding, for research, 60

G

Gaze
    functions of, 145
    in social skill, 139
Gestures, 145–146
    cultural differences in, 180
Gift exchange, verbal, 28

H

Headshaking, cross-cultural comparisons of,
    24
Heart rate, emotion and, 34
Hyperexplanation, 101–102

I

Ideas, social interaction and, 153
Illocutionary force, 100
Inclusiveness, 206
Individual differences, in communicative be-
    havior, 12–13
Infant(s), social interactions and
    face as social stimulus for, 37–38
    smiling and laughing and, 38–39
Infact–mother attachment, emotion com-
    munication and, 39–40
Information preserve, 214–215
Innate releasing mechanism, 25
Institutional behavior, of teachers, 199–200
Intelligence, see Cognitive ability
Interaction sequences, 146–147
    ethology and, 147
    failure and, 155
    linguistic models of, 147–148
Intimacy, 206

K

Kinesics, 160
Kiss, cross-cultural comparisons of, 22

L

Language, perception and, 74–75
Laughing
    development of, 38
    functions of, 38–39
    in infant–mother interactions, 39
Linguistic models, of social encounters, 147–
    148
Listening behavior
    in interrracial interviews1 105–115, 118–121
        implications of, 121–125
    regulatory functions of, 102–105

M

Meaning
    of nonverbal communication, 205–207
    of signals, 141–142
Metabehavior, change and, 13–14
Minority students, miscommunication with
        teachers by, see Teachers, miscommuni-
        cation with minority students by
Miscommunication
    circumstances and consequences of, 189–
        193
    context analysis of function of, 183–189
    school failure and, 175–177
    cause of, 177–182
Modeling, for psychological growth, 133–134
Modernization, perception and, 75– 76
Mother–infant attachment, emotion com-
        munication and, 39–40
Motivation, emotions as, 34–35, 37
    cognitively induced distress, altruism, self-
        gratification and conscience develop-
        ment and, 36–37
    delay of gratification and, 35–36
    face as social stimulus, 37–38
    mother–infant attachment and, 39–40
    in older children and adults, 40–41
    smiling and laughing, 38–39
Motor patterns, 29–30
    analogies in principle, 25–27
    homologous, 20–24
    inborn, 19–20
        cultural convention and, 24–25
    ritualized, 29

N

Negative expressions, 206
Neural organization, communicative fields
        and, 14–15
No, expression of, cross-cultural comparisons
        of, 24–25

Nonverbal communication, 141–142, 160, 161–162
  acquisition of, 160–161
  concept of nonverbal in, 2
  encouraging–restricting models of, 205–207
  failure of, 154–155
  functions of, 142–144
  importance of, 161, 210–217
  interest in, 209–210
  meaning of, 198
  reasons for use of, 146
  signals in, 145–146
Nonverbal Components of Communication (NVC) Newsletter, 57

O

Observation, of nonverbal communication, 203–205

P

Paralanguage, 160
Perception
  of attitudes, 143
  cultural variation in, 70–76
  in psychological assessment, 43–44
Perlocutionary effect, 100
Personal behavior, of teachers, 200, 201
Phallic threats, 26–27
Pidgins, 180
Pointing, 202
Political factors, in miscommunication, 178–182
Positive expressions, 206
Predication, 101
Profile of Nonverbal Sensitivity (PONS) Test, 69–70
  age and, 84–86
  cognitive correlates of, 87–90
  cultural variation in perception and, 71–76
  future research related to, 91–92
  interpersonal success and, 86–87
  norms and reliability for, 92–94
    still photo form, 94–96
  psychopathology and, 76–80
  self-.rating and, 86
  sex and, 80–84
Proxemics, 160
Psychodiagnosis, 128

  body movement and, 53–54
  research on, 129–130
Psychopathy, sensitivity to nonverbal communication and, 76–80
Psychotherapy, emotion control and, 45–46

R

Race, listening behavior and, 104–115, 118–121
  implications of, 121–125
Rapport, establishing, 132–133
Real truth, 6–9
Reductionism, 4–5
Reification, 5–6
Reinforcement, in social skill, 140
Resistance, in therapy, 129, 131–132
Responsiveness, 205–206
Ritualization, 144
  cultural and biological, 29
Rules, of situation, 150–151

S

Schizophrenics
  emotion perception by, 43–44
  facial expressions in, 44
  sensitivity to nonverbal communication, 79–80
Scholastic aptitude, sensitivity to nonverbal communication and, 84, 88
Self-adaptors, 131
Self-gratification, cognitively induced, motivation and, 36–37
Self-presentation, 144
  in social skill, 140–141
Self-ratings, of sensitivity to nonverbal communications, 86
Sensitivity, to nonverbal communications, 67–68, see also Profile of Nonverbal Sensitivity Test
Sex, sensitivity to nonverbal communication and, 80–84
Shame, attitudes toward, cross-cultural differences in, 41–43
Situations, 148–150
  components of, 150
  failure in, 155
  rules of, 150–151
Smiling, in infants, 38

Smithsonian Science Information Exchange
    (SSIE), 57
Social episodes, 148
Social interaction
    cross-cultural variation in
        accommodation and, 153
        ideas and, 153
        nonverbal communication and, 152
        rules of, 152–153
        training and, 153
        universals, 154
    emotion expression as motivation in, 37
    face as social stimulus, 37–38
    mother–infant attachment and, 39–40
    in older children and adults, 40–41
    smiling and laughing, 38–39
    strategies of, cross-cultural comparisons of,
        28–29
Social skill(s)
    failure of, 154–155
    gaze in, 139
    interaction sequences and, 146–148
    reinforcement in, 140
    self-presentation in, 140–141
    taking role of other in, 140
Social skill training (SST), 155–156
    modeling in, 134
Space, openness of, 206
Stranger awareness, cross-cultural compari-
    sons of, 24
Success, interpersonal, sensitivity to nonver-
    bal communications and, 86–87
Support, 206
Synchronizing, 144

T

Task behavior, of teachers, 200
Teachers
    alleviation of problems of immigrants by,
        165–166, 179–171

training and research in, 171–172
    expectations of, cross-cultural differences
        in, 164–165
    learning about culture by, 163
    miscommunication with minority students
        by, 175–177
    cause of, 177–182
    circumstances and consequences of,
        189–193
    context analysis of function of, 183–189
    model, nonverbal characteristics of, 163–
        164
    nonverbal communication and, 197–199
    cues in, 201–203
    dimensions of teaching and, 199–200
    feedback on, 203–205
    personal dimension and, 201
Therapy, nonverbal communication in, 127–
    128
    client-generated, 128–132
    implications for research and training, 135–
        136
    therapist-generated, 129, 132–134
Time, use of, 206
Touching, 184–185
Training
    misconceptions about, 210–217
    social interaction and, 153
    in social skills, 155–156
    for teachers, 171
    of therapists, 135–136

V

Values, in therapy, 134
Verbal clichés, 28
Verbal proficiency, sensitivity to nonverbal
    communications and, 90
Verbal utterances, completing and elaborating
    of, 143–144

Date Due